Widening Access to Higher Education in the UK

Widening Access to Higher Education in the UK

Developments and approaches using credit accumulation and transfer

Edited by
Wayne Turnbull and Harvey Woolf

Open University Press

Open University Press
McGraw-Hill Education
8th Floor, 338 Euston Road
London
England
NW1 3BH

email: enquiries@openup.co.uk
world wide web: www.openup.co.uk

and Two Penn Plaza, New York, NY 10121-2289, USA

First edition published 2022

Executive Editor: Eleanor Christie
Editorial Assistant: Zoe Osman
Content Product Manager: Ali Davis

A catalogue record of this book is available from the British Library

ISBN-13: 9780335250592
ISBN-10: 0335250599
eISBN: 9780335250608

Library of Congress Cataloging-in-Publication Data
CIP data applied for

Typeset by Transforma Pvt. Ltd., Chennai, India

Praise page

"Rarely does a text come along which tackles challenging, technical aspects of higher education and presents them in an accessible and creative way. What is most striking is the tone and content of this collection of essays perfectly befits the subject matter; facilitating wider access to the important debates, challenges and benefits that arise from widening access to higher education through the effective use of credit We explore, from both theoretical and practical perspectives, the value of credit recognition for the learner, the challenges presented by the different models in operation across the four nations of the UK, through to the benefits accorded to student mobility from sound, underpinning credit. This is nestled between a succinct history of credit and a conclusion offering a positive vista of global synergy. For those in the know, and those yet to be inducted, this is a must read."
Maureen McLaughlin, Academic Registrar, Northumbria University, UK

"This is a scholarly and timely analysis of the development of systems for recognising academic credit within the context of widening access to higher education. In presenting a range of UK based and international or organisational snapshots of policy and practice, the authors make clear that 'credit' is a slippery and contested construct that can be used creatively to empower and support new ways of learning. As such it will be of interest to historians, policy makers and those managing and developing credit based academic frameworks."
Dr Marie Stowell, Director of Quality and Educational Development, University of Worcester, UK

"This much needed investigation of credit and learner mobility is both timely and impactful. The editors have worked with an excellent set of contributors to explore how credit is used to support student achievement and enhance learning. It offers compelling reasons as to why credit is a crucial part of the wider higher education ecosystem, examines how credit relates to European and international contexts, and provides insightful commentary on the value of credit in a devolved educational policy landscape. This book is required reading for anyone interested in the future of higher education in a rapidly changing world."
Dr Andy W. Smith, Quality Assurance Agency for Higher Education

"It is hard to find enough words of praise for this excellent collection of essays on how the notion of credit and its wider ramifications help widening access to higher education, as demonstrated in a UK setting.

Acknowledgements

The idea for this book and support for the research underpinning it came from the Northern Universities Consortium for Credit Accumulation and Transfer (NUCCAT). We thank NUCCAT for their commitment not only to this project but their passionate advocacy for credit in all its forms and functions over the past three decades. We also thank the Student Assessment and Classification Working Group (SACWG) for continuing to explore regulatory and other issues relating to credit, even when such matters were unfashionable.

Our final thanks are to Professor Rigby for her Foreword and to the chapter authors, who have freely shared their experiences, knowledge and wisdom.

Wayne Turnbull & Harvey Woolf, August 2021

Contents

List of figures and tables

List of contributors

Professor Darryll Bravenboer, *Director of Apprenticeships and Professor of Higher Education and Skills, Middlesex University, UK*

Darryll is a Principal Fellow of the Higher Education Academy and has extensive experience of developing and researching professional, vocational, work-integrated higher education and higher and degree apprenticeships in response to the needs of a wide range of professional sectors in collaboration with employers. Darryll is Co-Chair of the Higher Education Employer Trailblazer Group for England; Trustee of the University Association for Lifelong Learning and Chair of the SEEC Credit Network; Board Director of the University Vocational Awards Council; a member of the Quality Assurance Agency Higher Education in Apprenticeships, Work-based Learning and Higher Education Credit Framework Advisory Groups; and a member of the Institute for Apprenticeships and Technical Education Provider Panel.

Professor Samantha Broadhead, *Head of Research, Leeds Arts University, UK*

Samantha is Head of Research at Leeds Arts University in the North of England and researches mature students' experiences in art and design education. She serves on the editorial board of the *Journal of Widening Participation and Lifelong Learning* and carries out review work for FACE (Forum for Access and Continuing Education).

Dr Ian Corrie, *Principal Lecturer in Transformative Learning & Healthcare Leadership, University of Cumbria, Institute of Health, UK*

Ian is a Principal Lecturer within the Institute of Health at the University of Cumbria, the Applied Health Research Theme Lead within the Centre of Research for Health and Society, and a Visiting Professor at the University of Sunderland. Ian is interested in transformative learning, coaching and disruptive pedagogical approaches in higher education.

Dr Erik Cownie, *Lecturer in Community Development, Ulster University, UK*

Erik has a long-standing research interest in educational disadvantage in working-class communities and in widening access to higher education.

Dr Anne Danby, *Course Director, College of Science and Engineering, University of Derby, UK*

Anne has navigated an eclectic career in quality, regulation, course design and teaching at (post-92) universities committed to widening participation and social mobility. She is also a farmer, beekeeper, ecological consultant and globe trotter, with a particular interest in African forestry projects.

Clare Dunn, *Senior Manager, Recognition of Prior Learning, Open University, UK*

Clare is passionate about widening access to higher education and promotes recognition of prior learning as a mechanism to achieve this. For almost 14 years Clare delivered higher education qualifications within further education colleges and supported students in their transition to higher-level study.

Sheila Dunn, *Head of Quality and International Development, Scottish Credit and Qualifications Framework Partnership (SCQFP), UK*

Sheila is currently Head of Quality and International Development at the SCQF Partnership, where she leads on activities relating to the quality and integrity of the national qualifications framework (SCQF) as well as its links to other national qualifications frameworks across the UK and around the world. She has worked in education in Scotland for 30 years, beginning her career as a researcher before moving into a range of quality assurance roles in both the higher and further education sectors before joining the SCQF Partnership in 2012.

Professor Volker Gehmlich, *Teacher in Business Management, Osnabrück University of Applied Sciences, Germany*

Volker is involved at an institutional level with the development and management of innovative study programmes. He has international experience of the development and implementation of University-Enterprise Training Partnerships; University Cooperation; the European Credit Accumulation and Transfer System; and European, national, sectoral and institutional qualifications frameworks.

Rev Dr Isy Hawthorne-Steele, *Senior Lecturer, Director of Research, Ulster University, UK*

Isy has been involved with community and youth work since the mid-1970s as a teacher, youth and community worker, and lecturer at Ulster from 1995. She is passionately involved in faith-based social action projects.

Professor Catherine Hayes, *Professor of Health Professions Pedagogy & Scholarship, Faculty of Health Sciences and Wellbeing, University of Sunderland, UK*

Catherine is a National Teaching Fellow and Principal Fellow of the Higher Education Academy. A podiatrist by original profession, she has worked extensively within higher education curriculum development and pedagogy in health professions for the past 20 years.

James Keevy, *Chief Executive Officer, JET Education Services, South Africa*

James is an experienced policy researcher who has worked in South Africa, Africa and internationally for the last 25 years. His specific areas of expertise include qualifications, the recognition of learning, digitalisation and the professionalisation and migration of teachers.

Dr Liz Marr, *Pro-Vice-Chancellor (Students), The Open University, UK*
Liz has over 30 years of experience in teaching and learning in UK higher education, with a particular interest in social justice and social mobility, and is passionate about opening opportunity for all who wish to participate in learning, both formally and informally. She is currently Vice President of the European Association of Distance Teaching Universities, having recently completed a term as President.

Dr Bob Morgan, *Visiting Professor, Nurtingen University, Germany*
Bob was a lecturer in international business/economics and is currently a consultant in the construction of international university networks. He has published widely on the Welsh economy and taught in several European and American universities.

Dr Rosemary Moreland, *Senior Lecturer/Community Development Subject Lead, Ulster University, UK*
Rosemary has been involved in teaching and researching adult and community education since 1989 at Ulster University. She previously held the role of Access Partnership Manager for Social Sciences at Ulster University and is currently Chief Editor of the *Adult Learner Journal.*

Beverley Oliver, *Emeritus Professor (Institutional Affiliations), Deakin University, Australia*
Beverley is a higher education consultant and former Deputy Vice Chancellor at Deakin University, Australia. Beverley researches and publishes in areas related to higher education quality and curriculum reform, graduate attributes and employability, emerging digital education models and micro-credentials.

Maeve Paris, *Senior Lecturer and Partnership Manager, Ulster University, UK*
Maeve is a Senior Lecturer in Computer Science, and Partnership Manager for Computing, Engineering and the Built Environment. She supports regional HE in Further Education partners in the delivery of high-quality validated provision to around 1,500 students enrolled on Foundation degrees and Access to HE Diplomas across Northern Ireland.

Dr Wayne Turnbull, *Liverpool John Moores University and the Northern Universities Consortium for Credit Accumulation and Transfer, UK*
Wayne is an historian with over a quarter of a century of experience of academic policies and administrative processes. He is an adviser, author and authority on higher education policy and the history of the UK university sector.

Harvey Woolf, *Honorary Research Fellow, University of Wolverhampton, UK*
Harvey was Head of Academic Standards at the University of Wolverhampton, where he also taught history. He has researched and written on modularity, external examiners, assessment in the workplace and reflective learning, and academic regulations.

Foreword

When you think about it, how is it possible to compare a unit of learning in maths with one in nursing or fine art? The content is not only different, but requires different learner skills; the purpose of denoting a pass is different (you don't die from messing up a painting); and the time it takes an individual to complete a unit of learning will depend on them as much as on the work being required. Any solution will, in effect, be a decision to agree, not the solution to an insoluble problem.

Take the qualifications we assume are comparable – are all GCSEs the same? Really, are you sure? Crucially, how do you know? A-levels? Is an HNC the same as the first year of an undergraduate degree? At the risk of becoming existential, what do we mean by parity?

Of course, this is the external view. Inside a university system, any experienced lecturer has a good sense of what a unit of learning looks and feels like, and is adept at designing such a unit. But then again, they generally do it within one discipline and can simultaneously stop worrying about parity across disciplines and rely on a whole set of implicit learning from peers to ground-truth their designs. Does this result in parity of learning demand for qualification gain? I don't think we can be sure.

This is where credit and notions of credit attribution come into play, and where this book does great service in opening up the complexity and ambiguity of this rather simple idea. Credit doesn't solve the problems I have highlighted, but it offers a way to provide an agreed consistency to something emergent and inherently inconsistent. By dividing learning into credit-bearing courses, it is possible to break down the amount of time and effort that a learner puts into the sub-disciplines of their work. By assigning an expectation of effort to a unit of credit, it is possible to gain a view of the work required to attain a qualification. By considering the award of credit for prior learning which may have been informal, it is possible to allow a more experienced learner to start at the right place for them within a qualification.

But at the end of the day, credit is a construct that provides the appearance of consistency in the profoundly inconsistent space that is learning. It matters, it helps, but it is also a fudge. This book explores, with much more nuance than this foreword, these intellectual challenges and ambiguities. It should be required reading for anyone who wants to understand how value can be linked to study and how a qualification can be pinned down, if only through a rather convoluted process of abstraction. This is a timely and effective contribution with much to commend it.

Professor Sue Rigby
Vice Chancellor, Bath Spa University
Chair, 2021 Credit Framework for England Advisory Group

Introduction

Wayne Turnbull and Harvey Woolf

Alright, but apart from widening participation, recognising prior attainment, quantifying study, facilitating equivalence of learning, embedding flexibility, expediting student mobility, rewarding achievement and promoting transparency of systems, processes and outcomes ... what has credit ever done for us?

This is not a book about credit *per se*, but about the plethora of manifestations, applications and outcomes that arise from the use of credit, particularly but not exclusively in UK higher education. It is at heart a book about the relationship between learners and the contexts in which they learn, mediated through multiple lenses and expert perspectives on credit policy and practice. As befits a concept as multi-faceted and flexible as credit, the critical light cast by the authors of this book is refracted into diverse and perceptive analyses. Credit is both local and global, embedded within institutional curricula and an international currency for mobile learners. The story of credit is one without end, following a complex narrative in which credit is variously championed, rejected and indeed ignored.

Emerging as if from the ether in the UK higher education sector with the launch of the Open University in the summer of 1969, credit was *borrowed* from the college system in the United States of America.[1] Although Lin-Manuel Miranda depicted founding father Alexander Hamilton as having 'my honour, a tolerance for pain, a couple of college credits and my top-notch brain' (Miranda 2016), such a claim is sadly anachronistic. It was over 100 years after Hamilton matriculated from King's College in New York when the Carnegie Unit of quantifying study time was introduced into the US college system (Turnbull 2020). By the turn of the twenty-first century, credit had become an international phenomenon, articulated in numerous forms in multiple locations.

Alongside the quantification of learning achieved in UK higher education (especially in flexible- or distance-modes), credit was also initially perceived as a valuable mechanism for quantifying experiential learning and widening access. Early UK credit practitioners therefore supported university applicants lacking traditional A Level entry qualifications and brokered the movement of learners between contexts. Notwithstanding the positive outcome of the feasibility study by the Department for Education and Science published in 1979 in the Toyne Report (DES 1979), the expansion of credit policy and practice in the UK higher education sector was piecemeal and spasmodic throughout the 1980s. Indeed, credit may have remained peripheral and inconsequential but for the rapid expansion of UK higher education in the 1990s in which the costs of sectoral enlargement would in part be met by increased efficiency in academic delivery.

Almost overnight, credit in the UK higher education sector ceased to be associated with episodic acts of benevolent learner support and instead became tarnished by association with the managerialism in which university curricula were hastily modularised to facilitate expansion of student numbers in pursuit of mass higher education. It is unfortunate that at the point where opportunities for offering flexible study modes, multi-disciplinarity and student-focused curricular provision became realised in the higher education sector in the UK, academic communities largely opposed the proposition (Trowler 1998). In the mid-1990s, an ambitious manifesto for re-orienting higher education provision around the needs of learners, *Choosing to Change* (HEQC 1994), was rejected amidst criticism of the commodification of higher education embodied in the dystopian rendering of *pick and mix degrees* awarded by McDonald's University. A once-in-a-generation opportunity lost, credit policy and practice in UK higher education drifted into fragmented variation. Whilst most of the outcomes of the National Committee of Inquiry into Higher Education in 1997 (the Dearing Report) were implemented by the Blair administration, the clear recommendation for 'a framework of qualifications based on agreed credits and levels of achievement' (Dearing 1997: 160) was left to wither on the vine.

Over the course of the twenty-first century, the administrative landscape of the UK higher education sector has evolved to comprise a multitude of professional, statutory and regulatory bodies, with prominent roles also played by the devolved administrations of the nations within the UK. At the time of writing, universities in England are subject to regulation by the Office for Students, Scottish universities are regulated by the Scottish Funding Council, the Higher Education Funding Council for Wales regulates Welsh universities, whilst universities in Northern Ireland are subject to regulation by the Department for the Economy. In accordance with the Higher Education and Research Act (HERA 2017), the regulatory authorities are obliged to designate a quality body to safeguard academic standards, a role currently fulfilled by the Quality Assurance Agency for Higher Education. Depending upon location, credit can either be an integral feature of the academic infrastructure, as in the Scottish Credit and Qualifications Framework, or an advisory ancillary adjunct, as in the Higher Education Credit Framework for England (QAA 2021a).

Shortly before publication of this book, the UK higher education sector's designated quality body completed a formal review of the Higher Education Credit Framework for England, initially published in 2008 (QAA 2008). A revised version, now titled *Advice on Academic Credit Arrangements*, has been published alongside a supporting document, *Making Use of Credit: A Companion to the Higher Education Credit Framework for England* (QAA 2021b). This document occupies a liminal space between sectoral regulation and institutional autonomy. For example, whilst the document incorporates a tabular representation of a Credit Framework for England 2021, this is a not the framework of qualifications based on *agreed credits and levels of achievement* envisaged by

Dearing but rather *advice* that 'allows higher education providers the freedom to adopt and adapt elements as appropriate to their needs and circumstances' (QAA 2021b: 5).

The *Advice on Academic Credit Arrangements* includes a summary of guiding principles for the use of credit: clarity, consistency, flexibility and creativity. Within the *clarity* theme, credit supports transparent learner progression and codifies academic standards via credit levels. *Consistency* and *flexibility* are expressed through notional learning time and the promotion of common curricula structures, although the 'currency' of 10 hours per credit is now presented as a 'typical' measure (as discussed in the ensuing chapters, 'common currencies', rather than heterogeneity, facilitate learner mobility). The *creativity* of credit supports innovative academic programme design (including interdisciplinarity) and the creation of responsive products (such as microcredentials) within the UK higher education marketplace. Yet, as will be explored within this book, much of this remains aspirational, as credit's latent potential has largely been unrealised and will be likely to remain so south of Hadrian's Wall whilst credit 'operates outside the regulatory framework in England' (QAA 2021b: 5).

Governments of various political hues in recent decades have taken steps towards the creation of a UK higher education market, in which the student is positioned as a customer. If the higher education sector is to operate as a marketplace, then credit will be its currency. Yet the flexibility, mobility and self-determination offered to customers within a marketplace do not characterise the relationship between UK students and their universities. Other than study abroad, there is little capacity for demand-led learner mobility in this *market*. However, not only has the UK de-coupled from the European Union, it has also withdrawn from participation in the ERASMUS student exchange programme in which students transferred credits *sans frontières* as they broadened their educational horizons. A replacement *Turing Scheme* is under development at the time of writing, which may offer a new chapter to credit's ongoing story (Staufenberg 2021).

In the context of these changes, it is timely to capture a series of snapshots of credit policy and practice. We are indebted to our chapter authors for their insightful, expert contributions. All chapters in this book are written in a personal capacity and the views expressed herein are the authors' own. The book is structured around three sections, each exploring a different aspect of UK credit practice: recognition of learner achievement, credit practice in the four nations of the UK and learner mobility. Observations on the synergies between chapters – and between sections – are explored in the concluding chapter. A brief summary of each of the chapters is provided below.

It is fitting that a book such as this should begin with a chapter about the Open University (OU). Since the launch of the OU in 1969, when it essentially established the use of credit in UK higher education, it has led the field in the provision of accessible, flexible, distance-taught higher education in the UK. Long before the expansion of higher education in the UK, the OU championed the participation of students whose pathways had not followed the traditional

A Level route. Such is the distinct character of its academic delivery, the very existence of the OU challenges other universities to orient their curricula around students. However, the OU is a magnificent manifestation of the principles underpinning widening access, learner-centred education and the centrality of credit. In *Credit where credit's due – the role of the Open University in credit recognition*, Clare Dunn and Liz Marr of the Open University reflect on over 50 years of credit practice at the OU and the process through which credit is awarded in respect of prior learning. Clare and Liz also look forward to future credit developments, building upon the principles established by the credit pioneers who sought to widen access to a higher education system run by and for a privileged few.

Ian Corrie and Catherine Hayes explore the relationship between learners and education providers in *Tripartite innovation as a bridge to transformation: UK military medical services and university credit transfer systems.* This chapter provides an insight into the practical function of accreditation of prior learning from the perspective of reciprocal needs of a higher education institution and Army Medical Services, highlighting the challenges and opportunities of accrediting current and veteran military personnel. The chapter considers issues such as parity in the award of credit for prior experiential learning, and the mapping of transferrable skills between contexts.

Credit provides a means of formally recognising previously attained learner achievement, as the Army Medical Services case study demonstrates. Such recognition can either be integrated within a programme of study or may serve as a bridge between study at different settings. The majority of UK higher education students fit a traditional demographic mould, although a commitment to lifelong learning supports the participation of mature learners alongside school-leavers. Non-traditional participation has been facilitated over time by the Open College movement, which pioneered the use of credit and the brokerage of formal reciprocal recognition agreements. Many mature students progress to higher education via bespoke programmes of learning, which are the subject of the chapter entitled *The Janus of the Access to HE Diploma: Rethinking qualifications, units, credits and levels.* In her chapter, Sam Broadhead draws upon evidence from access practitioners and their students to analyse the impact of credit within the Access to HE Diploma qualification.

Any reader who assumes that credit policy and practice are consistently managed between UK universities will be disabused of such a notion in reading the fourth chapter of this book. The chapter *Variations in the award of credit in UK higher education* emerges from research undertaken within UK universities on their academic regulations governing student achievement and progression. Wayne Turnbull and Harvey Woolf also drew upon the canon of research published by the Student and Classification Working Group (SACWG) on this theme (see, for example, Yorke et al. 2004; Stowell et al. 2016). They map the different regulatory positions occupied by UK universities in the award of credit, including the ability of a student to gain credit following re-assessment in light of initial failure. They demonstrate how, by subjecting the same student profile to the regulatory frameworks of multiple universities, student performance alone does not determine whether that student is deemed to be successful in the attainment of credit. The authors explore the implications of such inconsistency of credit regulation and practice for the sector, particularly for learners.

It would be remiss of any study of credit policy and practice in the UK to ignore the diversity of credit practice between the four nations of England, Northern Ireland, Scotland and Wales. The middle section of the book offers an overview of contemporary credit practice within the four nations, each of which is the subject of a discrete chapter. Alphabetically, we begin with a chapter on England authored by Darryll Bravenboer. One of Darryll's roles is as Convenor of the SEEC network of the Universities Association for Lifelong Learning in Higher Education, in which universities and HE providers collaborate to advance the use and practice of academic credit. His chapter, *The official discourse of academic credit in England*, provides a detailed analysis of the environment in which credit policy with an impact on students in England has been debated and developed.

Colleagues from Ulster University have collaborated to produce the chapter *Widening access and participation in Northern Ireland*. The unique political, social and cultural environments in which the further and higher education institutions in Northern Ireland operate prioritise and value the ethos of widening participation. This chapter offers a clear demonstration of the ethical underpinnings of facilitating wider access to higher education, as well as the collective economic benefits of public investment in a skilled, stable society. Rosemary Moreland, Erik Cownie, Isobel Hawthorne-Steele and Maeve Paris provide an overview of governmental and institutional policies over time, in which to contextualise current developments. They illustrate their theme with two case studies: Foundation degrees (an intermediate-level qualification) and the operation of the Accreditation of Prior Learning in further education colleges in Northern Ireland.

Credit policy and practice is unevenly managed amongst all of the nations of the UK, but the most complete and comprehensive expression of credit as an integrated element of a consistent framework can be found in Scotland. In *The role of credit in the Scottish Credit and Qualifications Framework*, Sheila Dunn of the SCQF Partnership Executive Team reviews two decades of progress in which the Framework has embedded credit in lifelong learning. In the context of the SCQF, the credit framework is presented as a means of planning an individual's learning journey. It also provides a mechanism for explaining the equivalences between qualifications of different types offered in different settings. In her chapter, Sheila outlines the underpinning principles of the Framework, offering an expert analysis of the benefits and challenges arising from the Scottish approach.

Over the past quarter of a century, the political map of the United Kingdom has been unevenly transformed by the initial introduction and progressive extension of the devolution of powers to the respective nations, as illustrated by the example of Wales. Bob Morgan taught in the Welsh university sector for many of these interesting years, enjoying a front-row seat in the theatre of developing events. His chapter, *Credit and curriculum in Wales, devolution, Bologna and Brexit: An eclectic journey*, navigates the reader through the many and varied developments in Welsh education policy and (in common with the later chapter by Volker Gehmlich) explores relationships with the European Higher Education Area. Bob's chapter is timely in commenting on the aftershocks of Brexit and the potential impact of this change upon the higher education landscape in Wales.

Most of the chapters in this book are written about the UK higher education sector from a UK higher education perspective. However, our final section focusing on learner mobility varies the perspective through regional, European and trans-global lenses. This approach reflects the inherent flexibility of credit, focusing on the potential for realising opportunities for technology-enabled, twenty-first-century universal learners. In her chapter, *The use of credit in institutional collaboration: The example of the Midlands Enterprise Universities' Credit Compass Initiative*, Anne Danby chronicles how a partnership of English universities has responded to the requirements enshrined in the 2017 Higher Education and Research Act (HERA) for Student Protection Plans and student transfers. Anne illustrates how a working group drawn from the member universities produced a co-ordinated plan for dealing with the consequences for students of course closures, developing a service to facilitate and promote student mobility with recognition of prior learning between members and which has the potential to significantly exceed HERA's formal requirements.

Proof, should it be needed, that we do not intend to ignore the elephant in the corner of the room can be found in the chapter authored by the leading German expert on credit systems and lifelong learning, Volker Gehmlich of Osnabrück University. In *Brexit – its impact on learner mobility and recognition of qualifications from the perspective of learners and providers of education and training programmes*, Volker considers the implications for numerous stakeholders in higher education of the withdrawal of the UK from the European Union and from the flagship ERASMUS programme. The aftershocks of withdrawal were still being felt as the chapter was being written. Balancing analysis of the implications of past actions with an element of future-gazing, Volker provides an informed overview of the likely impact of Brexit on credit and learner mobility in the UK.

The final chapter of the book extends our perspective even further, incorporating references as wide-ranging as the Australian Qualifications Framework, credential verification services in the USA and the UNESCO Institute for Lifelong Learning. *Credit and recognition in a more interoperable global context: Implications for data privacy, certification and the recognition of prior learning* is written by Beverley Oliver and James Keevy. They examine the complex context in which recognition of learner achievement operates. This chapter not only places the UK higher education sector into a global context, but it demonstrates the synergies between the operation of credit systems in widely different contexts. Perhaps most importantly, it offers a gentle and reassuring reminder to anyone engaged in the operation of credit systems in the UK that we are not alone in the struggle.

Note

1 There were parallel developments in the UK's further education sector.

References

Dearing, R. (1997) *Higher Education in the Learning Society.* Report of the National Committee of Inquiry into Higher Education (The Dearing Report). London: HMSO. Available at: http://www.educationengland.org.uk/documents/dearing1997/dearing 1997.html (accessed 2 July 2021).

Department of Education and Science (DES) (1979) *Educational Credit Transfer: Feasibility study.* London: HMSO.

HERA (2017) *Higher Education and Research Act.* Available at: legislation.gov.uk (accessed 1 June 2021).

Higher Education Quality Council (HEQC) (1994) *Choosing to Change: Extending access, choice and mobility in higher education, the Report of the HEQC CAT Development Project: Executive Statement & Summary.* London: HEQC.

Miranda, L.-M. (2016) *Hamilton: An American Musical* [Musical], Warner/Chappel.

Quality Assurance Agency (QAA) (2008) *Higher Education Credit Framework for England: Guidance on academic credit arrangements in higher education in England.* Gloucester: QAA.

Quality Assurance Agency (QAA) (2021a) *Higher Education Credit Framework for England: Advice on academic credit arrangements,* 2nd edn. Gloucester: QAA. Available at: https://www.qaa.ac.uk/quality-code/higher-education-credit-framework-for-england (accessed 2 July 2021).

Quality Assurance Agency (QAA) (2021b) *Making Use of Credit: A companion to the Higher Education Credit Framework for England.* Gloucester: QAA. Available at: https://www.qaa.ac.uk/quality-code/higher-education-credit-framework-for-england (accessed 2 July 2021).

Staufenberg, J. (2021) How does the Turing scheme compare to Erasmus?, *FE Week,* 9 March.

Stowell, M., Falahee, M. and Woolf, H. (2016) Academic standards and regulatory frameworks: Necessary compromises?, *Assessment and Evaluation in Higher Education,* 41 (4): 515–31.

Trowler, P. (1998) What managerialists forget: Higher education credit frameworks and managerialist ideology, *International Studies in Sociology of Education,* 8 (1): 91–110.

Turnbull, W. (2020) *A Brief History of Credit in UK Higher Education: Laying Siege to the Ivory Tower.* Bingley: Emerald Publishing.

Yorke, M., Barnett, G., Evanson, P. et al. (2004) Self-help in research and development relating to assessment: A case study, *Assessment and Evaluation in Higher Education,* 29 (4): 389–99.

Part 1

Credit and the recognition of learner achievement

1 Credit where credit's due: the role of the Open University in credit recognition

Clare Dunn and Liz Marr

The establishment of the Open University (OU) in 1969 has arguably had a significant impact on credit accumulation and transfer systems (CATs) in the UK, although Pollard et al. (2017) point out that the concept of credit pre-dates this, noting the significance of the Robbins Report (Parry 2014) in highlighting the opportunities for flexibility and movement between institutions. Despite this relatively long history, however, and the efforts of several networks (e.g. SEEC, NUCCAT), credit mobility as envisaged by the OU is not yet main-streamed in the sector and flexible progression through and between qualification frameworks is still under-developed. Furthermore, devolution of responsibility for higher education to the four nations of the UK has resulted in a diversity of practice in relation to the free movement of credit which varying funding models render difficult to replicate – articulation between higher national and degree qualifications is positively encouraged and funded in Scotland, for example, but less common in England, which is somewhat prob-lematic for a four-nation university.

Successive initiatives in England have toyed with CATs, although policy drivers have varied. As Bekhradnia notes, the agreement between the Council for National Academic Awards (CNAA) and the OU to create a joint credit transfer system was established to 'allow students to apply for credit for work already completed' (2004: 22) and to transfer between OU and CNAA courses. He goes on to cite the Robertson Report (1994), *Choosing to Change*, as another attempt to convince a sceptical sector of the need for such schemes. Similarly, Schuller and Watson (2009) identified a national system of CATS as a priority for the New Labour government, distilled from three influential 1997 reports – Kennedy, Dearing and Fryer (Tight 1998). Schuller and Watson go on to point out, however, that this was 'sadly unrealised' (2009: 146) and provide a still-recognisable list of reasons for failure.

In 2017, work on the Higher Education and Research Act brought renewed attention to credit transfer but as a mechanism to allow students to trade up universities, ostensibly to drive up standards (Dent et al. 2017; Marr and Bravenboer 2017). And as we write, a Skills White Paper (DfE 2021) envisages a revised approach to loan entitlement, usable for modules at higher technical and degree levels regardless of whether they are provided in colleges or universities. The intention is to allow greater flexibility for learners – allowing them to space out their studies, transfer credits between institutions, and partake in more part-time study. Whether this ideal, which should go a long way in breaking down the systemic and artificial divide between technical and academic higher-level learning, is ever realised remains to be seen. It is, however, something the OU has long lobbied for.

In this chapter, we look back and forwards, focusing on the OU's approach to the use and value of credit. We consider the role it can play in part-time learning, the opportunities and constraints the University encounters, relating these to sector issues around CATS, credit transfer and recognition of prior learning, both certificated and experiential. We also describe some current developments in micro-credentials and the OU's innovative Open box curriculum which extends the possibilities of the use of credit in lifelong learning.

What is credit and why does it matter?

The use of credit in higher education (HE) enhances the transparency of qualifications and facilitates the notion of fair recognition that has been one of the core objectives of the Bologna Process since its launch in 1999 (Chaparro et al. 2017). Through this process, academic credit brings parity to learning irrespective of where it has been achieved, bridging the gap between formal, non-formal and informal learning opportunities. Of importance here is the notion that academic credit, in the form of either 'prior educational qualifications or HE credit awarded and recognised for the purpose of entry to or transfer between HE institutions' is a form of 'market currency' (Marr and Bravenboer 2017: 1). It can be used to 'buy' entry to an institution with advanced standing (e.g. directly into Level 5 or 6) or into employment and it is, or should be, an absolute measure of equivalence of learning. However, although the Higher Education Credit Framework (QAA 2008, 2021) seeks to promote a common understanding of the value of credits, their perceived worth might differ between higher education institutions (HEIs) and in different contexts. As Schuller and Watson point out: 'Individual institutions … have for various reasons (especially perceptions of relative status) been reluctant to accept the judgements of other institutions about the achievement of students and its relationship to that of those that they have admitted to the beginning of their own courses' (2009: 146).

The review of literature by Pollard et al. (2017) suggests that, as a tool, credit can provide HEIs with a 'common language' that helps to compare and recognise learning that has been achieved in different institutions and contexts. Bekhradnia explains that 'credits are quite simply a means of attaching relative values to the different components of a course' (2004: 5), those components most commonly being modules. Credit itself is measured as time spent on learning, thus some modules may be longer than others and carry more credit but there is agreement on the overall quantity of learning which constitutes a qualification.

However, Blackman has argued that the premise that academic credit can be viewed as common currency should be questioned when the UK higher education sector is 'differentiated by radically different degrees of academic selection' (2017: 6). This is an issue of which the OU is only too aware. Although the University's credit transfer process is designed with the view that all credit is equal, this is clearly not reciprocated in some institutions, which list OU credit as entry for Level 4 study, despite operating equally in a quality and standards framework that relies on peer review through the external examiner system.

And herein lies the rub. Credentials, as Gallagher (2016) notes, are important signifiers in the job market and degrees are unlikely to become less significant in the near future, even when new credentials emerge. Market insight obtained for the OU (unpublished) in relation to employer appetite for micro-credentials[1] reveals that although the award of credit to allow stacking for a credential was not a primary driver for them, it was an important badge of quality. Research with students conducted by Pegg and Di Paolo (2013) identified learning to obtain credentials as a key theme in their motivation to pursue credit transfer as the means to complete what they described as 'unfinished business'. In the context of an economic imperative where rapid technological development requires constant re- and up-skilling, the possibility of making every credit count in a lifelong learning journey becomes more acute. Thus, the role of credit and its recognition are important foundations for lifelong learning journeys (Giddens 1991, cited by Harris et al. 2014).

Credit recognition and sector challenges

Despite being practised in the UK for several decades (Harris et al. 2014) and providing a plethora of benefits to learners, HEIs and employers, the lack of a unified system for the implementation, monitoring and reporting of recognition of prior learning (RPL) makes it difficult to identify the scale at which RPL is utilised across the sector (Atlay and Turnbull 2017). At the OU, recognition of prior learning is defined as the identification, assessment and formal acknowledgement of learning and achievement that occurred at some time in the past that is taken into account when admitting a student to a course of study. It is viewed as an umbrella term to encompass different ways to recognise an individual's prior learning, including the recognition of prior certificated learning (RPCL), the recognition of prior experiential learning (RPEL) and direct entry or, as often defined within the sector, entry with advanced standing.

The devolved nature of higher education in the UK means that HEIs cannot be held accountable for the level to which they recognise prior certificated or experiential learning and contribute to student mobility. Similarly, the delegation of ensuring quality and standards to individual institutions also presents challenges. For credit recognition to be fully embedded across the sector, mutual trust in each other's quality assurance processes is essential and institutions need confidence in assessment decisions. Although the presence of the Quality Assurance Agency (QAA) and UK Quality Code help to instil this trust, barriers still exist (Pollard et al. 2017). Taking the example of RPEL, Pokorny (2006) points out that processes which seek equivalence in our established curricula and pedagogies result in us only recognising learning that is familiar to us. These are all challenges the OU faces in managing its credit recognition processes.

Although the majority of HEIs will have an institutional policy for recognising prior learning, the autonomous nature of higher education in the UK in terms of curriculum design can challenge implementation of such policies and the recognition of credit. Institutions are therefore free to develop qualifications without regard for RPL, which can make it difficult to award credit for prior learning when a close match in learning outcomes[2] and content is required. Although subject benchmark statements exist to 'describe the nature of study and the academic standards expected of graduates in a specific subject area' (QAA 2020), institutions have the autonomy to determine the actual content and associated learning outcomes at qualification and modular level. This can lead to inter-institutional differences in content, resulting in difficulties in mapping credit to qualifications with the same title but in a different institution. This, counter-intuitively, may result in differential recognition of qualifications that exist together on qualification frameworks. The perceived equivalence of any learning is thus in the hands of individual HEIs and the rules that underpin their RPL policies and ultimately with the academic assessors that are making the decisions on what does or does not fit. Learners might then find themselves being offered different levels of recognition by institutions for the same prior qualification. Even within the OU, it is possible for an applicant's prior credit to be assessed differently, depending on the qualification they apply for.

Credit at the Open University

The mission of the OU is to be open to people, places, methods and ideas. The reasoning behind its establishment was clearly summarised by Geoffrey Crowther, the first Chancellor, when he stressed that the University's 'most urgent' priority was 'to cater for the many thousands of people, fully capable of a higher education, who, for one reason or another, do not get it, or do not get as much of it as they can turn to advantage, or as they discover, sometimes too late, that they need' (1969: 1). He further noted that, 'Only in recent years have we come to realise how many such people there are, and how large are the gaps in educational provision through which they can fall. The existing system, for all its expansion, misses and leaves aside a great unused reservoir of human talent and potential' (1969: 1).

The open entry approach which derives from the mission and purpose of the University means that for most courses there are no formal entry requirements.

In its early manifestation, many students were teachers seeking to acquire hitherto unrequired credentials in the form of qualifications and the University had only one degree, a general BA, to which a BSc was later added in 1996 (Cooke et al. 2018). Although not formally defined in credit terms, each course, beginning at foundation level, was seen as one credit and six were required for an ordinary degree, eight for an honours degree. With the introduction of the UK credit framework in 2004, credit systems stabilised around 120 credits for the equivalent of a year of study and the OU adopted the sector norm of 360 credits for an honours degree and 300 without honours. Unlike much of the sector, however, the OU moved to credit sizes of 60 and 30, with some 15- and some 10-credit modules. This was designed to facilitate the acquisition of credit at flexible rates, allowing for part-time study and recognising that students within this system could collect credit and then cash in for a qualification. At the same time, the OU began to expand its subject-specific degrees but maintained the general BA/BSc, rebranding as the BA/BSc (Honours) Open degree in 2005. The BA/BSc (Honours) Open degree is still one of the most popular qualifications for direct entrants as it allows the construction of a personalised programme of study, but is also popular with credit transfer students as it will accept general[3] as opposed to specific credit. We might consider this as catering to another unused reservoir – that of the many people who begin study but for one reason or another do not complete it.

Credit recognition at the Open University

Credit recognition is fundamental to the OU's mission and through RPL provides a mechanism to achieve the vision of reaching 'more students with life-changing learning that meets their needs and enriches society'.

The OU formalised its approach to RPL in a policy approved by its Senate in 2015. Subsequent changes were made to the policy in 2018 to widen the University's approach to direct entry and in 2020 in response to the COVID-19 pandemic. This latter change sought to ensure that students applying for credit transfer did not have to repeat any unnecessary learning if compensation[4] or condonement[5] was used by the awarding institution in response to the pandemic. Substantial effort was devoted to the development of this policy in order to ensure that it met the needs of students, the University and other stakeholders, that it protected quality and standards, and was future-proof in anticipating innovation, particularly around recognition of non-formal, informal and experiential learning. Our initial research and consultations reflected the many benefits identified in the literature. For learners it reduces unnecessary duplication of learning and can accelerate progression to employment. When prior certificated learning has been completed, the mechanism of credit transfer can enable and provide an opportunity to top up sub-qualifications to a full honours degree. The OU also found, in line with Pollard et al. (2017), that it can support learner mobility, reduce the risk of drop-out because the time commitment required to complete study is less, and offer greater choice and flexibility for learners.

For the University itself, it was clear that the provision of RPL opportunities made us more responsive and accessible to the student market, contributed to our widening access goals, and provided an opportunity to build partnerships with other institutions, employers and the wider community. As we will show, opportunities to bridge the gap between formal, non-formal and informal learning opportunities were identified as a result of working on the policy and there is now wider acknowledgement that higher-level learning can take place outside traditional university settings (Marr and Bravenboer 2017). We also found, like Pollard et al. (2017), that our credit transfer students contribute to an increase in retention and completion.

The OU recognises prior certificated learning that has been awarded academic credit through a process of credit transfer and awards either module, stage or general credit exemption. Prior certificated learning that has taken place at higher education level but does not bear academic credit (for example, professional development awards) is also recognised by the OU through a credit assessment process which evaluates the level, credit value and quality of the prior learning and assessment. Through the operation of a credit rating panel, the University previously offered a credit rating service for non-credit-bearing courses that were offered by professional organisations. The limitation of this approach was that the panel did not *award* credit but *rated* it in credit terms. The value of the credit could therefore only be recognised in OU qualifications. Furthermore, the process itself was expensive thus, despite several providers using the service, the number of learners seeking to cash in their credit towards an OU qualification was very low and the OU took the decision in 2016 to disband the panel. In partial compensation to employers who had found the service valuable, credit assessment was formalised as an operational process to ensure a mechanism continued to exist for the recognition of non-credit-bearing prior certificated learning as part of a qualification.

The University's RPL policy is operationalised centrally through the credit transfer centre, a dedicated administrative team within the University's student recruitment and fees unit that receives and processes applications for RPL. The presence of the credit transfer centre enables the institution to work at scale through streamlined processes for the administration and recognition of credit, liaising with academics in faculties where mapping is required. These processes allow the augmentation of a knowledge base to reduce the repeated mapping of frequently used qualifications, such as Higher National Certificates (HNCs) and Higher National Diplomas (HNDs). Although still referred to as the credit transfer centre, the team has wider responsibility, including processing RPEL applications for apprenticeship qualifications. Between 2014/15 and 2019/20, the centre has, on average, received applications from approximately 7,000 applicants each year. Of these, just under 5,900 on average per year have received an award of credit transfer. It should be noted that the OU does not make any charge for credit transfer and given that there is never full take-up of awards, return on investment is uncertain, although it is aligned to the mission of openness. The most common study type for recognition is incomplete degrees followed by HNCs and HNDs. In line with its mission, the University's RPL policy provides an inclusive offer to students, allowing up to a maximum of two-thirds of a qualification to be achieved through RPL, and recognising prior study completed up to a maximum of 16 years prior to the start of study on an OU qualification, subject to limits set in individual qualification regulations. Although most qualifications permit the maximum volume of prior learning, some variations do exist across the institution. In some cases, this is to meet professional, statutory or regulatory body requirements but in others the structure of the qualification and size of modules makes the award of two-thirds challenging. As noted above, it is quite possible that the amount of credit awarded for the same prior learning might differ between qualifications. Using a centralised as opposed to localised recognition process does, however, enable the institution to monitor the type of study being transferred into OU qualifications and ensures that the agreed principles of the RPL policy that have been approved for each qualification are applied. These include the maximum amount of credit that can be awarded in recognition of prior learning, the age of prior learning and the award of either module or general credit exemption.

The credit transfer centre holds an administrative role within this process but the decision-making responsibility for the recognition of prior learning (certificated or experiential) lies with the academic assessor. Once the credit transfer centre has confirmed that the prior learning is eligible for recognition and meets the core principles of the RPL policy, the designated academic assessor(s) within faculties is required to evaluate the suitability of the prior learning for recognition against specified modules within their qualification. For some qualifications, the existence of an approved precedent award, which formally endorses the award of module, stage or general credit exemption, allows the credit transfer centre to make an award of credit transfer without the need for individual academic assessment. Precedent awards are subject to annual review, but once in operation increase the speed at which a student can receive their award of credit transfer.

The RPL policy is mission aligned in being open to a wide range of qualifications, including those achieved within the European Higher Education Area and internationally. Although operating across borders can present challenges for the recognition of prior learning, the presence of the European Credit Transfer and Accumulation System (ECTS) supports the recognition of European higher education qualifications within the University.

A unique offering of the University's RPL process is the choice and flexibility it allows. Learners can apply to have their prior study recognised against three qualifications and will in addition to this be automatically assessed against the BA/BSc (Honours) Open degree. This qualification is interdisciplinary in nature and allows a learner to personalise their study path to meet their personal as well as professional needs, which is particularly desirable if learners are looking to change their study or career path. Consequently, the BA/BSc (Honours) Open degree attracts the largest number of students with credit transfer in their profile.

Future developments at the OU

Building on the University's commitment to RPL, there are several innovations both in train and in plan. The emergence of degree apprenticeships has, in recent years, raised the profile of RPEL by making the assessment of prior learning and experience central to the application process. Not only does the presence of RPEL here push 'the boundary of what higher education actually is' (Blackman 2017: 7), it fundamentally acknowledges that 'higher-level learning does not only take place in universities or higher education institutions' (Marr and Bravenboer 2017: 2).

Within the context of prior learning, the use of credit has an important role to play in the recognition of prior experiential learning. By recognising an individual's experiential learning, the use of credit moves beyond the scope of formal certificated study to more informal, naturally occurring learning that takes place at work, during voluntary activity and throughout key life experiences. As Garnett and Caveye (2015) point out, drawing on Mumford and Roodhouse (2010), this provides an avenue for individuals to engage in higher education study 'who might otherwise be excluded by a lack of formal qualifications' (2015: 29).

The mechanism for recognising informal or experiential learning for online and distance universities like the OU is, however, far from straightforward and requires innovative solutions to operationalise at scale. If not achieved, the risk as Harris (2000, cited by Pokorny et al. 2017) found was that the very process could become a lone one for learners, which could deter some from applying – 'particularly individuals who have had limited interaction with formal education and who lack confidence to go through what appears to be a highly confusing process' (Bowman et al. 2003: 27, cited by Claridge and Felce 2017: 93). This could result in learners having to repeat study of knowledge or skills that they have already achieved and paying again for the privilege.

Although various models have been used to recognise experiential learning at the OU, the current RPEL offer is still in its infancy. To enhance the delivery of degree apprenticeships, the University has recently piloted two approaches to recognising prior experiential learning: a traditional portfolio-based approach, and the use of a knowledge- and skills-based test followed by written assessment tasks. Early, tentative conclusions suggest that the method used to assess experiential learning is likely to differ depending on subject matter and the content of the module for which recognition is sought. The development of a 'one-size-fits-all' approach is unlikely to meet the needs of all qualifications.

In order to successfully implement RPEL processes, a shared understanding of what constitutes university-level learning is needed between the learner and assessor (Pokorny et al. 2017), which might be better enabled through the award of general credit (Blackman 2017), facilitating the benchmarking of learning against relevant level descriptors such as those presented by the Southern England Consortium for Credit Accumulation and Transfer (SEEC 2016). The use of general credit as a mechanism to recognise and formally accredit prior experiential learning could help to build parity between learning experiences that have taken place in different contexts and subject areas, as well as provide a more streamlined approach across qualifications. An accreditation wrapper could be a possible mechanism for capturing generic skills and capabilities that are developed through experience. Within this model, learners could map their experiential learning against level descriptors as opposed to specific module learning outcomes. Subsequent completion of a formal assessment to accredit the learning could then provide the basis for awarding general credit exemption. Such a model could move the focus away from the experience itself to the learning that has been derived from such experience. The context in which the learning has been achieved then becomes somewhat irrelevant because it is the capturing of learning that is of most importance.

The OU has also been piloting the use of Open box modules as a means of recognising non-formal learning. Inspired by Talbot's (2017) survey of institutions awarding credit for MOOC (Massive Open Online Courses) study, the University began to explore ways to provide a credit wrapper in which students could be assessed on their reflection on learning from other sources against an agreed set of learning outcomes. The 30-credit Level 4 module, *Making Your Learning Count*, is an offer on the BA/BSc (Honours) Open degree where students draw on 150 hours of Open Educational Resources (free learning resources such as those available through the University's Open Learn platform), MOOCs and other non-accredited courses. The module is also available as an option in a small number of other qualifications and numbers have increased dramatically since its launch in 2017, with approximately 400 registrations in 2019. Students are supported by a tutor to plan their learning and complete the assessment, whilst developing skills for interdisciplinary study.

In 2021, a postgraduate version of the Open box module, *Advance Your Independent Learning*, was launched as an option in the MA/MSc Open and the use of both under- and postgraduate models are beginning to be adopted in other programmes of study. There is also work underway to use the same approach to assess voluntary work experience in health and social care programmes. A key advantage for learners is that fees for these modules are set at approximately half the usual 30-credit fee at undergraduate level and at approximately two-thirds at postgraduate level, to recognise that the students effectively bring the content themselves.

RPL concepts are also being applied at the OU in relation to the relatively new field of micro-credential production. Developed from the MOOC concept and MOOC platforms such as Coursera or edX, micro-credentials are small, accredited 'chunks' of learning of 10–15 credits for which a fee is paid. Under the Common Microcredential Framework (CMF) developed by the European Association of Distance Teaching Universities (EADTU) working with the European MOOC consortium, these certificated courses carry credit, meet the needs of continuing professional development and preferably have employer endorsement. They should also be 'stackable' into whole qualifications – certificates, diplomas or degrees – although they do not necessarily have to be stacked. The OU is offering micro-credentials on its commercial Futurelearn platform and may consider recognition within OU qualifications, whether they be produced by the OU or other universities. The new European University Alliances are taking similar approaches in offering recognition of credit from all partners to create a single Alliance qualification. These are major steps forward in using RPL principles to effectively realise lifelong learning.

Conclusion

In the ever-changing higher education context, with an increased focus on, and provision for, lifelong learning that meets professional and personal needs, it is increasingly clear that *'what* makes universities unique is not teaching or research but their function of formally recognising learning achievement' (Garnett and Caveye 2015: 30). Through RPL this could, as Marr and Bravenboer (2017) suggest, disrupt the control universities have on higher-level credentials and enable other stakeholders such as employers to have a role in the development of learning pathways. Recognising RPL as a 'specialised pedagogic practice' and sharing conditions that underpin this will be an important mechanism to moving this forward (Pokorny et al. 2017: 19) and ensuring that students are enabled not only to reach their learning goals but also fulfil their potential. Through the way it uses and recognises credit, the OU continues to lead the way in this endeavour.

Notes

1 Short (100–150 hours) sector-endorsed credit-bearing courses designed to help build professional skills and pursue further specialised study.
2 A statement of 'what a learner is expected to know, understand and/or be able to demonstrate after completing a process of learning' (QAA, 2018).
3 Awarded on the basis of the quantity of learning and level demonstrated against the learning outcomes of a qualification as a whole or the learning outcomes of a stage within a qualification, rather than on the detailed learning outcomes of individual modules. This is most commonly allowed against the BA/BSc (Honours) Open degree.
4 The allowance of a marginal failure in a limited number of modules on the basis of an overall performance that is sufficient to merit the award of the qualification concerned. Credit for the failed module is normally awarded but the mark stands.
5 The process that allows a stage to be passed despite failure to achieve 120 passed credits in the stage, provided that a stage average of at least 40% has been achieved over the 120 credits of assessment, including the marks for any failed modules. Credit is not normally awarded and the student is exceptionally awarded the stage.

References

Atlay, M. and Turnbull, W. (2017) *Aspects of Credit Practice in English and Welsh Universities*, UKCF Report #2. London: UK Credit Forum.

Bekhradnia, B. (2004) *Credit Accumulation and Transfer, and the Bologna Process: An overview*. Oxford: HEPI.

Blackman, T. (2017) Recognising prior learning: A window onto what is wrong with higher education, *Widening Participation and Lifelong Learning*, 19 (3): 6–17.

Bowman, K., Clayton, B., Bateman, A. et al. (2003) *Recognition of Prior Learning in the Vocational Education and Training Sector*, Research Report. Adelaide: NCVER.

Chaparro, T.S., Ros, C.E., De Labastida, E.F. et al. (2017) *Current Practices on External Quality Assurance of Academic Recognition Among QA Agencies*. Brussels: ENQA.

Claridge, M. and Felce, A. (2017) Raising awareness, facilitating access, creating opportunity, enabling achievement: Making RPL accessible, *Widening Participation and Lifelong Learning*, 19 (3): 85–97.

Cooke, H., Lane, T. and Taylor, P. (2018) Open by degrees: A case of flexibility or personalisation?, in C. Stevenson (ed.) *Enhancing Education Through Open Degree Programs and Prior Learning Assessment*. Hershey, PA: IGI Global.

Crowther, G. (1969) Speech by Lord Crowther, first Chancellor of the Open University at the presentation of the Charter [Transcript]. Available at: https://www.open.ac.uk/library/digital-archive/pdf/script/script:ous_clip3 (accessed 30 January 2021).

Dent, S., Nightingale, J., Mather, H. et al. (2017) *Should I Stay, or Should I Go?: Student demand for credit transfer and recommendations for policy and practice*. Sheffield: The University of Sheffield.

Department for Education (DfE) (2021) *Skills for Jobs: Lifelong learning for opportunity and growth*. Available at: https://assets.publishing.service.gov.uk/government/uploads/system/uploads/attachment_data/file/953510/skills-for-jobs-lifelong-learning-for-opportunity-and-growth.pdf (accessed 30 January 2021).

Gallagher, S. (2016) *The Future of University Credentials: New Developments at the Intersection of Higher Education and Hiring*. Cambridge, MA: Harvard University Press.

Garnett, J. and Cavaye, A. (2015) Recognition of prior learning: Opportunities and challenges for higher education, *Journal of Work-Applied Management*, 7 (1): 28–37.

Giddens, A. (1991) *Modernity and Self-Identity: Self and Society in the Late Modern Age*. Cambridge: Polity.

Harris, J. (2000) *RPL: Power Pedagogy and Possibility, Conceptual and Implementation Guides*. Pretoria: HSRC Press.

Harris, J., Wihak, C. and Kleef, J.V. (2014) *Handbook of the Recognition of Prior Learning: Research into Practice*. Leicester: NIACE.

Marr, L. and Bravenboer, D. (2017) Editorial: Widening participation, lifelong learning and the role of higher education credit, *Widening Participation and Lifelong Learning*, 19 (3): 1–5.

Mumford, J. and Roodhouse, S. (eds.) (2010) *Understanding Work Based Learning*. London: Gower.

Parry, G. (2014) Robbins and advanced further education, *Higher Education Quarterly*, 68 (2): 187–209.

Pegg, A. and Di Paolo, T. (2013) Narrating unfinished business: Adult learners using credit transfer to re-engage with higher education, *Studies in Continuing Education*, 35 (2): 209–23.

Pokorny, H. (2006) Recognising prior learning: What do we know?, in P. Anderson and J. Harris (eds.) *Re-theorising the Recognition of Prior Learning*. Leicester: NIACE.

Pokorny, H., Fox, S. and Griffiths, D. (2017) Recognition of Prior Learning (RPL) as pedagogical pragmatism, *Widening Participation and Lifelong Learning*, 19 (3): 18–30.

Pollard, E., Hadjivassiliou, K., Swift, S. et al. (2017) *Credit Transfer in Higher Education: A Review of the Literature*. London: Department for Education.

Quality Assurance Agency (QAA) (2008) *Higher Education Credit Framework for England: Guidance on academic credit arrangements in higher education in England*. Gloucester: QAA.

Quality Assurance Agency (QAA) (2018) *QAA Glossary*. Gloucester: QAA.

Quality Assurance Agency (QAA) (2020) *Subject Benchmark Statements*. Available at: https://www.qaa.ac.uk/quality-code/subject-benchmark-statements (accessed 10 February 2021).

Robertson, D. (1994) *Choosing to Change*. London: Education Quality Council.

Schuller, T. and Watson, D. (2009) *Learning Through Life: Inquiry into the Future for Lifelong Learning*. Leicester: NIACE.

SEEC (2016) *Credit Level Descriptors for Higher Education*. London: SEEC.

Talbot, J. (2017) Repurposing MOOCs for the accreditation of prior learning: A survey of practice in University Work Based Learning departments, *Widening Participation and Lifelong Learning*, 19 (3): 113–36.

Tight, M. (1998) Education, Education, Education! The vision of lifelong learning in the Kennedy, Dearing and Fryer reports, *Oxford Review of Education*, 24 (4): 473–85.

2 Tripartite innovation as a bridge to transformation: UK Military Medical Services and university credit transfer systems

Ian Corrie and Catherine Hayes

Introduction

Globally, the incidence of serving and retired military veterans enrolling on higher education programmes is increasing exponentially (Coll et al. 2009). This is supported by the UK Armed Forces Extended Learning Credit (ELC) scheme that enables a significant number of those veterans access to education opportunities (Cable et al. 2021). The scale of such enrolments and the context of a unique professional identity of military personnel pose direct challenges and opportunities for higher education institutions (HEIs) in the constructive alignment of transfer pathways to provide optimal choices for veterans and serving members of the military. In a neoliberalist educational system, these populations are identifiable as a critical source of recruitment, regardless of the academic disciplines or signature pedagogies within which they choose to complete their studies. The wider civic impact[1] of providing education and training for service personnel and veterans is tangible. Tailoring programmes to address individual needs will ensure a demonstrable impact at both personal and professional levels. The tripartite relationship between key industrial sectors, HEIs and the Ministry of Defence (MoD) is crucial in ensuring that students undertaking a liminal shift in career trajectory as part of either lifelong learning or a complete change of career is a valid and reliable opportunity to gain a purposeful qualification, which leads to gainful employment and consequently civic and societal impact. This chapter seeks to explore the barriers and enablers of optimal credit transfer systems operational within the UK higher education sector, with a view to providing a window into the potential issues faced by industry, HEIs and the MoD as a tripartite collective.

Theoretical lenses for accreditation providers

A key issue in the award of accreditation for prior experiential or work-based learning is that of parity and equity within and between educational institutions and the value they place on the attainment of service personnel (Armsby et al. 2006). Highly bureaucratic in terms of official process, the credit transfer systems for serving and veteran military personnel can be unwieldy to implement and lack the parity and equity of decision-making that ought to characterise academic administration and regulatory procedures (McCready 2017). Whilst the credit transfer system for these personnel is complicated by the mapping of transferable skillsets from military to civic scopes of practice, the theoretical basis of this is far less complex. In its most simplistic sense, bureaucratic issues can be understood through a theoretical lens which incorporates both administrative process and the policy underpinning it – that is, the system of Accreditation of Prior Experiential Learning (APEL). Organisationally, within HEIs, there remains a degree of consistency in bureaucratic process, which lends itself well to the theoretical perspectives posited by Selznick (1994) in *The Moral Commonwealth*. What is highlighted are the levels at which reciprocal working practices can be used as a mechanism of co-existence and potential enrichment for all parties (Pouget and Osborne 2004). Neoliberalist business perspectives have commodified education into packages, thereby challenging traditional approaches to governance and accountability in higher education admissions policies (Giroux 2010). This inherent flex has enabled many veterans to become students upon completion of their military service.

The fourfold framework Selznick implements in providing a lens through which administrative processes around which APEL is administered can be divided into:

1 Character attribution
2 Formality versus informality in institutionalisation
3 Thick institutionalisation
4 Lack of institutionalisation.

Selznick's observations on the significance of informal structures pre-existing within formal organisations are that these create a degree of complex ambiguity. Directly linked to processes of APEL, this means that there can be tensions among those facilitating the process whose functional roles may be an embedded part of wider administrative duties. The covenant relationships are individually negotiated between UK HEIs, and the Armed Services have served to transform a functional mapping exercise into one of a moral civic obligation, which can ultimately impact on processes of formal decision-making. In turn, this can impact on the established reciprocal relationships that exist between the military and HEIs (Harvey et al. 2020).

Learning and learners – the challenges of pedagogical mapping

Those frameworks specifically designed to map transferrable skillsets and make tacit issues tangible for formal evaluation can also provide a mix of challenges in administrative practice. One of the main issues is the extent to which constructive alignment of curricula in the form of learning outcomes, mechanisms of teaching, learning and assessment are articulated and have been formalised in practice. Being able to capture military learner experience and align it to pre-set criteria can prove challenging, not least because of the disparate activities and the types of experiences that are to be evaluated and categorised in relation to formal academic awards. Within this context, military learners ought to be delineated into whether they are now veterans or whether they have existing vocational or academic qualifications upon which to build their academic portfolio.

Vignettes from reciprocal praxis

The following vignettes articulate the three alternative perspectives of the university, a lecturer and a student, examined through the lens of narrative inquiry, providing illumination of both the social and personal stories that frame the human aspects of experience, as posited by Webster and Mertova (2007). This approach ascribes the experiences through the eyes of a university lecturer in an Institute of Health, a student from the Army Medical Services, and provides the perspective of the university through the eyes of the authors.

The first vignette explores the university's approach to working with the MoD, in this case Army Medical Services, justifying the application of its policies and procedures and academic regulation to enabling the formalisation and justification of Army curriculum into university credit. The second vignette illuminates the experience of the lecturer in delivering programmes of study to Combat Medical Technicians, and the challenges that this presented for both the student and the lecturer. The third and final vignette ascribes the experiences of a personal journey from the perspective of a student progressing from being at high school, to joining the British Army, achieving the role of Combat Medical Technician and Registered Paramedic, finally completing the journey through becoming a seconded lecturer. Army Medical Services and the university have been collaborating in practice for a significant period of time, educating military Combat Medical Technicians through assigning credit for Army Medical Services qualifications, teaching students on a Certificate in Pre-hospital care, and latterly a Diploma in Paramedic Practice. Those students who successfully complete the Diploma register with the Health and Care Professions Council as paramedics.

Vignette 1: Framing collaboration in practice – the challenge of perspectives

The recognisable discourses and narratives of both higher education and the military are vehicles for the cultural semantics which can potentially also drive miscommunication and misunderstanding, due to complex and ambiguous issues. The processes of language socialisation and the consequential semantic differences, in these bounded contexts, have the potential to set the parameters of belonging of those immersed in formalised cultural and professional identities. Fully understanding the requirement and the context of the setting in which Army Medical Services train was key to comprehending the agency afforded to military personnel and the infrastructure within which this agency can be operationalised. This agency is central to the military training process and the development of professional identity, cultural acclimatisation and in fostering a sense of belonging to a specific role in the military. Military learners are taught in a traditional way that has altered minimally over a century; this initial training is based on the requirement of the service to firstly train recruits as soldiers. Standard-entry soldiers, typically people aged between 18 and 36 years, begin their initial Phase 1 training on direct entry to the Army. Upon completion of this phase, soldiers are awarded their first cap badges, which is followed by disciplinary specific training at Phase 2, in order to prepare recruits for their specific occupational duties as they work as an integral part of the military.

In this study, we specifically examine and illuminate training as a Combat Medical Technician (CMT). Three levels of Combat Medical Technician exist within current military infrastructure. Class 3 CMT is the initial recruit qualification, followed by Class 2 CMT qualification. Soldiers graduate from Phase 2 training as Class 2 CMTs. Personnel then spend a year in the field army, which consolidates their experiential learning and provides them with the opportunity of building a portfolio of clinical evidence. This portfolio and evidence of an enhanced skillset from the experiential learning they undertake provides a set of evidence which enables progression on to their Class 1 CMT, where once formally qualified they are employed/deployed according to need across the Armed Services and relative to the formal level of qualifications they have gained.

Understanding this context provided a curriculum design blueprint for the technical, experiential and academic progression of Combat Medical Technicians at the various developmental milestones of their military trajectories. Thus, the university was able to construct an overview of the alignment between the milestones and academic policy, procedure and regulation to facilitate the award for academic credit for prior learning. This mapping also provided a valuable insight for aligning the requirements of the professional statutory regulatory body, in this case the Health and Care Professions Council (HCPC), with the formal requirements of university validation processes and the context of Army Medical Services. Multiple mapping exercises were undertaken which constructively aligned the requirements and learning outcomes from the university's module and programme outcomes with the existing Army Medical Services Combat Medical Technician training and education pathways. This initial scoping exercise provided delineation of the experiential aspects of the learning, including any placement requirement, from the formal academic aspects, which in turn enabled a formal process of mapping to the academic requirements of the university for formal validation and for approval from the HCPC.

The Framework for Higher Education Qualifications (FHEQ) informs the university process of awarding its validated programmes of study, including that of the accreditation of prior learning (APL). APL is divided into two fundamental components: the first, credit for the 'Accreditation of Prior Certified Learning' (APCL), which in practice is a learning qualification already certified; and secondly, credit for the 'Accreditation of Prior Experiential Learning' (APEL), gained from the active processes of life/work experience. To be awarded the latter, a student must be able to demonstrate that the prior learning proposed for formal accreditation is equivalent to/at the standard of learning required as part of the intended programme of study in respect of skills, subject knowledge, understanding and professional competence. The university Academic Quality Department (AQD) advised and guided the process, with credit being awarded through the formal university processes of accreditation. This entailed mapping subject-specific learning outcomes with formal or experiential learning, depending on whether APCL or APEL was being sought. Throughout this process, close negotiation with the military was maintained; advice and guidance were sought with the subject matter experts (SMEs) in Army Medical Services in order to enable the mutual co-creation, co-justification and co-development of these programmes of study. This ensured a duality in ensuring that both military and higher education vocational training and academic requirements were being met.

In developing a needs-led curriculum and being able to translate and formalise the core knowledge and skills required by Combat Medical Technicians into practice, core assumptions have to be challenged, deconstructed and reassembled in a manner that is reflective of a programme with both academic credibility for validation purposes but more significantly fitness for purpose across a whole array of situated contexts of emergency care provision. Central to this is the capacity for interactive dialogue, which is reciprocally understood and mutually constructed. Stakeholder relationships such as this are centred on trust, respect and the open regard for the need to question, interrogate and being able to test decisions regarding strategic curriculum development proposals. More important than the development of curricula in this sense are their justification and constructive alignment with the need for optimal performance of Combat Medical Technicians in practice. It is the degree of reciprocal agency that both academics and military leaders are afforded in developing this interactive dialogue that ultimately determines the quality and authentic efficacy of the resultant curricula in military education and training.

Vignette 2: The lecturer's perspective on semantics and agency

In most cases, military students receive detailed and individually tailored feedback when undertaking any practical placement element of a formal programme of study. This feedback occurs through the triangulation of formal observations made by academic staff, clinical placement providers and observations and feedback from their practice educators and mentors in clinical practice. In terms of understanding the concepts of personhood and authenticity, military students bring with them a multiplicity of transferable skills, experience and learning for which there is no perceptible equivalency in the civilian world. Formal military training is undertaken in a hierarchical and disciplined context; it exposes soldiers to a values and standards system based upon the right to life and liberty, the underpinning philosophy of British democratic society. Army values and standards are founded upon, and characterised by, the principles of courage, discipline, respect for others, integrity, loyalty and selfless commitment. Military doctrine provides a scaffolding structure within which military students can be supported and facilitated in understanding the world within the military environment. However, military doctrine, once decontextualised outside of the institution, holds minimal currency within the civilian or NHS environments and its overriding influence is often regarded as an active source of distraction during this transition phase (McCormick et al. 2019).

Lecturing staff at the university are well placed through their experience and knowledge of teaching and learning to support the military student transition. They are able to provide cognitive buffers in terms of their academic teaching so that the integration of military and civilian students is as seamless as possible. This requires a subtle nuancing of the approach to the military student induction, contextualising it to take account of the identified cognitive and cultural differences that these students bring. One exercise used early in the teaching to prepare military students for the higher education/NHS environment, is mapping their personally articulated values to those of the NHS. The lecturing team facilitate the students in aligning their own values with the NHS values to demonstrate the relative degrees of consensus or identifiable tension between them. This process is then consolidated during the student's time with their practice educator facilitators (PEFs) within the NHS Trust, establishing a deeper understanding of how the NHS operates based upon these values and how their individual personhood aligns with them in this context.

Since university academics are non-military personnel, lecturers need to create a non-judgemental, safe, positive and constructive learning environment, which derives from their subject knowledge, authenticity and openly recognised positionality and allows the students to be challenged. This creates opportunities for open discourse and a platform for dynamic debate, which encourages the recognition of personal versus professional perspectives and removes the fear of being judged by peers. This often resulted in a reported and tangibly observable transformative learning experience for the students, specifically as their awareness was raised of their capacity to exercise agency in both formal higher education and NHS settings (Hayes and Corrie 2020; Corrie 2021). As students' awareness and regard for their own levels of epistemic cognition further developed during the programme, they were generally more able to recognise the agency they held within the NHS environment as clinical practitioners.

One reported facet of learning that emerges from the process of learning in higher education, is that of the concept of imposter syndrome. Whilst military professional identity is not an issue, many personnel report struggling to align their personal identity with that of a university student, and a clinician within an NHS setting. Once recognised as a potential barrier to engagement with processes of learning, this was formally addressed in the curriculum in terms of integrating an element of training in transitioning into higher education, via facilitating them in their understanding of multiple identities within the role of Combat Medical Technician and the impact of this on becoming an HCPC-registered paramedic. In establishing key communities of professional practice, these military students were supported in acknowledging their identity within their current roles, which were uniquely situated within the context of higher education. This provided an anchor point for the transition from military identity, the liminal shift to higher education student identity and consequently to NHS clinical practitioner identity. This new perspective on their multiple identity provided a further transformative learning experience, enhancing their understanding of the degree of agency they were afforded and how it could be applied across multi-dimensional contexts of working practice.

Concurrently, military students use the tacit knowledge they have acquired and developed from military contexts and consciously or unconsciously apply this to their new civilian environment, sometimes unsuccessfully due to key differences in situational contexts and settings. In addition to this, some of these students struggle in relation to their working vocabulary, since they have become entrenched in institutionalised learning characterised by acronyms and expressions specific to the military and even individual military contexts. Whilst these contribute to a sense of belonging and frame the culture and context of military life during service, their role beyond veteran camaraderie in civilian life is limited. This may even extend as far as the language used to describe everyday items. An example of this would be the civilian reference for 'a cup of tea', called 'a brew' in the Army and 'a wet' in the Navy. This is a direct legacy of Phase 1 and Phase 2 training, both of which are characterised by instrumental instructions and a series of cultural norms. Lecturers actively challenged students on their use of language, supporting and facilitating them through academic debate to recognise and understand how the civilian lexicon differs, and potential linguistic equivalency in that different context.

Vignette 3: Reflections on a learning journey – going full circle

This vignette is based on a personal reflection from a member of academic staff. The insight the case study provides is one that details the active processes of epistemic cognitive adjustment that accompany a transition into the context of higher education. Whilst not generalisable in any sense, the lens of illumination that this case study provides is such that a window into the world of one such Combat Medical Technician is opened. She reflects that at the perceived young age of 15, I was very aware that university was not the intended path for me at that moment in time. A few weeks into my A-levels I made the decision to withdraw from college and join the military, much to my parents and teachers' dismay. I was advised on multiple occasions that this was an unwise decision, and that school/university should be my priority; encouraged by parents, friends and faculty to continue my studies before making any decisions. Leaving with just my GSCEs, I had no visions of studying at university in the future, let alone qualifying into a new profession and later returning to university as academic staff.

During military Phase 1 training and becoming a Combat Medical Technician, I knew I had made the right decision; however, I was very aware that at the time, my new profession was not transferable to life outside the military and offered me no recognised accredited qualification. With this in mind, and the desire to enhance my opportunities and abilities, gaining a place on the paramedic course was now my main goal. To get accepted onto the course, certain qualifications were required, which my military training did not provide. Luckily, the university took our military experience into account and we were given the opportunity to meet the rest of the requirements through the provision of some Level 4 modules at university to bring us up to the desired level.

The CertHE was an intense and insightful introduction into a level of academia that was completely new to me, and to the majority of my military colleagues. With three short weeks of campus delivery and multiple written assignments later, I successfully completed the Level 4 top up and was able to apply for the paramedic DipHE. The paramedic course felt like a significant step up from the CertHE, however this was made slightly easier due to the experience gained on the top-up. The DipHE consisted of 750 hours of placement, 10 weeks of scheduled delivery and an array of written and practical assessments. I worked hard throughout the year to achieve consistently high marks and positive feedback on all tasks and assessments requested of me throughout the programme. One of those assessments was a poster presentation on a condition provided by the lecturing staff. It was after this presentation that the staff began to ask if I had ever thought about teaching and whether I would be interested in helping at the university; I took the positive feedback but never thought it would come to fruition.

After qualifying, I was sent back to a medical regiment within the Army and deployed for seven months as a Medical Emergency Response Team (MERT) paramedic. I was sent home to interview for the lecturing position and was successful. I was originally seconded to the university for one year, however I am now starting my third year as a member of staff. I began helping where possible and then gradually gained more responsibility; I am now acting as a senior lecturer, module lead for trauma and programme lead for the military cohort. Being a member of the university has enabled me to gain experience and significantly develop each year, enhancing my knowledge and leadership, in addition to conducting regular shifts with a local Ambulance Service. Additionally, I am currently completing my Level 6 dissertation to achieve my degree in paramedic science.

It is clear from these reflections that there are liminal shifts from education and training to active service as a Combat Medical Technician and the active transitioning from military to civilian contexts. The process of being able to integrate both life worlds provides an insight into the complexity of experience felt during such a pivotal time of active learning and adaptation to new opportunities in the context of emergency response work.

Conclusion

In terms of needs-led educational provision, accessible pathways into higher education, which acknowledge the prior formal qualifications and experiential learning of potential students, are pivotal in both diversifying new cohorts and facilitating and equipping armed services personnel to gain qualifications with currency in both military and civilian contexts. As illustrated, this has ramifications not only in the construction of unique professional identities but also in the challenges that this process poses to HEIs and the military where liminal shifts in transitioning for staff have to be addressed to ensure parity of support and equity in educational provision for whole cohorts. Needs-led educational development is dependent on the relationship between stakeholders and educational institutions, the success of which is largely dependent on optimal and effective communication skills and the interactive dialogue which provides the basis for the building of trust and respect in reciprocal working relationships. It is not merely curriculum development – the key outcome of this relationship – that matters but rather the firm basis of justification and mutual regard for the integration of democratic principles, which provides the keystone for optimal partnership working.

The vignettes incorporated within the chapter have provided a clear basis for the consideration of how tripartite partnership working between industry, the military and HEIs also contributes to civic and societal impact by the collective capacity for integration and change that needs-led curriculum development affords all three contexts. The assurance of the quality of academic programmes validated by HEIs and formally approved for delivery by the HCPC necessitates a clear constructive alignment between the standards evidenced within the MoD and those from HEIs as an integral part of the recognition that students can attain as part of their individual lifelong learning trajectories. The paralleled mirroring of these tripartite relationships is also reflected in the placement opportunities that students are afforded, where the dynamics of partnership working is harnessed for the benefit of all students learning at the front line of patient care.

This chapter has also considered the concept and impact of neoliberalism in terms of how the commodification of educational provision has necessitated the packaging and marketing of academic programmes in a manner which is both accessible and easily attainable. The capacity of HEIs to design access routes to adjunct career transitions and the uptake of continuous learning for the majority of adults working across all sectors may well accelerate in the post-COVID-19 pandemic era. This illustration from practice regarding the need for seamless collaborative partnership working and reciprocal multi-professional agency trust is central to the optimal development of the next generation of military combat technicians and civilian paramedic practitioners.

Note

1 Key terms and definitions can be found at the end of the chapter.

Acknowledgement

This work would not have been possible without the unconditional support of Tom Davidson, Director of the Paramedic Centre of Excellence Paramedic Practice, University of Cumbria, UK, for whose support and contributions to this chapter we are both, as authors, immensely grateful.

References

Armsby, P., Costley, C. and Garnett, J. (2006) The legitimisation of knowledge: A work-based learning perspective of APEL, *International Journal of Lifelong Education*, 25 (4): 369–83.

Cable, G., Cathcart, D. and Almond, M. (2021) The case for veteran-friendly higher education in Canada and the United Kingdom, *Journal of Veterans Studies*, 7 (1): 46–54.

Coll, J.E., Oh, H., Joyce, C. et al. (2009) Veterans in higher education: What every adviser may want to know, *The Mentor: An Academic Advising Journal*, 11 (2): 1–5.

Corrie, I. (2021) *Facilitating of Epistemic Knowledge Construction: Transformational change perspectives and the facilitation of meaning making.* Unpublished doctoral thesis, University of Sunderland.

Giroux, H.A. (2010) Bare pedagogy and the scourge of neoliberalism: Rethinking higher education as a democratic public sphere, *The Educational Forum*, 74 (3): 184–96.

Harvey, A., Andrewartha, L., Sharp, M. et al. (2020) *From the Military to the Academy: Supporting younger military veterans in Australian higher education.* Melbourne: La Trobe University for Higher Education Equity and Diversity Research. Available at: https://www.latrobe.edu.au/__data/assets/pdf_file/0007/1127149/La-Trobe-final-report-From-the-military-to-the-academy-2020.pdf (accessed 2 June 2021).

Hayes, C. and Corrie, I. (2020) Learner-centred pedagogy framing authentic identity and positionality in higher education, in Y. Inoue-Smith and T. McVey (eds.) *Optimizing Higher Education Learning Through Activities and Assessments.* Hershey, PA: IGI Global.

McCormick, W.H., Currier, J.M., Isaak, S.L. et al. (2019) Military culture and post-military transitioning among veterans: A qualitative analysis, *Journal of Veterans Studies*, 4 (2): 287–98.

McCready, S. (2017) Using technology to overcome barriers to APEL, *Widening Participation and Lifelong Learning*, 19 (3): 98–112.

Pouget, M. and Osborne, M. (2004) Accreditation or validation of prior experiential learning: Knowledge and savoirs in France – a different perspective?, *Studies in Continuing Education*, 26 (1): 45–66.

Selznick, P. (1994) *The Moral Commonwealth: Social Theory and the Promise of Community*. Berkeley, CA: University of California Press.

Webster, L. and Mertova, P. (2007) *Using Narrative Inquiry as a Research Method: An Introduction to Using Critical Event Narrative Analysis in Research on Learning and Teaching*. Abingdon: Routledge.

Further reading

Boyd, V. (2020) Work-based learning for enabling social responsibility: The benefits of university-to-business partnerships – a case study, in E. Sengupta, P. Blessinger and C. Mahoney (eds.) *Civil Society and Social Responsibility in Higher Education: International Perspectives on Curriculum and Teaching Development*. Bingley: Emerald Publishing.

Chargualaf, K.A., Elliott, B. and Patterson, B. (2021) Student veterans in higher education, in B. Elliott, K. Chargualaf and B. Patterson (eds.) *Veteran-Centered Care in Education and Practice: An Essential Guide for Nursing Faculty*. New York: Springer.

Chen, J.I., Cameron, D.C., Laliberte, A.Z. et al. (2021) Assessment of suicidal intent in self-directed violence and subsequent care received among military veterans: A national study of gender differences, *Medical Care*, 59: S17–S22.

Chiara, N.A., Chiara, M. and Ashlock, M.Z. (2020) What is impacting the military-affiliated learner experience in higher education?, in V. Mcdermott, L.H. Hernández and A.R. May (eds.) *Supporting the Military-affiliated Learner: Communication Approaches to Military Pedagogy and Education*. Washington, DC: Lexington Books.

Fullerton, A., Hatch-Tocaimaza, D.K., Synstelien, S.S. et al. (2020) Professional military education in the Marine Corps Reserve: A narrative inquiry, *New Horizons in Adult Education and Human Resource Development*, 32 (3): 5–19.

Hawkshaw, R. and O'Neil, C.N. (2020) Military professionalism and the British Army, in K.K. Hachey, T. Libel and W.H. Dean (eds.) *Rethinking Military Professionalism for the Changing Armed Forces*. Cham: Springer.

Kim, J.-H. (2016) *Understanding Narrative Inquiry: The Crafting and Analysis of Stories as Research*. Thousand Oaks, CA: Sage.

McCready, S. (2020) Accrediting prior learning: Tensions between its social inclusion and widening participation intentions and current practice, in R. Papa (ed.) *Handbook on Promoting Social Justice in Education*. Cham: Springer.

Medvid, M., Dem'yanyshyn, V., Chernichenko, I. et al. (2021) The development of readiness for the educational activities in teachers of higher military educational institutions, in S.A.R. Khan and T. Hauer (eds.) *2020 3rd International Seminar on Education Research and Social Science (ISERSS 2020)*. Dordrecht: Atlantis Press.

Salmi, J. and D'Addio, A. (2021) Policies for achieving inclusion in higher education, *Policy Reviews in Higher Education*, 5 (1): 47–72.

Turnbull, W. (2020) *A Brief History of Credit in UK Higher Education: Laying Siege to the Ivory Tower*. Bingley: Emerald Publishing.

Key terms and definitions

Civic impact: the empowering of society through the sharing and construction of knowledge, education, training and research, and active collaboration.

Equity: the quality or value of being fair and impartial.

Needs-led education: curricula specifically designed to address the needs of society in relation to what is expected from people in order to fulfil the obligations of any context-specific labour market demand.

Neoliberalism: neoliberalism in the context of this chapter refers to the commodification of higher education via competitive markets, which have an active influence on regional, national and global economies.

Parity: for the purposes of this chapter, parity refers to the state or condition of being equal, especially with regard to opportunity or the attribution of academic credit.

Professional statutory regulatory bodies: external organisations which formally accredit, approve and recognise university programmes, setting standards for and regulating entry into particular professions.

Stakeholder: a person or organisation with a vested interest or concern with a particular issue.

Transferrable skills: core sets of skills and abilities that can be generically transferred to a broader contextual range of career trajectories.

The Janus of the Access to HE Diploma: Rethinking qualifications, units, credits and levels

Sam Broadhead

This chapter explores the impact the underpinning thinking around credit accumulation and transfer had on the Access to HE Diploma (AHED). At the time of writing, AHED courses are validated by Access Validation Agencies (AVAs). The Quality Assurance Agency for Higher Education (QAA) licenses the AVAs across England and Wales (Busher et al. 2012; DfE 2020).

It is argued that although Access education and the unitisation of curricula are seen by many as supporting adult learning and widening participation, there are tensions and contradictions that have never been resolved. This has resulted in a qualification which, for some, is overly complex, bureaucratic and heavily assessed. Reflections from Access practitioners, managers and students are drawn upon to see how they experience and perceive the AHED.[1] The flexibility and responsiveness to adults' needs of unitisation, credit value and credit level are reconsidered within the context of the AHED.

There are more bespoke Access programmes situated in higher education institutions (HEIs) throughout the UK that have different approaches and structures to the AHED and are validated inhouse (Broadhead et al. 2019). No AVAs are regulated by the QAA based in Northern Ireland or Scotland. Access to HE courses are delivered in the devolved nations but very few are validated by the QAA in Northern Ireland and there are none from Scottish colleges (Access to HE 2019).

The AHED is the current iteration of previous Access to HE qualifications that are often delivered within further education (Busher et al. 2015). It is designed for those adults who for many social, cultural and practical reasons wish to return to study later in life. Initially, Access courses were not only concerned with preparing students for higher education (Kearney and Diamond 1990). They also aimed to develop students both academically and personally so they could confidently follow their dreams to study a particular subject(s), continue to further study or enter/advance a new career. Access courses often foster a love of learning in a person as part of living a fulfilling life (Broadhead and Gregson 2018).

Access courses were recognised as the third route to higher education in the White Paper, *Higher Education: Meeting the Challenge* (DES 1987). Since then, the number of courses and, more importantly, the number of students accessing higher education has increased sporadically (Layer 1993).

As the Access course has developed, it has become more focused on progression to higher education. As a Level 3 credit-based qualification for students wishing to go to university, the AHED makes the intended aim of Access education more explicit in its title. The AHEDs are specialised – for example, Law, Medical Sciences, Education, Social Sciences. Diamond (1999) has argued that Access started out as a radical educational movement that was practitioner-led and responsive to the needs of local communities. However, it has been transformed through monitoring and standardisation into a qualification that is now prescriptive and similar to conventional forms of education such as A Levels (Broadhead et al. 2019).

Access to HE Diploma and the validation of credit-based programmes

Proposed AHED specifications along with information about student support, institutional resources and advice and guidance are considered by a panel of peers that comprises members from the AVA, higher and further education, subject specialists and other AHED providers. If successful, the course would be validated for a prescribed period of time up to five years. External moderators employed by the AVAs visit the AHED providers twice a year to ensure the quality of the provision and assessment. AHED managers or course leaders recognised by some AVAs (for example, CertaAccess) have an opportunity to revise the units at annual validation events run by the AVA (CertaAccess 2019). The validation process is informed by similar processes in higher education. Other AVAs such as Ascentis operate differently, offering qualifications and resources that are designed by the organisation whilst listening to the needs of the provider (Ascentis 2020).

AVAs are recognised by the QAA and often have historical links to the Open College Networks (OCNs) that were very influential in developing credit accumulation and transfer for adult learners in the 1980s and 1990s. The OCN model of credit-based learning and assessment was acknowledged in *A Basis for Credit* (FEU 1992, 1993). The OCN approach sought to recognise learning through the assessment of units. A unit comprises a credit value, credit level, learning outcomes, assessment criteria, guided learning hours and expected assessment evidence (essay, artefact, portfolio, presentation, project, examination, etc.) (Tait 2003). Accreditation based on units implies a curriculum that is modularised.

The 2003 White Paper, *The Future of Higher Education* (DfES 2003), invited the QAA to come forward with proposals to modernise the criteria for Access courses so that they were 'sufficiently flexible and attractive to meet the needs of today's adult learners'. The White Paper had recognised the importance of Access to HE education but noted that numbers had not increased during the previous years. The QAA became responsible for managing the quality and standards of an Access to HE qualification. It sought to standardise some of the diverse practices and approaches to assessment of Access providers so that those in higher education and other stakeholders could be assured of the qualification's quality.

All approved AHEDs are now made up of 60 credits, of which at least 45 must be at Level 3. Before 2008, Access to HE certificates were ungraded and Access tutors had some control over the structure of their courses. However, higher education admissions departments claimed that they could not select students based on their ability or merit because the Access to HE certificate was a pass/fail qualification (Karadia and Mizon 2018). Since 2008, the 45 units of the Access to HE Diploma have been graded. It is interesting – and some would say problematic – that individual units were graded rather than the final qualification. This fundamental change was led by the QAA in collaboration with the AVAs, AHED providers and HEIs. The grading scheme was designed to accommodate the flexibility of the qualification, so that it could be applied to all AHEDs, whatever their subject or structure. These changes meant that in 2017 the AHED could be aligned to UCAS tariff points. It could be argued that standardisation made the AHED more visible and meaningful to higher education admissions staff. Grading made it easier for HEIs to select 'the most able' students on to degree courses (Karadia and Mizon 2018).

Unitisation is good for adult learning

Underpinning the structure of the AHED is an acceptance that unitisation and modularisation associated with credit accumulation and transfer frameworks are beneficial for adult learning. This understanding can be seen in the 1972 Russell Committee Report, which was influenced by the work of the Open University (Parry 1996). The Committee called for qualifications that were suitable for adults. Importantly, approaches to assessment should be appropriate for adults. Layer (1993) describes how in the 1980s the Manchester Open College Federation (MOCF) pioneered the 'Manchester model' that established four characteristics of an accreditation framework:

1 It constructed four levels of learning from basic skills to access to higher education.
2 It conceptualised the notion of credit value as based on hours of study to give an indication of the volume of learning.
3 It encouraged practitioner-led curriculum design and development while promoting peer-review panels for the scrutiny of submitted courses.
4 It certificated the achievement of students by the means of credit awards that were logged in a Study Passport, a portable record of personal success (Sanders and Whaley 2007).

The MOCF was one of the first Open College Networks. As OCNs grew in the 1990s under an umbrella organisation, the National Open College Network (NOCN), the process of credit transfer could be more easily facilitated. The first national Credit Accumulation and Transfer Agreement (CATA) was signed in Manchester Town Hall on 6 July 1990 (Sanders and Whaley 2007). This OCN approach was very influential and was taken up more widely within further education (FEU 1992, 1993; Layer 1993). At the same time, Access courses were growing in number, becoming the third way to university (DES 1987). Very often, Access programmes were validated by OCNs that ascribed to the Manchester model (Sanders and Whaley 2007).

Credit accumulation and transfer continued to be seen as an important means of facilitating the education of adults. This was reiterated in the Kennedy Report (1997), which recommended the introduction of a national credit framework. It explained the benefits that such a system would have for adult students: 'Learners are able to collect credit for each unit studied and to build up a record of achievement, which counts towards their overall qualification. If a student has to leave, it is possible for them to come back at a later date and to build on existing credits' (Kennedy 1997: 35). Kennedy also noted that 'Learners offer each other mutual support. Adults bring with them a great wealth of experience and they are encouraged to draw on this experience for their own and for others' benefit. Learners are taught the skills necessary to work in groups and on their own' (1997: 35).

Credit-based assessment aimed to be transparent, equitable and empowering for mature learners. Its advocates believed that the credit accumulation and transfer system should be open, flexible and enable students to make choices about their learning; in other words, treating them as responsible adults (Tait 2003).

These ideals were seen as achievable because when curricula were unitised with the relevant credit value and level, students could choose to study small volumes of credit at their own pace and level. Coady et al. (1997) argued that credit-based mechanisms could enable students to progress vertically and horizontally. Adult learners could study units at higher credit levels when they were ready to do so. Theoretically, if a student required a breadth of learning experience, they could also study different subject areas but at the same credit level. There could also be greater flexibility in the mode of study, where adult students could switch to part-time study when required or take their credits with them if they moved to a new institution (Layer 1993).

All forms of learning could be recognised if the focus was placed on units rather than the qualification. *A Basis for Credit* (FEU 1993) maintained that older students could gain confidence by accumulating credit without being bound to a whole qualification for a long period of time. Students could drop in and out of learning depending on what was happening in the rest of their lives. A personalised learning programme could be designed to comprise many levels so a student need not be held back by their weakest subject. So, for example, a student may be studying Level 3 in cake-making and Level 1 in English language concurrently.

When credit accumulation and transfer frameworks are recognised across institutions, sectors and even national boundaries, they drive student social and geographic mobility. Different kinds of learning could be bridged so that previous experiential and work-based learning could be recognised and accredited (Pollard et al. 2017).

The Association of Colleges (AoC 2014) argued that credit accumulation and transfer systems and corresponding modular structures are central to Access courses for adults, promoting lifelong learning, access and widening participation.

Evidence from the experiences of Access students suggests that the unitisation of the AHED and the associated credit values did help them organise their work and reflect on their progress. Paul studied his Access to HE Diploma as a residential student. He said, 'I never really thought about credits as time – I would just complete each piece of work without really thinking about the amount of time I had spent on it'. However, Paul later described how he used the modularised structure of his course to his best advantage, clarifying that 'I was aware of the sort of modules I would be good at such as creative modules and made sure that in these modules I would do work that would gain me the maximum credits'. It seems that Paul was able to retain some agency about where he focused his attention based on his perceived aptitudes and interests: 'This would then counterbalance modules that I struggled at such as coding and programming where I would not get many if any credits. We were constantly made aware of how many credits we had earned during tutorials and on the online learning space'.

Rosa studied her Access to HE Diploma over two years (2009–2011) at the point when the AHED model was becoming established and the grading of units embedded in the qualification. She recounted how she had not been aware of the meaning of credits at the time, but took a pragmatic approach to study: 'I am not sure that I was aware of this [credit as notional 10 learning hours]. However, I did ensure that I put aside the time to do what was needed and more. For example, I didn't work Fridays – so this was mainly my day but I always used some time in the evenings or my lunch hour'.

It seems that the credit system did give the students some control and ownership of the learning process. What is less clear is how flexible the Diploma is, even though it comprises units. Naomi, an access practitioner with over ten years' experience, articulated the diminishing opportunities for students to select the units they want to study as part of the AHED due to pragmatic reasons. She stated, 'It is a myth that students can pick and choose units. The tutor selects the units with the required credit levels and values. If the students picked the units, they would be all doing different learning outcomes and there would have to be a margin for error'. Commenting on limitations to flexibility, she noted that 'Choice is an ideal but it never happens in practice because of the process of management of pedagogy. There can be too much choice and that could add stress (am I picking the right units?). You need structure and planning from teaching staff'. While reflecting on her experience, she stated: 'Only massive programmes could facilitate pathways and choices; most Access courses are small scale [and that t]here are rules of combination and also mandatory units that tend to be the written ones'. Naomi concluded, 'Credits are at the periphery of student experience; it is the qualification as a whole that is the focus. The units don't register on the horizon'.

Naomi's comments illustrate the tensions that exist between a standardised and prescribed qualification that is structured with many units. The students did not appear to be fully cognisant of the way their courses were organised according to credit value, but they did find the unitised structure useful in tracking their progress and organising their work. In Naomi's experience, Access to HE programmes are small and cannot provide much scope for students choosing units or pathways. However, this may be dependent on where the AHED is situated and the subject area; for example, Health, Public Services and Care Access courses attract large numbers of students (Access to HE 2019).

Critique of unitisation

From the point of view of Access practitioners, there are some criticisms of unitisation when it is applied to AHED courses. Linda is a member of the senior management team of a sixth-form college that also provides adult education. She explained, 'We had a foundation year zero that was a university award, then we moved over to the Access to HE Diploma (Health). The Access to HE Diploma is made up of 60 credits over nine different units'. In her view, 'Access is overly burdened with administration to do with credit and it doesn't help learning. It's just madness – credit values of 3, 6, 9 – 45 graded 60 all in all'.

Linda felt she was in a good position to compare the in-house foundation programme with the AHED because it was aimed at the same groups of students and taught by the same staff and covered the same subject area. However, the difference in how the qualification was structured caused some concern. According to Linda: 'It doesn't mean anything to the students; they are only interested in assignments and how these relate to UCAS points. AHED is very complicated. With foundation there was not as much assessment, there were larger modules, treated more like a university would'.

She reflected on the possible reasons for the complexity: 'Access is hampered by FE bureaucracy, the worst bits of BTEC – it takes so much of staff when they should be teaching. It is unnecessarily complex and makes learning performative: done that – next – hoop jumping'. Linda's account of her experience with AHED stems from a sense of frustration that the means of assessment is not in sympathy with the way she believes adults should be taught or how they learn. Marton and Säljö (1976) argued that a unitisation approach to learning could encourage surface and atomised learning. Some of Naomi's comments mirror the ones made by Linda, who stated that 'The volume of 45 credits can get very bitty. The units written to provide the credits could be simplified because people can get stressed over too many deadlines'. She felt '12 units is ridiculous, you don't need lots of separate bits. Students find multiple hand-ins increase their stress levels. Also, there is the tutor's time to collate and give summative feedback when they could be doing more formative assessment'.

Due to the evolution of the AHED within the method of accreditation pioneered by the Open College movement, the Diploma is a qualification made up of units with small credit values (Lester 2011). Browning (1991) had previously raised questions about the bureaucratic control of Open Colleges and small unit sizes contribute to this. Units with larger credit values are discouraged through the validation process because that could threaten the flexibility associated with units. There is also a belief that larger units are risky for the student if they fail or get a low grade.

Notional learning time as a means of establishing credit value

Education understood in terms of time became more relevant from the 1960s onwards when there were adjustments to schools' temporal organisation according to economic factors. Research was conducted during the following years that found positive correlations between time on task and achievement. Alhadeff-Jones claimed that, 'The results of the studies conducted during that period progressively shifted the perspective adopted by educational researchers, moving their focus from schooling to learning' (2017: 105).

Carroll's (1963) model of instructional time defined most variables of the learning in terms of time, a unit of analysis that could be used at different levels: years, months, weeks, days, hours, minutes. Students were now defined as fast or slow, rather than bright or dull, gifted or disabled. This line of thinking can be seen in the construction of credit as the notional time it takes an 'average' student to learn something. One credit in Access to HE education was originally aligned to 30 notional learning hours and then later in 2004 it was changed by the National Open College Network (NOCN) to 10 notional hours to align with higher education's model of credits.

Alhadeff-Jones (2017) critiqued this model of quantifying learning: 'With Bloom's (1968) "mastery learning" model, Carroll's notion of aptitude was later used to predict time required by an individual to reach a determined level of competency and manipulate teaching variables so most students could reach it' (2017:106). He argued that staff and students struggle with the normative hybridity and heterogeneous temporal positions. By linking time to learning, two antagonistic principles appear to be addressed: (1) 'the logic of efficiency dictated by economic rationality' – auditing time as a commodity; and (2) 'the value of equity responding to a democratic and humanist ideal' (2017: 113).

By quantifying learning into credit values that are then attached to units of assessment, adults are able to study smaller 'chunks' of the curriculum within a time that is appropriate to them. Wilson (1994) argued that the exact value of credit in terms of hours should not be an area of concern for educators or students: 'The figures 10, 20, 40, 50, etc. might have been substituted for 30 and would have formed an equally arbitrary (and therefore equally sound) basis for such a definition'. However, underpinning the credit approach was a notion of what an 'average' student could learn in a prescribed amount of time, as if learning could be disentangled from the temporal complexities of students' lives. When thinking about the diversity of Access students – of all students – it is questionable whether the construct of an 'average' student is helpful or desirable.

Wilson says that ascribing credit value to a unit is not an exact science and is dependent on professional judgement: 'It therefore follows that the wider the group which is asked to confirm the reasonableness of this credit value, the more rational the approximation will be' (1994: 59). He goes on to say, 'In other words, the greater the variety of perspectives on the particular credit value of a unit, the closer we can get to the idealised notion of the average learner' (1994: 59).

Some Access practitioners are critical of ascribing time as a measurement (volume) of learning. Naomi's comments also resonate with those of the students, where there is a certain amount of ambivalence towards notional learning time:

> *Credit as 10 notional hours of learning, people do not engage with that. They understand that you may need to put in more hours.*

> *This way of looking at learning and assessment does not apply to subjects like the arts that are driven by process, where it may take more time to learn the craft of creating something. They enjoy learning so they will put the time in.*

> *Time is money if people are slow, take more time then there is more cost. It's all about consumerism. That is why slow crafting is so radical – it subverts the notion of achievement and success is about being quick.*

Naomi's comments illustrate how credit-based learning appeared to unify Alhadeff-Jones' (2017) antagonistic principles of learning time as a commodity and the drive towards equitable education. Bert also made the point that unitisation only suited some subjects. He said there is an 'issue with time. Sennett [2008] has said it takes 10,000 hours to master a skill, you may need to do another 1,000 hours before you take the next step, or you may need 500 hours; practical subjects are not like academic learning, which is about learning facts!' He further stated: 'When we were developing the Access course the model was an Access to law course. Law development was totally different. Law fitted credit accumulation and transfer. Those students were articulate and you could easily show a student had an awareness of law at different levels'.

Even though credit values defined by notional learning hours were deemed to be an arbitrary measure and a pragmatic solution to recognising learning, it seems that some Access practitioners continue to be uncomfortable with this approach. Both Naomi and Bert highlight the temporal complexities around adult learning, pointing out that the time taken to learn is dependent on context and subject area.

By looking at how the ideas that were initiated in the 1960s were developed during the ensuing five decades, it can be seen that quantifying learning in terms of time became a dogma within educational policy and practice that was difficult to question. The impact of this model of learning was beneficial for adults as it provided a basis for the flexibility they required (Davies 1999). However, the tensions between unitisation (and the corresponding fragmentation of learning time) and the need for a nationally recognised Access qualification culminated in the complexities of the Access to HE Diploma. Practitioners report that the AHED has lost its original responsiveness to individual student temporal needs while overly burdening staff and students with assessment bureaucracy and the dividing up of knowledge (Broadhead et al. 2019).

Are Access levels helpful?

Units are defined by credit values based on the notional hours an 'average' student would take to study them; they are also ascribed a credit level. Initially, Access courses were aligned with the NOCN Level 4. Later, as part of the Qualification and Credit Framework (QCF) and to fit in with higher education levels, the AHED was classified as a Level 3 qualification. The FEU (1993) argued that credit values and credit levels were a pragmatic response to accreditation. However, the imposition of credit levels on Access education could be seen to be in conflict with its approach to adult learning. Kearney and Diamond (1990) believed any flexibility in the application of levels to Access education was limited by the need to align Access levels to NVQs. Avis (1991) was very critical of applying levels to Access education as it undermined the radical forms of pedagogy employed by the pioneering Access teachers that were developed in the 1970s and 1980s (Diamond 1999; Broadhead et al. 2019): '[t]his leaves unchallenged a number of dichotomies: The academic/vocational, practical/applied, mental/manual. A critical education should interrogate these divisions. Credit levels parody these dualities echoing traditional academic distinction' (Avis 1991: 49).

Avis was further concerned that the underpinning ideas of credit-based learning and assessment were based on a developmental model of learning proposed by Piaget which should be contested: '[w]e should in our practice as Access tutors use credit levels pragmatically and be aware of their anti-educational consequences, particularly the dangers of exclusion that can arise around basic skills.' (Avis 1991: 49). These ideas and assumptions about pedagogy and learning were under-theorised because educators did not have the time and space to fully consider the political and ideological implications of these assessment structures. Avis went on to argue that, 'We should be aware of the consequences of attributing critical ability only to higher levels and the way such a model constructs lower level learners as irrational' (1991: 50). In practice, adult learners may not fit neatly into a defined level, and may not progress through the levels in a linear manner suggested by a developmental model of learning.

As has previously been stated, Access education had wider objectives than just preparing people for university. People could be learning together in the same Access cohort who had very different motivations and learning goals. Bert, who began working in Access education 40 years ago, remembers he 'was asked to be part of a pilot open college project led by the head of West and North Yorkshire Open College Network (WNYOCN)'. The project 'started by looking at what was already out there. A credit was initially decided to be 30 hours of notional learning time, which fitted in with 3 hours per week on an evening course that ran for 10 weeks. However, there were all sorts of levels in one class, so we started separating them out into beginnings, intermediate and advanced'. Bert 'did not agree with this because a mix of levels meant that students helped each other out and people were not stigmatised for being in the lower end. It looked nice though, entry level, 1, 2, 3, 4 ... But as soon as these levels were implemented they were separated out because of funding'.

In the 1990s, Access to HE delivered in organisations aligned to NOCN was then characterised as Level 4 provision existing within a wider framework where Access to adult and further education was catered for by credit levels that included entry, 1, 2 and 3 levels. This drove a rationalisation and narrowing of Access education where Access to HE courses became a distinctive provision with a prescribed purpose that was differentiated from other forms of Access.

Nationally recognised Access provision

In order for a credit accumulation and transfer system to work, there needed to be the consistency provided by a national credit or qualifications framework (Layer 1993). At the same time, such a framework, underpinned by the developmental model of education, applied to many if not all qualifications would be hard to challenge. It seems ironic that credit-based learning which was promoted as being designed to meet the needs of adult students ultimately led to Access education becoming more like A Levels because of the drive to find an equivalence with other qualifications.

The Qualifications and Credit Framework (QCF), which was officially launched in 2008 (Lester 2011), replaced the National Qualifications Framework in 2011 (AoC 2014). The QCF aimed to capture learning regardless of volume or where it took place and was based on unit specifications. The Office of Qualifications and Examinations Regulation (OfQual) in England was now ultimately the central authority responsible for approving units and qualification structures. Units rather than qualifications were the primary currency. All units now had a credit rating as in higher education, where one credit is equivalent to 10 notional learning hours. The Open College Network approach that considered units first and then combined them into qualifications was carried over to the QCF (Wilson 1994). Units were standardised to comprise learning outcomes, assessment criteria, a credit rating and a level.

On 1 September 2004, NOCN changed the value of credits from one credit equals 30 hours of notional learning time to one credit equals 10 hours of notional learning time. This also applied to all the Access to HE courses that were recognised and validated by AVAs. The Access to HE qualification was now aligned to the higher education credit values.

The impact of the QCF for Access courses was the continued standardisation of the qualification. It became a Level 3 diploma rather than a certificate because it had a value of over 37 units and was an alternative qualification to A Levels or BTECs (Level 3 qualifications) for applications to university. The Access to HE Diploma was born and AVAs needed to ensure that all the diplomas they validated were approved by QAA. The notion of nationally recognised credits was important to Rosa who said, 'to me it was a measure of how well I was doing'. She continued, 'This was a new subject area for me and the fact that it was nationally recognised was important in making the decision to pursue the qualification'. Yasmina, another AHED student, was very informed about where the diploma sat with other qualifications: 'I was aware that the Access course was A Level "level", so to speak, although I don't think I knew what Level 3 meant when I started'. She reflected that 'it was important to me that it was properly accredited by a recognised body, but I think you would expect that when taking a course at an institution such as the then-College'.

Naomi, an Access tutor, reflected that 'Level 3 people like the fact that it is equivalent to A Levels – it levels the playing field'. However, Linda did not agree with Naomi. Even though AHED and A Levels are an equivalent level, Linda believes the work load is not comparable: 'Who decides the size of it? There was less content in the foundation year and progression was amazing. Who decided? It's funded like two A Levels but it feels like they are doing three or four. And we need to integrate study skills and not have separate modules'.

Linda pointed out the issues with unitisation, that small units increase assessment points and therefore increase the time on assessment rather than learning. She was also critical of how different types of knowledge and skills are separated out instead of being integrated. The expectations on AHED students to achieve high grades in many small units could be seen to be unfair compared with the volume of work expected from A Level students (Broadhead et al. 2019).

Conclusion

The development of the Access to HE qualification is entwined with the history of credit accumulation and transfer. This is partly because the Open College movement was so influential in creating a system of accreditation that led to the unitisation of qualifications and modularisation of curricula. At the same time, Access to HE courses were often validated by AVAs, which were also part of OCNs.

The OCN approach to accreditation was pragmatic but it did not address the fundamental tensions that existed between the philosophy of Access education and the concept of credits. There were issues such as credit values as notional learning hours, access levels and a focus on units rather than the qualification. Access practitioners now claim the qualification is overly complex due to the number of units and the amount of assessment points that increase workload unnecessarily. Unitisation may work for academic learning but for those subjects that are about learning practical skills or developing creative projects, a more holistic assessment process would be beneficial.

The underpinning philosophy of education that is implicit in credit-based learning has gone unquestioned. For example, is it educationally sound to measure the credit value in terms of notional learning hours? Or, is this a means of accounting for time and its associated cost on a programme? Similarly, the construction of a framework based on levels draws strongly upon developmental theories of education. These theories contradict the notion of lifelong learning. This is because they assume people learn in a linear manner from one level to another (Avis 1991). It has been argued that adults may have aptitudes in different areas and may need or wish to study across subjects rather than one subject at a progressively higher level (Layer 1993; Coady et al. 1997). Or, a student may be learning on a basic skills course, but operating with complexity and criticality in certain parts of the curriculum and in their day-to-day lives (Avis 1991).

Because such a strong case is made that credit-based learning is good for adult learning, it is hard to imagine a form of AHED that is not modularised. Students have reported that they value the AHED as being nationally recognised and equivalent to A Levels. However, the AHED is now a discrete qualification rather than a more fluid portfolio or 'passport' of credits that has been chosen by students and studied at their own pace. Students are now encouraged to complete the AHED in one academic year and meet assessment deadlines that are set by the AHED providers and regulated by the AVAs. Unfortunately, the flexibility of units has been lost, but the fragmentation of knowledge and assessment overload for staff and students remain.

The Janus is a god from Roman mythology, and is symbolic of gates, doors, doorways, beginnings and endings, a fitting metaphor for Access education (Briggs 2010). However, it is depicted as having two faces looking in opposite directions and these can represent the tensions of the AHED units and qualification that are underpinned by contradictory educational principles.

Note

1 Access practitioners and people who had been awarded the AHED were contacted and asked if they would give their informed consent to participate in a small project about AHED and credit-based education. Three Access tutors (two had managed

Access programmes), a senior manager and three people who had been awarded an AHED agreed to contribute. They were given the option to email their thoughts or to take part in a video call interview that was transcribed and the subsequent text confirmed with the participant. The participants' identities were protected through the use of pseudonyms and details about their organisations were generalised.

Acknowledgements

I would like to thank Professor John Diamond, Garry Barker, Christopher Graham, Jo Fletcher-Saxon, Frances Norton, Ann Barass, Ingrid Bale and David Jowett for their insights and guidance.

References

Access to HE (2019) *Data Report.* Available at: https://www.accesstohe.ac.uk/docs/access/regulating-access-documents/access-to-he-data-report-19.pdf?sfvrsn=47d1c781_6 (accessed 19 January 2021).

Alhadeff-Jones, M. (2017) *Time and the Rhythms of Emancipatory Education: Rethinking the Temporal Complexity of Self and Society.* Abingdon: Routledge.

Ascentis (2020) *Access to HE.* Available at: https://www.ascentis.co.uk/qualifications/access-to-higher-education (accessed 19 January 2021).

Association of Colleges (AoC) (2014) *Making Credit Accumulation and Transfer Work: Final report on research and evaluation of the Credit Accumulation and Transfer Scheme (CATS) pilot projects.* Available at: https://www.aoc.co.uk/sites/default/files/CATS.PDF (accessed 8 January 2021).

Avis, J. (1991) Not so radical after all? Access, credit levels and the student, *Journal of Access Studies,* 6 (1): 40–51.

Bloom, B.S. (1968) Learning for mastery: Instruction and curriculum. Regional education laboratory for the Carolinas and Virginia, topical papers and reprints, *Evaluation Comment,* 1 (2): 1–12.

Briggs, D. (2010) Janus-like policymakers and health managers urgently required, *Asia Pacific Journal of Health Management,* 5 (2): 4–6.

Broadhead, S., Davies, R. and Hudson, A. (2019) *Perspectives on Access to Higher Education: Practice and Research.* Bingley: Emerald Publishing.

Broadhead, S. and Gregson, M. (2018) *Practical Wisdom and Democratic Education: Phronesis, Art and Non-Traditional Students.* Cham: Palgrave Macmillan.

Browning, D. (1991) Are Open Colleges too bureaucratic?, *Journal of Access Studies,* 1: 72–79.

Busher, H., James, N. and Piela, A. (2015) 'I always wanted to do second chance learning': Identities and experiences of tutors on access to higher education courses, *Research in Post-Compulsory Education,* 20 (2): 127–39.

Busher, H., James, N. and Suttill, B. (2012) *Access to Higher Education: Student perspectives of access courses as sites of transformation of their learning identities.* Available at: https://www.researchgate.net/publication/282764053_James_N_Busher_H_Suttill_B_2012_Access_to_Higher_Education_Understanding_Access_Students'_perspectives_on_the_transformations_of_their_Learning_Identities_and_Careers_in_Changing_Policy_contexts_ (accessed 8 January 2021).

Carroll, J.B. (1963) A model of school learning, *Teachers College Record*, 64 (8): 723–33.

CertaAccess (2019) *Provider Handbook*. Available at: https://certaaccess.co.uk/wp-content/uploads/2019/09/Provider-Handbook-2019-20.pdf (accessed 19 January 2021).

Coady, S., Tait, T. and Bennett, J. (1997) Give us the credit: Achieving a comprehensive FE framework, *FE Matters*, 1 (20): 4–34.

Davies, P. (1999) Mickey Mouse or Michaelmas: A false dichotomy for an inclusive framework of qualifications, *Widening Participation and Lifelong Learning*, 1 (2): 33–40.

Department for Education (DfE) (2020) *Review of Post-16 Qualifications at Level 3 in England. Second stage: Government consultation*. Available at: https://consult.education.gov.uk/post-16-qualifications-review-team/review-of-post-16-qualifications-at-level-3/supporting_documents/Consultation%20document%20%20Review%20of%20post16%20qualifications%20at%20level%203.pdf (accessed 19 January 2021).

Department for Education and Science (DES) (1987) *Higher Education: Meeting the challenge*. White Paper. London: HMSO.

Department for Education and Skills (DfES) (2003) *The Future of Higher Education*. London: HMSO. Available at: http://www.educationengland.org.uk/documents/pdfs/2003-white-paper-higher-ed.pdf (accessed 2 January 2019).

Diamond, J. (1999) Access: The year 2000 and beyond – what next?, *Journal of Access and Credit Studies*, 1 (2): 183–91.

Further Education Unit (FEU) (1992) *A Basis for Credit? Developing a post-16 credit accumulation and transfer framework: A paper for discussion*. London: FEU.

Further Education Unit (FEU) (1993) *A Basis for Credit? Developing a post-16 credit accumulation and transfer framework. Feedback and Developments: A paper for discussion*. London: FEU.

Karadia, A. and Mizon, J. (2018) Collaborating on grading developments: Refining the method to ensure quality of opportunity, Paper presented at FACE Conference, *Transformative Higher Education: Access Inclusion and Lifelong Learning*, University of Worcester.

Kearney, K. and Diamond, J. (1990) Access courses: A new orthodoxy?, *Journal of Further and Higher Education*, 14 (1): 128–38.

Kennedy, H. (1997) *Learning Works: Widening participation in further education (Kennedy Report)*. Coventry: The Further Education Funding Council. Available at: https://dera.ioe.ac.uk/15073/2/Learning%20works%20-%20widening%20participation%20in%20further%20education%20(Kennedy%20report).pdf (accessed 8 January 2021).

Layer, G. (1993) Credit accumulation and credit transfer, in J. Calder (ed.) *Disaffection and Diversity: Overcoming Barriers for Adult Learners*. London: Falmer Press.

Learndirect (2019) *Access to HE Diploma: Go to university without A-levels*. Available at: https://www.learndirect.com/blog/access-online-faq-an-alternative-route-to-university-without-a-levels (accessed 8 January 2021).

Lester, S. (2011) The UK qualifications and credit framework: A critique, *Journal of Vocational Education and Training*, 63 (2): 205–16.

Marton, F. and Säljö, R. (1976) On qualitative differences in learning: I – Outcome and process, *British Journal of Educational Psychology*, 46 (1): 4–11.

Parry, G. (1996) Access education in England and Wales 1973–1994: From second chance to third wave, *Journal of Access Studies*, 11 (1): 10–33.

Pollard, E., Hadjivassiliou, K., Swift, S. et al. (2017) *Credit Transfer in Higher Education: A review of the literature*. London: Department for Education.

Sanders, J. and Whaley, P. (2007) *Celebrating Achievement: 25 years of Open College Networks*. Leicester and Sheffield: National Institute of Adult Continuing Education (NIACE) and National Open College Network (NOCN).

Sennett, R. (2008) *The Craftsman*. New Haven, CT: Yale University Press.

Tait, T. (2003) *Credit Systems for Learning and Skills: Current developments*. LSDA Reports. London: Learning and Skills Development Agency.

Wilson, P. (1994) Towards a credit culture in further education, in C. Flint and M. Austin (eds.) *Going Further: Essays in Further Education*. Bristol: The Staff College.

4 Variations in the award of credit in UK higher education

Wayne Turnbull and Harvey Woolf

Introduction

Unique among the nations of the United Kingdom, credit policy and practice are defined wholly within each awarding institution[1] in England. The absence of an integrated credit and qualifications framework in England renders the QAA's Credit Framework for England merely advisory (QAA 2008, 2014, 2020, 2021), thereby tolerating (and indeed encouraging) inconsistency of credit policy and practice in academic regulation between awarding institutions. This variety both reflects and is reflected in the ways in which universities are protective of their autonomy over all aspects of academic regulation, including the criteria for the award of credit. Thus, describing credit, learner achievement and academic progression within the English context may be considered akin to decoding audio frequencies or refracting light through a prism.

Although the other UK nations operate within regional frameworks of credit and qualifications, in England the detail of the requirements for the award of credit may differ between universities. Each awarding institution's academic regulations manage credit in a manner that is unique to their context. This means that appearances of common practice or principle, such as an honours degree comprising 360 credits, are deceptive. This is because the basis upon which such credit is awarded and the rules governing credit-based progression of students towards an award all differ.

Even a principle as apparently generic as the award of credit based upon successful attainment of learning outcomes may be undermined by the particular local conditions and caveats in determining when an outcome has been met. For example, awarding institutions may determine that credit release is triggered once a student attains a pass mark in a module, and/or require that a pass mark is achieved in all assessments in the module, and/or require that all assessments be attempted, and/or impose an attendance requirement. The pass mark may be the same for the module as for the assessed components within the module, or these may differ. Awarding bodies may develop and apply regulations at the institutional level or may permit constituent academic departments to create their own, or indeed allow variation on a local basis.

Beyond consideration of a student's initial assessment attempt, the variations in the management of re-assessment and facilitated progression (for example, compensation, condonement and trailing) are legion.

It follows that any discussion of credit in the UK carries a major health warning: all credit is not the same. Recently articulated concern over honours degree grade inflation in the UK has drawn critical public attention to the existing cornucopia of degree classification algorithms, with successive short-lived universities ministers pledging to clean up the mess.[2] Yet inconsistencies between algorithms represent just the tip of the iceberg; there is much greater (deeper and wider) variation of policy and practice at the level of the award of credit. The days of the secluded regulatory priesthoods who hold responsibility for devising and implementing institutional credit frameworks and regulations may be numbered.

The lottery of student progression

Students failing to meet credit requirements for progression enter a lottery in which the vagaries of academic regulation employed by their institution determine their entitlements to re-assessment or articulate the boundaries within which discretion may be applied (a rich soil for the germination of institutional idiosyncrasies). The extent of regulatory variation has been a cause of concern for NUCCAT[3] and SACWG[4] for many years. From 2016, the two groups collaborated on a series of surveys of UK credit policy and practice, with the respective projects jointly led by Wayne Turnbull and Harvey Woolf. The data underpinning this chapter are derived from our findings.

NUCCAT and SACWG worked with a group of UK universities to analyse both their institutional regulations and progression data. Nine universities submitted results for nearly 20,000 students.[5] Although a small sample, the institutions reflect the range of regulatory practices occurring in English universities. It is our understanding that this type of analysis has not been undertaken previously or since. Snelling and Fisher (2020a), however, discuss some aspects of module re-assessment in section 4 of their report.

Our research was rooted in the principle that assessment regulations should promote and embed fairness and equity. We investigated the extent to which serendipitous choices by students over what and where to study were likely to enhance or impede their chances of being awarded credit. We explored whether academic progression (especially progression following initial failure) is little more than a lottery in which the rules are obscured from the players. We argued that we should create credit/regulatory frameworks that promote both fair and equitable assessment outcomes by re-casting regulations to remove ambiguity, inconsistency and (often unfettered) discretion.

Regulations do not, of course, exist in a vacuum, nor do they have any agency. As we have argued elsewhere (Stowell et al. 2016), assessment regulations are socially constructed artefacts that are derived from, and reflect, institutional cultures. Beyond that, the way regulations are applied will be influenced by a myriad of factors. These include the structure of the institution's decision-making processes, the membership of the examination board, the precise mechanisms and practices adopted by the board, the training of board chairs and officers and the protocols for and quality of board minutes. When considering the award of credit in respect of students' performances, boards will also be operating in the context of the institution's learning, teaching and assessment strategy, its student support systems and a sometimes overlooked factor – the advice given to students about their programme of study.

Mapping and understanding variations in the award of credit

In a series of projects undertaken from 2016, we investigated institutional regulation and practice to determine whether variations are evident in the criteria for the award of credit, the award of credit following initial failure, the award of credit by compensation/condonement and the trailing of credit between levels. In our sample of nine universities, five operated institution-wide regulations for the award of credit when the module pass mark[6] had been attained without any further requirements. Two universities used an institution-wide criterion based on the above principle, but each had an additional criterion: '... and where an attempt has been made at each summative assessment within the module'; '... and where a mark for each summative assessment within the module is equal to or greater than a given threshold, which may be below the module pass mark'. One university had an institution-wide criterion which discounted the module mark altogether and awarded credit when a mark of at least 40% was attained for each summative assessment within the module.[7] One university did not operate institution-wide criteria for the award of credit but permitted variation at the programme level where general criteria (an aggregated pass and an attempt at each summative assessment within the module) may be supplemented by a further local criterion (passing each assessment).

In relation to regulations governing the award of credit after initial failure, all universities in the sample permitted the students to be re-assessed. Six universities permitted a single re-assessment attempt only, one provided two opportunities, one offered a second opportunity on condition that performance criteria were met, and in one it was left to the discretion of the examination board to decide how many re-assessment opportunities a student should be allowed. This (limited) variation on the number of permitted opportunities to attain credit following initial failure masks a more complicated picture regarding eligibility for re-assessment.

In our sample of nine universities, three regarded students as automatically eligible for re-assessment. Each of the remaining six universities put in place qualifying criteria. Two universities judged eligibility on the basis of the extent of initial failure; one set the limit at 60 credits per level, whilst one set the limit at 40 credits per level. Two universities judged eligibility on the basis of prior performance; one required that the initial failed assessment was attempted, and one required that all initial assessments were attempted and that any attendance requirements were met. One university in the sample regarded all students as automatically eligible for re-assessment and judged certain students as eligible for an additional re-assessment based upon their performance against criteria. We also discovered that one university in the sample did not regard re-assessment as a right, but an opportunity offered at the discretion of an examination board.

Most UK universities employ mechanisms for facilitating student progression through the award of credit via condonement or compensation of failure (Atlay and Turnbull 2017). For the research, we adopted the following definitions: *condonement* is forgiveness of failure, requiring latitude in interpreting credit requirements for awards, whereas *compensation* is a deliberative balancing process, determining whether elements of performance elsewhere can offset elements of failure within fixed award credit requirements. *Trailing* is the process of allowing students to take failed assessments/modules in a subsequent level or year of study. To introduce some standardisation of terminology across the sector, Snelling and Fisher (2020b: 27) defined compensation as 'a way of mitigating poor performance in a module or modules, where poor performance is offset by considering the score against satisfactory performance in other modules', and condonement as 'institutional acceptance that the failure of a module does not disqualify the student from eligibility for the target award'. However, despite the differences in meaning, for the purpose of this research project, the terms 'compensation' and 'condonement' were considered interchangeable, as institutions do not use the terms consistently. If condoned students have been forgiven their failure and are not required to redeem those credits, then these students are counted as compensated, alongside students for whom credit was awarded by compensation.

Like snowflakes, no two of our universities were the same in their regulations governing facilitated progression. Five universities compensated but did not condone failure, two universities condoned failure but did not compensate, one university did both, while one university did neither. The total volume of credit that may be compensated/condoned within an honours degree ranged from no credits (0%) to 90 credits (25%). The lowest compensatable mark ranged from 0 to 35%. Five universities set a credit-attained trigger, ranging from 75% of credits passed to 83%. Four universities set a qualifying level average mark threshold, ranging from 40% to 50%. Three universities set bespoke additional criteria: 'all assessment must have been attempted', 'compensation applies to initial assessment only', 'compensation applies to referral assessment only'. Three universities designated specific modules as non-compensatable.

Academic programmes within the UK may be designed as distinct, linear constructs (entire unto themselves) or developed within a curricular framework that facilitates specialisation of award, often based upon deferred learner choice. Even within a standalone, self-contained academic programme, students progress through levels of attainment by accumulating the required number of credits. In the event that a student falls short of the credit total required for progression, institutional regulation may permit a student to progress trailing credit from a prior level. In such circumstances, the student must make good their credit shortfall whilst attempting a new diet of credit.

Every university in the reporting group presented a different set of regulations governing trailing credit between levels. In only one university was trailing regarded as an automatic right of the student, compared with three universities that regarded students as automatically eligible for initial re-assessment. Three universities permitted students to trail on the basis of mitigation only. The number of credits that must be passed at each level before a student can trail ranged from 75 to 100 credits. Board discretion and/or subject variation had a role to play in determining eligibility to trail in three universities. Such was the range of variables at play within regulations governing trailing credit between levels that it is very difficult to summarise or categorise these into a meaningful schema.

By way of comprehending the extent and nature of such variation in regulations governing the award of credit, we suggest that such rules and regulations are either articulated as *enshrined entitlements* (that is, credit is granted when $x = y$), *earned rights* (credit may be granted, if specific additional criteria are set and met) or *discretionary advantages* (credit may be granted, if the examination board decides to do so). The typology reflects a continuum of clarity and complexity for students: there is greatest clarity and simplicity where regulations comprise enshrined entitlements, and almost total obscurity where regulations are grounded in academic discretion and decisions are (entirely, or even largely) in the gift of individuals or boards. Enshrined entitlements may be readily codified in administrative systems to facilitate the recording of credit and the smooth and consistent processing of student progression; earned rights can be codified provided they are not too complex, whereas discretionary advantages cannot be systematised.

Enshrined entitlements, unless they are obscurely communicated, may be easily understood outside the university, whereas the opacity of regulations grounded in discretionary advantage may be understood only by the individual or board in which the power is vested. With earned rights, the extent to which these may be easily comprehended will depend upon the complexity of the criteria that the student must satisfy. Some aspects of an institution's academic regulations may be unavoidably complex (for example, where phased change results in multiple versions of regulations). In such cases, care must be taken to ensure clarity of exposition to students so that they understand the rules that govern their programme. By their very nature, enshrined entitlements are equally available to all students within a given setting. Provided that earned rights are consistently applied within a university, they are also grounded in equality of treatment and access for all students. Where decisions require an exercise of discretion over and above the performance of students, they then become veiled in obscurity and embedded in the secrecy afforded by the indemnity of academic judgement.

Implications for learners of regulatory variation in the award of credit

In terms of our typology, all universities in our sample consider the release of credit on the basis of passing a module as an earned right. However, that is where the commonality ends. What a student must do to pass a module would seem to be straightforward: to those unfamiliar with the byzantine nature of university regulations, asking such a question might seem to be otiose. For those on the inside, however, it is a question that is likely to have been debated for many a long hour in academic development committees.

The five survey universities that simply required a student to score an overall pass mark for the module to trigger credit release would seem to be adopting an unambiguous approach to determining whether students have demonstrated competence in the modules they have just studied. Students at these universities were aware that so long as they achieved an overall pass mark (usually 40% or a non-numerical equivalent), they would pass the module and attain the credit. However, one issue arising from this model is the relationship between the achievement of a module's learning outcomes and the mark(s) awarded. In the overall approach in multiple assessment modules, a student who scores well on one (or more) assessment can compensate for a poorer performance in other assignments. Thus, unless every learning outcome is assessed in every assignment, a student could pass a module having failed to meet at least one of its learning outcomes. This is also a model that advantages students taking multi-assessment modules, as in these modules students have several opportunities to achieve the pass mark.

A counter to this what might be called purist learning outcome position is that internal module compensation allows curriculum designers to develop flexible and developmental assessments *for* learning by combining formative and summative assignments. Intra-module compensation, therefore, ensures that a weak performance in a relatively small piece of summative work undertaken early in a module does not demotivate students for the remainder of the module. Specifying that each assignment must be passed with a mark of at least 40% satisfies concerns about learning outcomes being missed, provided 40% signifies achievement of all the intended outcomes. There is, though, a danger that such an approach stifles experimentation and risk-taking as everything has to count, no matter how minor the assignment. Non-summative *formative* tasks can, of course, be set, but these cannot contribute to the award of credit, and the effectiveness of such assessments is very much open to debate (Gibbs and Simpson 2005; Bennett 2011; Longcroft 2017).

The requirement that not only must students obtain an overall pass module mark but must also score a given threshold mark on each assessment that is *below* the pass mark for the award of credit again raises the question of whether all a module's learning outcomes have been achieved. It is an approach that places the same value on all assessments irrespective of their weighting and makes it explicit that students are expected to make a substantive attempt at a module to pass. In contrast, the rule that in addition to achieving an overall module pass mark students should attempt each summative assessment in the module, leaves what constitutes an 'attempt' open to interpretation. Does turning up to an exam, for example, and writing one's name correctly count as an attempt? Unless an attempt is clearly defined, students will be confused about what they must do to qualify for a pass and it will be left to the judgement of examination boards to decide whether an attempt has been made.

The universities in the survey reflect all three typology categories in relation to re-assessment after initial failure in pursuit of credit attainment. While four institutions opted for an earned right approach to eligibility, there was only the loosest agreement on what students should do to qualify for that right. The two that chose volume of credit passed as the criterion differed in requiring 30% vs. 50% of the level to be passed. Two institutions had variants of the seemingly elastic notion of attempting assessments. One university made re-assessment a discretionary advantage with examination boards responsible for the decision about eligibility, which inevitably raises questions about consistency of practice. Of the four institutions that enshrined the entitlement to be re-assessed by permitting failure of any kind to be re-assessed, one gave its board the power to grant some students the gift of a second re-sit. Applying the typology, this approach conflates aspects of discretionary advantage and enshrined entitlement.

Inherent in the whole re-assessment process is the unspoken assumption that everyone deserves a second chance, subject to the rules discussed above. The six universities that limited the number of re-sits to one took that maxim literally. Two other institutions adopted a more liberal stance and recognised that there may be good reasons why a third chance should be granted, though in one of the two, students had to satisfy stringent criteria. Only one university operated on the principle that the number of re-assessments was a discretionary advantage bestowed on students by the examination board.

All the rules relating to the release of credit by compensation and condonement are predicated on students meeting certain criteria – that is, students should earn the right to be compensated or condoned. Interestingly, although there is enormous variation in the criteria to be satisfied, no university decided that compensation should be a discretionary advantage conferred by examination boards. Given the extent to which other regulatory decisions are delegated to boards, it is somewhat surprising that here all the institutions opted for criteria-driven models. The reason for this is unclear. Is compensation, or condonement, too precise an intervention to be delegated to the vagaries of academic judgement? Perhaps, in a triumph of the technicists, it is only those experienced in crafting regulations who can determine which students should be compensated or condoned. Or, is there an inherent tension between academic judgement (that the student has failed a module) and the algorithmic determination that such a student may progress notwithstanding that failure (via compensation or condonement)?

Just one surveyed institution enshrined the entitlement to trail credits from one level to another, up to a specified credit limit. All the other universities imposed a variety of criteria and two of these gave their examination boards the authority to make the final decision about trailing. In that way, an earned right is transformed into a discretionary advantage. It could be argued that whether a student can cope with the demands of the additional workload of trailing modules can be best established by an examination board, whose members are likely to have some knowledge of the students. This has particular relevance when considered alongside the findings of parallel research into student attainment. The top three universities from the sample of nine, in terms of the proportion of trailing students who completed in time (that is, within three years of first registering), all regarded trailing as a discretionary advantage. Students in universities where trailing was an earned right fared poorly by comparison with those in which trailing credit was the gift of the board. Is it a coincidence that in the only university where trailing credit was an enshrined entitlement, none of the students who trailed Level 4 modules into Level 5 completed in time, and in the university where 'the board must have reason to be confident in the student's competence to progress', their in-time completion rate for trailers was 71%? The management of trailing credit as a discretionary advantage may be weeding-out students who would not be equipped to recover from failure in previous levels whilst attempting new modules. Thus, discretionary advantage may be seen in this context as a judicious mitigation of risk.

To what extent can the variations in regulations governing the award of credit be justified?

Throughout the debates on the Higher Education and Research Bill,[8] the institutional autonomy of universities was loudly championed. Nowhere can the consequences of that autonomy be as clearly seen as in the variety of regulations governing the award of credit to which students are subjected. It is often argued (QAA 2013) that regulations governing the award of credit reflect an institution's educational and curriculum choices and, as no two institutions are the same, regulations will necessarily be different. However, how far does such an argument justify the diversity of regulations extant in UK higher education? For example, while *the intra-module compensation versus pass everything* rules for passing a module can be interpreted as a difference in encouraging experimentation in summative assessment practice, it is difficult to explain the other module pass requirements in purely curriculum terms. We would argue that they are different ways of managing students' engagement with their study and, as such, could be regarded as Sadler's 'transactional and bestowed ... credits and debits' (2010: 732), rather than a measure of a student's achievement.

The variations in the regulations governing eligibility for the award of credit by re-assessment, the number of re-assessments permitted, the award of credit by compensation and/or condonement, and trailing credit between levels, as well as for passing a module, are undoubtedly the product of individual institutional histories and cultures. However, the relationship between those histories and their underpinning pedagogic principles have frequently got lost over time as regulations have often been modified to satisfy conjunctural needs. In terms of natural justice, it cannot be right that some students because they serendipitously study at one institution should automatically be able to retake a failed module, while others at another university must wait on the decision of an examination board.

Harmonising assessment regulations across the sector would reduce some of the chance elements that surround assessment in the universities, without doing damage to institutional autonomy. The process of harmonisation would encourage institutions to compare their regulations systematically with other universities and help institutions to identify the obscurities, complexities, inequities and inequalities in their regulations. The process might stimulate institutional regulations makers to consider introducing more enshrined entitlements so that their rules are essentially binary statements, or to reduce the complexity of the criteria that students must satisfy to earn a right, or indeed to eliminate capricious advantage giving to increase consistency of decision-making.

The diversity of higher education providers, as well as the UK Government's commitment to institutional autonomy, precludes the likelihood of achieving a single set of assessment regulations for higher education courses. The extent to which institutions are modifying their degree algorithms to bring them in line with sector norms (Snelling and Fisher 2020b) indicates that change is feasible. However, to ensure consistency and equity in the treatment of students, there also needs to be a reduction of the variations that are present in the academic regulations that underpin the algorithms, based on the following principles:

- Assessment should be designed to maximise opportunities for students to demonstrate their attainment of learning outcomes, for which credit may be awarded. It follows that the volume and timing of summative assessment within a course should be designed to facilitate and not to impede progression.
- The assessment of academic performance in determining eligibility for the award of credit should not be conflated with local concerns over student behaviours, such as student attendance.
- The award of credit by compensation, where based on clear criteria that include a marginal fail and good overall performance within the level,[9] has been shown to provide the most effective method of allowing students unsuccessful in modules at Level 4 to complete in-time. In contrast, the

practice of condoning failure challenges the principle of consistency in defining awards by a volume of total credits.

* Any student who fails a module should be allowed an opportunity for re-assessment, whereas any subsequent re-assessment attempt should be permitted only on the grounds of mitigation. Trailing credit should be a managed intervention, based upon a judgement of the student's ability to cope with the additional workload, and should be limited to one module per level.

We do not pretend that making regulations more transparent and equitable is either conceptually (McArthur 2016; Grace 2017) or practically simple. Giving discretion to designated individuals and examination boards is one way of ensuring deserving *individual* students can get their just rewards – that is, decisions can be fair. However, being fair to some individuals may well entail the inequitable treatment of all the other students in the cohort. Exercising discretion can be likened to consuming alcohol. In small measures it can have positive outcomes for the user, as in the case of the institution that made limited use of discretion to determine whether students should be allowed to trail credits. Taken in large, uncontrolled quantities, the effects may be deleterious.

In 'crafting [harmonised] regulations' (Stowell et al. 2016: 516–17) for the award of credit, determining where on the continuum between enshrined entitlement and individual/board discretion regulations should be pitched will be more of an art than a science. Difficult though this will be, we believe that bringing greater consistency in regulatory practices within and across institutions is an enterprise worth undertaking.

Notes

1 Awarding institutions can award their own degrees.
2 For responses to these concerns, see, for example, Snelling and Fisher (2020b).
3 The Northern Universities Consortium (NUCCAT) 'provides a forum for higher education practitioners with an interest in the design, implementation and regulation of credit-based curriculum and its implications for the student experience and progression, reflecting the changing dynamics of the sector'.
4 The Student and Assessment Classification Working Group (SACWG), formed in 1994, is composed of academics and administrators who have a professional and personal interest in assessment.
5 $N = 19,828$.
6 The term 'mark' covers both numeric and non-numeric scales.
7 In practice, this would have the same outcome for students as the university that awards credit where a module pass has been attained and where a mark for each summative assessment within the module is equal to or greater than a given threshold, provided that the given threshold is 40%.
8 Royal Assent was given on 27 April 2017.
9 Thereby ensuring that Level Learning Outcomes have been met.

References

Atlay, M. and Turnbull, W. (eds.) (2017) *Aspects of Credit Practice in English and Welsh Universities*. UKCF Report #2. Sheffield: UK Credit Forum.

Bennett, R.E. (2011) Formative assessment: A critical review, *Assessment in Education: Principles, Policy and Practice*, 18 (1): 5–25.

Gibbs, G. and Simpson C. (2005) Conditions under which assessment supports students' learning, *Learning and Teaching in Higher Education*, 1: 3–31.

Grace, C.C. (2017) Exploring the potential for and promise of incorporating distributive and procedural justices into post-secondary assessment of student learning, *Teaching in Higher Education*, 22 (3): 304–17.

Longcroft, A. (2017) *Consider the balance between formative and summative assessment* [blog]. Available at: http://tinyurl.com/nyopedb (accessed 10 December 2020).

McArthur, J. (2016) Assessment for social justice: The role of assessment in achieving social justice, *Assessment and Evaluation in Higher Education*, 41 (7): 967–81.

Quality Assurance Agency (QAA) (2008) *Higher Education Credit Framework for England: Guidance on academic credit arrangements in higher education in England*. Gloucester: QAA.

Quality Assurance Agency (QAA) (2013) *UK Quality Code for Higher Education – Part A: Setting and maintaining academic standards*. Gloucester: QAA.

Quality Assurance Agency (QAA) (2014) *The Frameworks for Higher Education Qualifications of UK Degree-awarding Bodies*. Gloucester: QAA.

Quality Assurance Agency (QAA) (2020) *Higher Education Credit Framework for England: Guidance on academic credit arrangements in higher education in England*, 2nd edn. Draft for consultation. Gloucester: QAA.

Quality Assurance Agency (QAA) (2021) *Higher Education Credit Framework for England: Advice on academic credit arrangements in higher education in England*, 2nd edn. Gloucester: QAA.

Sadler, D.R. (2010) Fidelity as a precondition for integrity in grading academic achievement, *Assessment and Evaluation in Higher Education*, 35 (6): 727–43.

Snelling, C. and Fisher, R. (2020a) *Degree Algorithm Practice in 2020*. Research Report. London: UKSCQA.

Snelling, C. and Fisher, R. (2020b) *Protecting the Value of UK Degrees: Reviewing progress one year on from the Statement of Intent*. London: UKSCQA.

Stowell, M., Falahee, M. and Woolf, H. (2016) Academic standards and regulatory frameworks: Necessary compromises?, *Assessment and Evaluation in Higher Education*, 41 (4): 515–31.

Part 2

Credit practice in the four nations of the UK

5 The official discourse of academic credit in England

Darryll Bravenboer

Introduction

The fortunes and popularity of academic credit have waxed and waned since the Quality Assurance Agency for Higher Education (QAA) published the Higher Education Credit Framework for England (QAA 2008). In the same year, the Office of Qualifications and Examinations Regulation (Ofqual) published the Qualifications and Credit Framework (Ofqual 2008), which was designed to support progression through vocational education and training routes. This chapter will provide an analysis or constructive description (Dowling 2009) of how academic credit has been positioned within official higher education discourse since 2008. In doing this, official texts such as governmental and other policy texts concerning higher education and academic credit will be considered as instances of socio-cultural action constituted as empirical objects for analysis. This chapter as text is also constructed as a socio-cultural artefact that it is hoped will be of value to its intended audience of higher education practitioners, leaders and policy-makers.

... where it stops nobody knows

In *Higher Ambitions: The Future of Universities in the Knowledge Economy* (BIS 2009), the credit system featured as a significant enabler for realising the UK Government's strategy for higher education: 'The use of academic credit supports flexibility in access to higher education, including portability – the ability of students to move on to a new institution to study new modules with formal recognition of what they have already achieved' (2009: 39). In seeking to respond to the demand for greater flexibility in higher education, the government noted that '[u]niversities can already claim funding for credit-bearing courses, and the Higher Education Credit Framework for England highlights the potential roles for credit in supporting progression into and within higher education, and transfer between programmes. Short, credit-based courses are already popular with employers' (2009: 39).

Fast forward through to 2011 and the mood music had changed. In *Higher Education: Students at the Heart of the System* (BIS 2011), academic credit is mentioned twice, once in relation to a case study where learners would gain academic credit through an internship and once listed as a component of the higher education achievement report (HEAR). The ambition to promote the use of 'the credit system' to promote flexible access and progression had vanished.

Government interest emerged again in the 2016 White Paper, *Success as a Knowledge Economy: Teaching Excellence, Social Mobility and Student Choice* (BIS 2016a). The White Paper once again set out the view that credit transfer can improve the life chances of students and increase social mobility but based upon maximising opportunities for student choice: 'We want to gather evidence on how credit transfer in particular can help enable flexible and lifetime learning, and drive up quality by giving students more choice' (2016a: 53). The White Paper noted that '[s]witching between institutions is possible in theory, but rare in practice: if students are unhappy with the quality of provision, they are unlikely to take their funding to an alternative institution' (2016a: 53). The White Paper's authors recognised that '[s]ome barriers to transfer are easy to fix – universities should, for example, present their policy on credit transfer clearly on their websites – but some will require significant and sustained attention' (2016a: 53).

Following on from the White Paper, *Accelerated Courses and Switching University or Degree: Call for Evidence* (BIS 2016b) was published. This consultation document had a section on the existing framework for credit transfer and readers were reminded that the QAA survey of higher education institutions in 2009 indicated that 93% 'confirmed they operated credit arrangements' (2016b: 5). However, while the higher education system is described as being 'designed so that the funding follows the student' (2016b: 5), the consultation sought to learn from the US experience where credit transfer is much more common than in the UK. The effective operation of the credit system is positioned as a matter of market access and the consultation has a second section on potential barriers to a successful credit transfer market. The potential barriers are listed as: a lack of information regarding opportunities to switch; inertia with regards to sticking with a provider regardless of quality, as we might with an energy provider, for example; credit not being a universal currency, as credit from one institution may be counted differently by another; the bureaucratic burden regarding the resource implications for credit recognition and transfer; and 'other' unintended barriers such as the impact on retention measures for the Teaching Excellence Framework (TEF) (Office for Students 2020).

This aligns with the positioning of higher education as a service commodity and students as consumers within the 2016 White Paper: 'Competition between providers in any market incentivises them to raise their game, offering consumers a greater choice of more innovative and better quality products and services at lower cost. Higher education is no exception' (BIS 2016a: 8). The transfer of academic credit is positioned in the same way that the ease with which consumers can switch between energy providers is intended to place competitive pressure on providers to raise the quality of service provided. In essence, the consultation on *Accelerated Courses and Switching University or Degree* (BIS 2016a) sought evidence about how the higher education credit system can better enable students to switch between universities and degree programmes so that their buying power can operate through the higher education market as an indicator of quality and value. Here, academic credit is positioned as a cultural capital currency that can be accrued and exchanged in the higher education market, then cashed in to secure a job or career progression.

At the heart of the credit system

Whilst the 2016 consultation represents a watershed moment for the re-emergence of credit, its positioning as a market access enabler is clearly aligned with the funding that follows the student driver established in 2011. As argued elsewhere (Bravenboer 2019), the Browne Report (2010) made the case for increased tuition fees based on the idea that since individual students are the main beneficiaries of higher education, they should bear the main brunt of the cost. In fact, Browne contrasted this student-led approach with an employer-led system, arguing that 'Asking businesses to contribute through a new tax is also likely to mean that the higher education system will have to be more responsive to their demands; and there is a risk that these may displace the choices made by students' (Browne 2010: 54).

However, in contrast, the germ of positioning employers at the heart of one area of the education system had started to take root following the reforms to apprenticeship policy heralded by the 2012 Richard Review. Richard argued for an employer-led system, where employers would define and determine the occupational standards that apprentices would be required to meet. The 2013 *Specification of Apprenticeship Standards for England* (SFA 2013) had already enabled apprenticeships to be delivered at Levels 6 and 7 and the introduction of degree apprenticeships in 2015 (BIS 2015) required the completion of a Bachelor's or Master's degree as a mandatory qualification.[1] So, an apprentice could undertake a degree apprenticeship and gain an honours degree through an employer-led system, but a non-apprentice student could only gain potentially the same honours degree through a student-led system. This bifurcated approach was further reinforced through the introduction of the apprenticeship levy in April 2017. The apprenticeship levy is a tax collected by the UK Government and it requires that all employers with a payroll of over £3 million must pay 0.5% of their payroll and that the funds collected can only be used to support apprenticeship training. By law, apprentices cannot not pay tuition fees while undertaking a degree apprenticeship; instead, the employer must contract with a higher education provider (for example, a university) and pay for provision through the levy (or contribute 5% if they fall below the £3 million payroll threshold). By contrast, non-apprentice students would need to pay tuition fees, either directly or indirectly through the student loan system.

The market access rationale is predicated on the idea that for the system to work effectively, students should be able to use their buying power flexibly across higher education providers and programmes. However, the rationale for credit recognition and transfer for degree apprentices cannot be based on market access as apprentices cannot, by law, pay for the tuition they receive or access tuition fee loans. The market access rationale that underpinned the 2016 switching university or degree consultation (BIS 2016b) is therefore disrupted by the advent of degree apprenticeships. This is because although the mandatory degree qualification will, in all but a tiny minority of cases, afford opportunities for credit recognition and transfer, apprentices are in no sense engaged in an economic exchange with a higher education provider, rather it is an apprentice's employer who is exchanging money for the opportunity for their employee (the apprentice) to gain academic credit, primarily through the apprenticeship levy. For non-apprentice students, they are individually paying for the opportunity to gain academic credit.

Interestingly, the same rationale is not deployed for employers who are using their buying power when purchasing apprenticeship training with regards to credit recognition and transfer. Rather, through the Education and Skills Funding Agency (ESFA), the government requires that levy funding is not used to develop knowledge, skills or behaviours that a prospective apprentice has already gained prior to starting their apprenticeship (ESFA 2019: 58–59).

All apprenticeship providers are required to conduct an initial assessment to ascertain if prospective apprentices have prior learning, measured against the specified knowledge, skills and behaviours (which are, in effect, learning outcomes) for the relevant Apprenticeship Standard. The Augar Report (DfE 2019) also noted that '… there are concerns that this is not happening: for example, the 2018 annual report of the Ofsted Chief Inspector highlighted that accreditation of existing skills remained a problem in spite of the reform programme' (2019: 153). While the requirement to assess prior learning does not in itself require that credit is awarded by higher education providers to account for learning evidenced through this assessment, in all other aspects it is equivalent. Prior learning is assessed against specified learning outcomes (knowledge, skills and behaviours); the resulting recognition of this prior learning will result in a reduction in the content, duration and price of the degree apprenticeship programme.

The rationale underpinning this is value from public investment, derived from the fact the apprenticeship levy operates as a tax. Using public money to fund learning that has already been achieved is not considered good value. However, it is also clear that the practice of requiring higher education providers to assess prior learning has the same benefits for learners that are identified for non-apprenticeship degree programmes. These include: supporting social mobility for under-represented groups; reduced risk of drop-out; attracting under-represented or disadvantaged groups; greater choice and flexibility supporting career progression; tracking progress and building confidence for further learning (Pollard et al. 2017: 14–15).

In one sense, the value from public investment rationale for degree apprenticeships is similar to the limitations on using tuition fee loan funding for 'equivalent or lower qualifications')[2] for non-apprentice students. It is not thought to be good value to add to the public tuition fee loan book to support learning at an equivalent or lower level that has previously been achieved (with some exceptions for medical and other priority areas). Beyond this, however, there is no funding requirement for higher education providers to assess an applicant's prior learning before undertaking a non-apprenticeship degree programme. As the 2008 Higher Education Credit Framework for England made clear, 'institutions' decision-making processes regarding academic standards and quality should, and will, remain properly and entirely the responsibility of each autonomous institution' (QAA 2008: 4). The QAA added that 'while all learning may be expressed in terms of credit values, not all credit can, or will, necessarily be accumulated towards a specific programme or award, and each higher education institution will determine what credit it will accept for purposes of accumulation or transfer' (2008: 4).

Thirteen years on, the draft Higher Education Credit Framework for England makes clear that the recognition of credit remains a matter of institutional autonomy, although there is a discernible shift in emphasis towards enabling the effective use of credit: 'In recognition of the autonomous status of UK higher education providers and the fact that not all providers in England use credit, the framework is not prescriptive; instead, it enables providers to make the most effective use of credit in the context of their own mission and values' (QAA 2020: 6).

While most higher education providers will have individual policies governing if and how they will recognise prior learning or recognise and transfer credit achieved elsewhere, Department of Education evidence suggests that in the UK these policies are not implemented in practice consistently (Pollard et al. 2017). As a consequence, individual students typically need to first find the relevant policies and then work out how to navigate through institutional systems themselves. No surprise, then, that the volume of credit transfer and recognition in UK higher education providers is reported as being small (BIS 2016a; Pollard et al. 2017).

How can this be squared with the ESFA requirement for all higher education providers of degree apprenticeship programmes to assess the prior learning of all prospective apprentices before starting their degree apprenticeship programme? How have we arrived at a situation where learners undertaking degree programmes in the same institution can be treated very differently with regards to credit recognition, solely because some learners may be registered on degree apprenticeships and others on other degree programmes? How does this square with individual institutional policies regarding credit recognition, let alone across the higher education sector? Given that all degree apprentices are at the same time students of the university or higher education provider awarding the degree qualification, it seems inequitable that non-apprentice students are not routinely afforded the opportunity to have their prior learning assessed and recognised.

Levelling up through credit

The *Independent Panel Report to the Review of Post-18 Education and Funding* (the Augar Report) (DfE 2019) made key recommendations regarding how academic credit could support the enhanced flexibility of higher-level learning: 'Learners should be able to access student finance for tuition fee and maintenance support for modules of credit-based Level 4, 5 and 6 qualifications' (2019: 40). The Augar Report also recommended that the limitations on funding equivalent or lower qualifications (ELQs) should be removed for learning at Levels 4, 5 and 6 and that in time emphasis should be placed on ensuring that qualifications meet employer-led standards.

Shift forward to 2021 and in response to the Augar Report's recommendations for flexibility, the *Interim Conclusion of the Review of Post-18 Education and Funding* (DfE 2021a) signalled a 'lifetime loan entitlement' to four years of post-18 education as part of a Lifetime Skills Guarantee. Also signalled is a move towards greater modularisation of higher education to support flexible opportunities for upskilling and career development. The Augar Report (DfE 2019) also highlighted the need for a change away from the market-orientated, competitive, student and/or employer as consumer model based on the underpinning principle that 'post-18 education cannot be left entirely to market forces' (2019: 122).

The Skills for Jobs White Paper (DfE 2021b) re-positions an effective credit system as a key requirement for realising a Lifetime Skills Guarantee. In addition to providing the skills the economy needs, a key driver for the proposed change in funding system is 'providing value for money for the taxpayer and levelling up across the country' (2021b: 52). Building on the employer-led approach for apprenticeships, the White Paper places 'employers at the heart of the system so that education and training leads to jobs that can improve productivity and fill skills gaps' (2021b: 5).

While *Skills for Jobs* (DfE 2021b) is focused on post-16 skills provision and signals major reforms for further education, many of the proposals have a direct impact upon the provision of higher education. This includes proposals to continue to grow apprenticeships, including higher and degree apprenticeships, and an increased focus on the recognition of prior learning to facilitate accelerated progression and career development. The White Paper also proposes the introduction of the lifetime loan entitlement, as a key part of a Lifetime Skills Guarantee, to 'make it easier for adults and young people to study more flexibly – allowing them to space out their studies, transfer credits between institutions, and partake in more part-time study' (2021b: 40). It will be able to be used by young people and adults to undertake modules or full years of study, higher technical qualifications and degrees at Levels 4 to 6 across further and higher education providers. The transfer of credit is positioned as key to underpinning the flexibility of the proposed new system. The White Paper proposed that '[t]o enable greater flexibility, we must ensure that high-quality provision is normally credit-bearing thereby enabling learners to accumulate and transfer credit where appropriate between institutions and to build up to meaningful qualifications over time fitting in with their personal and work circumstances' (2021b: 41). Crucially, the White Paper notes that '[c]urrently there is no systematic and widely used way for building up credit across different institutions. This poses a key barrier for flexible lifelong learning. We will take action to incentivise easier and more frequent credit transfer between institutions' (2021b: 41).

So, what has changed and what has stayed the same since 2008? How have the fluctuations in the official policy landscape positioned academic credit recognition and transfer within the higher education discursive field? How have the official texts referred to above operated by deploying technologies of truth (Simola et al. 1998) regarding the recognition and transfer of academic credit?

Reading credit recognition and transfer

For the purposes of this chapter, credit recognition and transfer is constituted as a specialist activity or practice that is described in texts produced in the higher education discursive field. The conception of the higher education discursive field draws on both Bourdieu's description of a social field of forces and struggles (Bourdieu 1988a, 1988b) as well as Foucault's description of discursive formation as 'practices that systematically form the objects of which they speak' (Foucault 1972: 49). The selected official texts are instances of sociocultural action within the higher education field and this analysis will seek to describe the discursive strategies and tactics at play. While the specific descriptions considered are historically contingent, they are also constituted by the strategic formation, maintenance and/or destabilising of oppositions and alignments within the selected texts. In other words, the descriptions of credit recognition and transfer that emerge in this reading of the selected official texts are constituted in dynamic relation to other descriptions within each text and within the wider field of higher education.

The selected official texts are constituted as empirical objects for analysis and while there are many other official texts that could be included, this analysis will focus on those referred to above. This will constitute a localising and bounding of the objects for analysis. The rationale for selecting the official texts chosen is that they exemplify differing discursive strategies deployed since the publication of the first Higher Education Credit Framework (QAA 2008), which illustrates how they are operating within the higher education discursive field. The specific approach utilised within this analysis draws on Dowling's (2009) conception of constructive description, which was further developed and applied by Bravenboer (2009, 2013) in the analysis of official higher education texts. The description of identified modes of strategic action can indicate the extent to which texts are operating to (re)produce or resist particular ideas about higher education, in this case the recognition and transfer of academic credit. The recognition and transfer of credit is, for the purposes of this analysis, considered as a form of exchange practice and this draws on Bourdieu's conception of cultural capital exchange (Bourdieu 1986, 1988a, 1988b).

It is important to note that the approach does not seek to uncover a hidden reality, nor does it seek to propose or critique any social or educational principle. Rather, it is intended to offer a re-contextualised constructive description as an artefact that provides a reading of how selected official texts are operating in the higher education discursive field to strategically position the recognition of and transfer of credit. A fuller description of the general methodology can be found in Bravenboer (2009) but it can be summarised as follows:

1 Localising and bounding of texts in the higher education discursive field as an object of analysis.
2 Identification of subjectivities and authorial/audience voices within object texts.
3 Identification of oppositions and alignments within a reading of object texts.
4 Construction of modes of action by re-contextualising identified oppositions and alignments.
5 Analysis of the dynamics of the strategic distribution and exclusion of textual objects in relation to the discursive space constructed as modes of socio-cultural action.

Authorial and audience voices

The official texts constitute a range of subjectivities (Simola et al. 1998) which include and/or exclude authorial and/or audience voices. For example, the Department of Business Innovation and Skills (BIS), the Department for Education (DfE), the Office for Students (OfS), the Education and Skills Funding Agency (ESFA) and the Quality Assurance Agency for Higher Education (QAA) have all been constituted as authors of official texts. Furthermore, the authority of these subjectivities has been constructed with reference to the exercise of legal and sovereign rights to act – for example, the Command status of White Papers. Other authoritative subjectivities, such as Ofsted, are referred to in the official texts in the scope of this analysis but not as authors.

Other subjectivities constituted within the official texts include universities, higher education providers, colleges and independent training providers, which are all described by the Augar Report (DfE 2019) as part of the institutional structure of post-18 education in England. These subjectivities are positioned as audiences, either as desired participants in consultation and review, as a means to establish greater authoritative weight to governmental decisions, or to give official notice of intended governmental actions that will impact on their operation and practice. In the case of QAA texts, providers of higher education are positioned as peers, selected representatives of which are themselves positioned as partial authorities to inform the production of texts. Processes of consultation and review further position higher education providers as contributors to the authorial process for guidance texts such as the Higher Education Credit Framework for England (QAA 2020).

Governmental texts, such as White Papers, commonly describe a key driver for intended actions as securing value from public investment or value for the taxpayer. The public or the taxpayer subjectivities are positioned as legitimising governmental action, although the rationale for this is not made explicit within the texts. Descriptions of why, for example, a taxpayer should be thought of as providing greater legitimation than those whose circumstances mean they do not pay tax, are absent within these governmental texts.

Students, learners, apprentices and consumers are also constituted as subjectivities by official texts in a variety of ways and the descriptions that are in alignment with these subjectivities can be read as indicative of how a text is operating in the higher education discursive field. For example, in *Higher Ambitions* (BIS 2009), access to higher education for students from underrepresented or disadvantaged groups is positioned as an entitlement to access higher education and the flexible use of credit described as a means to enable this. Similarly, in *Skills for Jobs* (DfE 2021b), learners are positioned as entitled to a Lifetime Skills Guarantee and the flexible use of credit as a means to realise this. In contrast, students are positioned as consumers of higher education in *Success as a Knowledge Economy* (BIS 2016a) based upon the premise that as the main beneficiaries of higher education, they bear the brunt of paying tuition fees (albeit through student loans). Here, credit is positioned as a matter of efficiently maximising consumer choice.

The apprentice subjectivity is interesting with regards to its positionality within official texts. In *Higher Ambitions* (BIS 2009), apprentices are not directly mentioned but the need for stronger ladders of opportunity through apprenticeships is part of the proposals to widen access to higher education. In *Success as a Knowledge Economy* (BIS 2016a), the growth and further development of degree apprenticeships is described as the means to enable 'apprentices to reach the highest level of technical and professional skills' (2016a: 13). However, the key thrust of the White Paper is that degree apprenticeships will entail employers working with universities to design programmes that meet needs and standards set by employers, incentivised by the forthcoming Apprenticeship Levy. The Augar report states that 'Apprentices are part of the employed labour force, although they and their employers are bound by very specific rights and duties, which are set out in legislation and/or formal sectoral agreements' (DfE 2019: 143). The legal context for employing and recognising an individual as an 'apprentice' includes the requirement to assess their prior learning 'to take account of prior learning and adapt content and price accordingly' (2019: 153). However, this is not presented as a learner entitlement but rather as a provider and employer responsibility.

The *Interim Conclusion* report (DfE 2021a) in response to the Augar Report (DfE 2019) talks about the Lifetime Skills Guarantee (which would be available for apprentices) but focuses on how apprenticeships meet the needs of employers. *Skills for Jobs* (DfE 2021b), however, does signal that apprentices should be entitled to have prior learning recognised 'to reduce the duration of their apprenticeship and reach occupational competence more quickly' (2021b: 22), and that for 'apprentices with considerable relevant experience, we want to support training providers so that they better recognise this experience during the prior learning assessment and account for this in the training' (2021b: 22).

The subjectivities that have been constituted for employers are also indicative of the discursive shifts that are evidenced within official texts, including increasingly being positioned as an authorial voice. *Higher Ambitions* (BIS 2009) positions the employer voice as channelled through representative bodies such as sector skills councils,[3] as well as partnerships with higher education institutions so that they can better understand their needs. This includes the provision of more flexible modes of higher education; for example, 'Short, credit-based courses are already popular with employers' (BIS 2009: 39). The proposals outlined are also designed to enable employers to 'make informed choices that increase competition between institutions' (2009: 4). *Higher Ambitions* also discusses further developing employer co-funded models, indicating that 'In future the burden of financing higher education's diversity of excellence will need to be more equitably shared between employers, the taxpayer, and individuals' (2009: 22).

Success in a Knowledge Economy (BIS 2016a) positions employers as beneficiaries from the competition and informed choice in higher education that the White Paper seeks to promote. Employers are positioned as taking the lead in the design of occupational standards for degree apprenticeships working with universities. This positioning is reproduced in the Augar Report (DfE 2019) and the employer-led approach adopted for apprenticeships is promoted for other technical post-18 provision, particularly at Levels 4 and 5: 'Employers play a vital role in post-18 education. They provide on-the-job training on a daily basis; they co-produce and deliver skills training with providers; they work with local and regional bodies to address skills needs; through their representative organisations, they have a fundamental role in setting the skills agenda' (2019: 19).

This key role for employers is also underpinned by the working principle in the Augar Report that 'the cost of post-18 education should be shared between taxpayers, employers and learners' (DfE 2019: 8), closely mirroring the position proposed in *Higher Ambitions* (BIS 2009) ten years earlier. The *Skills for Jobs* (DfE 2021b) White Paper goes further and explicitly describes putting employers at the heart of the system, developing local skills improvement plans, aligning provision to employer-led standards and growing apprenticeships so employers can benefit from the Lifetime Skills Guarantee.

Oppositions and alignments

The positioning of students at the heart of the system in official object texts can be read as a rationale for students, as the primary beneficiaries, paying for a higher education service. As consumers of this service, the rationale follows, students have a role to play in incentivising the raising of service quality through the buying decisions they make. If students can switch higher education provider and programme more easily, then the operation of the higher education market more effectively drives quality improvement of the service. The recognition and transfer of academic credit provides a key means by which students can enact their consumer preferences by switching provider and/or programme.

Aligned with this, the effective operation of the higher education market, driven by consumer choice, can be read as the means by which government secures value from public investment in higher education and an effective credit transfer system is a means to achieve this. Barriers or inflexibilities that impede the ability of students to switch providers or programmes, such as inconsistent recognition of academic credit by different providers, are positioned in opposition to consumer choice, service improvement and value from public investment. However, the institutional autonomy of higher education providers with degree-awarding powers is held as sacrosanct and this means that academic judgements about if and how credit is recognised and transferred is solely a matter for individual institutions.

More recently, official texts have positioned employers at the heart of the system rather than students. This can be read as a rationale for employers contributing to the costs of education and training where they set the standards and determine the needs that should be met. For example, for degree apprenticeship provision, employers design and set the occupational standards, they determine which apprentices they employ, and they support and contribute to required on-the-job learning. Employers who pay the apprenticeship levy also fund the provision of the required education and training, while smaller employers make a contribution to costs. In this context, the operation of the higher education provider market regarding employer choice for degree apprenticeships is restricted to the choice of provider, which includes consideration of price as well as quality. However, the benefit to employers regarding the recognition of prior learning before an individual starts an apprenticeship is aligned with enabling employers to deploy competent staff more quickly rather than as a driver of quality improvement of the provider service.

The conditions of higher education providers receiving apprenticeship levy funding from the ESFA include agreeing to assess prior learning for all prospective apprenticeship starts and adjusting both the content (i.e. the programme of on- and off-the-job learning required to reach competence) as well as the price. Recognition of prior learning for degree apprenticeships is arguably not primarily a matter of institutional autonomy, it is a matter of ESFA funding rules compliance. However, the alignment, in more recent official texts, between an efficient credit system and realising the Lifetime Skills Guarantee appears to emphasise the value of flexibility for the learner to better reflect changes to personal and work circumstances as a form of entitlement. *Skills for Jobs* (DfE 2021b) tells the reader that the government will incentivise easier and more frequent credit transfer but falls short of indicating that it will regulate, as is the case for degree apprenticeships.

Modes of credit recognition and transfer

Reading the oppositions and alignments described above, the legitimisation of recognition and transfer (of learning and/or credit) practice emerges as predicated on its value for either singular subjectivities, such as students and employers, or homogeneous subjectivities, such as taxpayers or the public. While it is of course entirely possible to think of 'students' or 'employers' homogeneously, the rationale for recognition and transfer described in *Success as a Knowledge Economy* (BIS 2016a) is predicated on the individual student consumer as the primary beneficiary of higher education. Interestingly, while individual employers who are large enough to pay the apprenticeship levy do constitute singular consumers of apprenticeship provision, the fact that the levy is collected as a tax simultaneously constructs a more homogeneous context. Similarly, apprentices seem to be primarily constructed as employees, that is, subject to contractual agreement with their employer, rather than singular subjectivities. Perhaps also, the fact that the recognition of prior learning is a regulated requirement for apprenticeship providers leads to an underplaying of the potential benefits this has for individual apprentices. This highlights a second key discursive opposition within the official object texts.

The practice of recognition of prior learning for prospective degree apprentices is highly regulated (as described above), as is the ability to award credit that can count towards higher education qualifications, which is limited to those organisations that have been afforded degree-awarding powers. However, official texts have indicated that this can present a barrier to flexibility, in terms of an individual's ability to 'accumulate and transfer credit where appropriate between institutions and to build up to meaningful qualifications over time' (DfE 2021b: 41). Similarly, the fact that recognition and transfer practice is closed creates barriers to credit recognition as a universal currency, which leads to it being counted differently by different higher education providers. In this sense, calls in official texts for a 'university currency' of academic credit represent both an opening up of recognition and transfer practice as well as the ascription of a more homogeneous value. By using the oppositions between value for singular or homogeneous subjectivities, cross-related with open or closed recognition and transfer practice, we can construct a conceptual space within which to map discursive instances that have emerged in this reading of official texts (see Table 5.1).

Table 5.1 Modes of credit recognition and transfer

Value	Practice	
	Open	Closed
Singular subjectivity	Consumer mode	Institutional mode
Homogeneous subjectivity	Commodified mode	Bureaucratic mode

The consumer mode represents where recognition and transfer are presented as of singular value and where practice is open. The rationale underpinning the positioning of academic credit as a matter of market access for individual consumers of higher education operates primarily in this mode. Of course, on this model, such consumers would need access to the higher education provider market to be able to enact their individual buying choices. At present, such a market would necessarily operate across 'commodified' and 'bureaucratic modes' as the provision of higher education is currently a regulated practice. Where employers are positioned 'at the heart of the system', however, the value of recognition and transfer is also simultaneously homogenised as value from public investment or value for the taxpayer, in the bureaucratic mode. Of course, employers who pay the apprenticeship levy are also taxpayers in this sense and the description of the requirement to assess and recognise prior learning, as required by the ESFA funding rules, is operating firmly in the bureaucratic mode.

The conception of levelling up described within more recent official texts positions credit as of homogeneous value aligned with statements that encourage an opening of recognition and transfer practice. It may also be the case that the descriptions of levelling up deployed in official texts seem of homogeneous value as they are applied in very general terms. The Lifetime Skills Guarantee is also generally described in more recent official texts, but the associated lifetime loan entitlement is more firmly positioned in bureaucratic mode as the facility to access funding to support flexible credit accumulation and transfer of credit-bearing learning activity. As indicated above, descriptions of a universal currency for credit are operating in the commodified mode, as the value of credit is presented as homogeneous and the practice of recognition and transfer opened if barriers to market access are to be addressed. It is the case, however, that such a system of universal credit currency would require a bureaucratic means to regulate the exchange rate, such as a national credit system.

The advent of levelling up within recent official texts has some echoes from descriptions of the need to recognise credit more flexibly to enable wider access to higher education in *Higher Ambitions* (BIS 2009). However, the context for such descriptions is more clearly placed within the 'institutional mode', where the singular value of recognition and transfer are solely a matter of the institutional autonomy of individual higher education providers. The requirements for Access Agreements and then Access and Participation Plans[4] construct a bureaucratic context but, to date, this does not entail any requirement to recognise prior learning or credit (with the notable exception of apprentices). As Pollard et al. (2017) pointed out, the fact that individual higher education providers will, more often than not, have policies that describe the means by which the institution will recognise and transfer credit, does not imply that such policies are commonly enacted.

The new draft Higher Education Credit Framework for England (QAA 2020) describes the Framework as enabling and directive, which is a departure from the 2008 version. The text describes many examples of credit recognition and

Figure 5.1 Mapping the official discourse of credit recognition and transfer

Consumer mode	Institutional mode
Singular value/open practice	*Singular value/closed practice*

Consumer Choice

Institutional Autonomy

Students at the Heart of the System

Institutional Credit Policy

Access to HE

Employers at the Heart of the System

HE Credit Framework

Commodified mode	Bureaucratic mode
Hologeneous value/open practice	*Homogeneous value/closed practice*

Levelling-up

Lifetime Loan Entitlement

Universal Credit Currency

Lifetime Skills Guarantee

National Credit System

ESFA Funding Rules

The HE Provider Market

Value from Public Investment

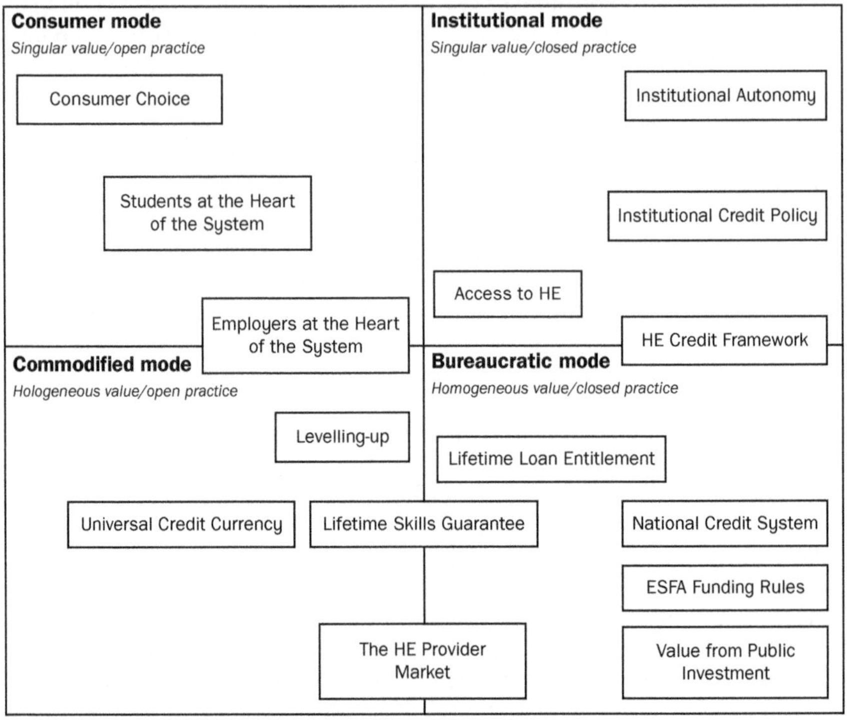

transfer practice, which are designed to provide guidance for higher education providers, employers and learners. The examples include the role of credit recognition and transfer for apprenticeships and micro-credentials, which further illustrate how practice can be constructively opened to accommodate these forms of higher education. This enabling and directive flexibility may indicate that the new Higher Education Credit Framework (QAA 2020) can serve as the underpinning for a national credit system.[5] For example, the outcome of the regulated assessment of prior learning for degree apprenticeships remains a matter for the higher education provider and, as such, a national bureaucratic approach need not be read as being in opposition to institutional autonomy. In this sense, the Higher Education Credit Framework straddles both institutional and bureaucratic modes.

Conclusion

It is clear that there have been strategic shifts in the positioning of the recognition and transfer of academic credit since 2008. While *Higher Ambitions* (BIS 2009), *Higher Education: Students at the Heart of the System* (BIS 2011) and *Success as a Knowledge Economy* (BIS 2016a) all maintain the primacy of institutional autonomy with regards to academic credit, the advent of degree apprenticeships potentially disrupts this orthodox position. At present, *Skills for Jobs* (DfE 2021b) promises to incentivise opening up of the practice of credit recognition and transfer, which might indicate funding incentives of some kind. However, if employers rather than students will be at the heart of the system, the rationale for securing value from public investment by introducing a regulatory requirement to assess prior learning does not seem impossible. Particularly given that the vast majority of universities in England are also signed up to the ESFA funding rules as apprenticeship providers.

It is of course also possible that the bifurcated model will persist and students will remain at the heart of the non-apprenticeship higher education system regarding the recognition and transfer of credit, while the 'skills system' will prioritise employers and, by extension, apprentices. Since, however, the Lifetime Loan Entitlement will apply to credit-bearing higher education modules, and if the clear intention that is signalled by *Skills for Jobs* (DfE 2021b) is to be realised, then some form of national system for the recognition and transfer of credit would be required. In any case, it is certainly worth another spin of the wheel!

Notes

1   The publication of the Specification of Apprenticeship Standards for England (SASE, 2013) followed a consultation to review the previous (2011) version of SASE that governed the approval and delivery of Apprenticeship Frameworks. SASE (2013) introduced Level 6 and 7 apprenticeships for the first time; increased the minimum credit values for Level 4 and 5 apprenticeships to 90 credits and for Level 6 and 7 apprenticeships to 120 credits; and incorporated the use and authentication of professional qualifications. These changes were designed to align apprenticeships with higher education qualifications.

2   'ELQ (equivalent or lower qualification) students are students who already hold a higher education qualification and are studying a course that leads to a qualification equivalent to or lower than one they already hold' (www.oficeforstudents.org).

3   Sector Skills Councils are independent, employer-led organisations licensed by the government to identify future sector skills needs. They are responsible for the design and approval of Apprenticeship Frameworks and National Occupational Standards.

4   Higher education providers required approval of their Access Agreement by the Office for Fair Access to be able to change higher-level tuition fees. The Office for Students undertook responsibility for these agreements after the Office for Fair Access was closed in March 2018. From 2019, higher education providers were required to produce Access and Participation Plans for the same purpose and to set out how they planned to improve equality of opportunity for under-represented groups to access, succeed in and progress from higher education.

5   At the time of writing, the author was referring to the consultative draft of the second edition of the Credit Guidance/Advice for England.

References

Bourdieu, P. (1986) The forms of capital, in J. Richardson (ed.) *Handbook of Theory of Research for the Sociology of Education*. Westport, CT: Greenwood Press.

Bourdieu, P. (1988a) *Practical Reason*. Cambridge: Polity Press.

Bourdieu, P. (1988b) *Homo Academicus*. Cambridge: Polity Press.

Bravenboer, D.W. (2009) *Commodification and the official discourse of higher education*. PhD thesis, Institute of Education, University of London.

Bravenboer, D.W. (2013) The official discourse of fair access to higher education, *Journal of Widening Participation and Lifelong Learning*, 14 (3): 120–40.

Bravenboer, D.W. (2019) The creative disruption of degree apprenticeships in the UK, in J. Talbot (ed.) *Global Perspectives on Work-Based Learning Initiatives*. Hershey, PA: IGI Global.

Browne, J. (2010) *Securing a Sustainable Future for Higher Education: Independent review of higher education funding & student finance* (the Browne Report). Available at: https://tinyurl.com/44h4skfu (accessed 30 March 2021).

Department for Business, Innovation and Skills (BIS) (2009) *Higher Ambitions: The future of universities in the knowledge economy*. London: BIS.

Department for Business, Innovation and Skills (BIS) (2011) *Higher Education: Students at the heart of the system*. London: BIS.

Department for Business, Innovation and Skills (BIS) (2015) *The Future of Apprenticeships in England: Guidance for trailblazers – from standards to starts*. London: BIS.

Department for Business, Innovation and Skills (BIS) (2016a) *Success as a Knowledge Economy: Teaching excellence, social mobility and student choice*. London: BIS.

Department for Business, Innovation and Skills (BIS) (2016b) *Accelerated Courses and Switching University or Degree: Call for evidence*. London: BIS.

Department for Education (DfE) (2019) *Independent Panel Report to the Review of Post-18 Education and Funding* (the Augar Report). London: DfE.

Department for Education (DfE) (2021a) *Interim Conclusion of the Review of Post-18 Education and Funding*. London: DfE.

Department for Education (DfE) (2021b) *Skills for Jobs: Lifelong learning for opportunity and growth*. London: DfE.

Dowling, P. (2009) *Sociology as Method*. Leiden: Brill-Sense.

Education and Skills Funding Agency (ESFA) (2019) *Apprenticeship Funding Rules for Main Providers*. Coventry: ESFA. Available at: https://assets.publishing.service.gov.uk/government/uploads/system/uploads/attachment_data/file/1007548/2021-07-28_-_2122_Provider_Rules_Version_Version_1.pdf.

Foucault, M. (1972) *The Archaeology of Knowledge*. London: Tavistock.

Office for Students (OfS) (2020) *About the TEF*. Available at: https://tinyurl.com/2vy5pa6b (accessed 19 March 2021).

Ofqual (2008) *Qualifications and Credit Framework*. Available at: https://tinyurl.com/ ywsu2xa5 (accessed 30 March 2021).

Pollard, E., Hadjivassiliou, K., Swift, S. et al. (2017) *Credit Transfer in Higher Education: A review of the literature*. London: DfE. Available at: https://assets.publishing. service.gov.uk/government/uploads/system/uploads/attachment_data/file/595633/ Credit_transfer_in_Higher_Education.pdf.

Quality Assurance Agency (QAA) (2008) *Higher Education Credit Framework for England: Guidance on academic credit arrangements in higher education in England*. Gloucester: QAA.

Quality Assurance Agency (QAA) (2020) *Higher Education Credit Framework for England: Guidance on academic credit arrangements in higher education in England*, 2nd edn. Draft for consultation. Gloucester: QAA.

Richard, D. (2012) *The Richard Review of Apprenticeships*. Available at: https://assets. publishing.service.gov.uk/government/uploads/system/uploads/attachment_data/ file/34708/richard-review-full.pdf.

Simola, H., Heikkenen, S. and Silvonen J. (1998) A catalog of possibilities: Foucaultian history of truth and educational research, in T.S. Popkewitz and M. Brennan (eds.) *Foucault's Challenge: Discourse, Knowledge and Power in Education*. New York: Teachers College Press.

Skills Funding Agency (SFA) (2013) *Specification of Apprenticeship Standards for England (SASE)*. Coventry: SFA.

6 | Widening access and participation in Northern Ireland

Rosemary Moreland, Erik Cownie,
Isobel Hawthorne-Steele and Maeve Paris

Northern Ireland has a substantial history of recognising achievement through credit accumulation and transfer. A working group set up in 1996 established guidelines for credit accumulation and transfer within Northern Ireland (NICATS 1999). These guidelines informed the foundation of credit accumulation and transfer across the UK, enabling educators to assign a number of credits, related to notional learning hours and level of credits pertaining to the 'demand, complexity and depth of learning and of learner autonomy' (1999: 53). In subsequent years, building upon this foundation, policy-makers and academic institutions have invested significant time and resources into widening access and participation in further and higher education for groups who have traditionally not benefited from post-compulsory education.

Both further and higher education providers have a distinct role to play in widening access to post-compulsory education. There are currently three universities operating in Northern Ireland: Queen's University Belfast, Ulster University and the Open University. There are two university colleges both based in Belfast – St. Mary's and Stranmillis, six regional further education (FE) colleges located across the province, and one specialist College of Agriculture, Food and Rural Enterprise (CAFRE). Since 2016, both further and higher education in Northern Ireland have come under the remit of the Department for the Economy (DfE); prior to this, responsibility fell to the Department for Employment and Learning (DELNI). As there is no specific higher education funding council in Northern Ireland, the DfE is tasked with formulating policy and administering funding to support education, research and related activities in further and higher education. Northern Ireland's universities are publicly funded and fully autonomous. DfE uses a funding formula to provide teaching grants, but it also applies a maximum student number (MaSN), an annual cost control on the overall number of full-time undergraduate students. The six FE colleges, on the other hand, are non-departmental public bodies operating at arms' length from the DfE to provide learning in essential skills, further education/secondary vocational training, as well as vocational higher education (the latter accounted for 9.2% of their activity in 2017/18) (OECD 2020: 19). (The specialist college CAFRE is funded by the Department for Agriculture, Environment and Rural Affairs, DAERA.) Hence, the further education sector offers an opportunity for the universities to diversify activity without affecting MaSN, effectively outsourcing sub-degree provision, and to offer progression pathways to honours degrees as part of a widening access remit. Each institution sets out its own policies with regard to widening access, credit accumulation and transfer.

This chapter will provide an overview of the key government policies that have provided the main impetus for widening access and participation to higher education. It will examine the information provided by each of the institutions in relation to the specific policies implemented at a local level. In order to illustrate the ways in which proactive implementation of these policies contributes to widening access, we will outline two case studies. The first will examine the partnership approach between further and higher education in delivering Foundation degrees, which have become the intermediate qualification of choice in Northern Ireland. As they integrate academic and work-based learning and are equivalent to two years' full-time study, these awards are particularly well suited to addressing regional employment needs and to widening access to higher education (QAA 2020). The second case study describes a unique Accreditation of Prior Learning (APL)[1] pathway, which enables adult learners to gain direct access to university.

Background

Northern Ireland has a strong track record in widening access and participation (WAP), with figures for participation in higher education by students from lower socio-economic backgrounds being consistently higher than the UK average (DELNI 2012, 2015). A key factor in this has been the Department of Employment and Learning's financial support to higher education students on low incomes, those with caring responsibilities and those with disabilities.[2] With the introduction of tuition fees for higher education in 2006, DELNI established Access Agreements with each provider, which set out its commitment each year to increasing participation from under-represented sections of society. Despite these positive measures, persistently high levels of unemployment and areas of low educational attainment prompted DELNI (2012) to develop a strategy on widening access and participation. The key objective of *Access to Success* (DELNI 2012: 5) was to 'widen participation in higher education by students from those groups which are currently under-represented', a commitment that was reiterated in the Higher Education Strategy (DELNI 2015). The 2012 DELNI report highlighted that this objective was not just about widening the higher education market, but also about up-skilling the workforce. Recognition was given to raising aspirations, promoting higher education across all providers; continuing further development of Access courses for adult learners and part-time students; and adopting student-centred approaches to support the successful retention and progression of non-traditional students.[3]

As part of this strategy, Access Agreements have been replaced with Widening Access and Participation Plans (WAPP), which each higher education provider is required to submit to DELNI on an annual basis. Based on the progress and achievements made in these plans, a premium is awarded to institutions towards the extra costs associated with recruiting and retaining WAP students. The Department provides additional special project funding, to enable the universities to engage with traditionally under-represented groups and schools, which normally have low numbers of students progressing to university. Despite these efforts, four main areas of under-representation persist: (1) those from socio-economic classes 5–7;[4] (2) low-participation neighbourhoods; (3) young Protestant males; and (4) persons with disabilities (DELNI 2012). Acknowledging the wider context of social and economic inequality, DELNI (2012) pledged support for programmes delivered by universities which seek to maximise the potential of students from disadvantaged backgrounds.

In order to tackle up-skilling of the workforce, the DELNI (2012) report urged HE institutions (HEIs) to make provision for suitable progression via advanced apprenticeships, Foundation degrees and other vocational programmes. In particular, the Department supported the wider promotion of Foundation degrees to employers and students; as well as supporting the implementation of a new framework to rationalise the qualification. The report also acknowledged the benefits of APL, although this is largely linked to up-skilling and re-skilling to meet workplace demands and is therefore identified as a useful additional entry to Foundation degrees. The Northern Ireland Strategy for Further Education (DELNI 2016) makes clear the role of further education in providing intermediate higher education, leading to established pathways of progression from Foundation degrees and Access programmes onto honours degree programmes. Adult Access programmes are well established across all the regional colleges in Northern Ireland and in line with England and Wales; QAA maintains and manages the scheme for recognising and quality assuring these programmes. Queen's University Belfast and Ulster University are licensed to validate and oversee Access diplomas in Northern Ireland and have established equivalencies, which allow achievement on the Access programmes to be measured against A Level grades, in order to create an equal playing field. The fact that FE colleges have a greater geographical reach into communities and provide qualifications from Level 1[5] upwards, means that they are better positioned than universities to enable those with few or no qualifications to progress to higher education. However, the Further Education Strategy (DELNI 2016) appears to place much greater emphasis on their role of up-skilling the workforce and enabling people to get into employment than on progression to higher education.

A similar theme is found in the strategy for higher education (DELNI 2015), whereby increasing access to such education is predominantly linked to the needs of the economy. Indeed, the restructuring of governmental departments in 2016, which led to the change from the Department of Employment and Learning to the Department for the Economy, signals a clear message that the focus of higher and further education should be predominantly on skilling the workforce. The recent Programme for Government Draft Outcomes Framework (NIE 2021: 21) highlights key outcomes relevant to higher and further education: improving educational achievement, tackling persistent underachievement, and '... alongside skills shortages, aligning Further and Higher Education to labour market demand'.

Whilst increasing individuals' opportunities to compete in the job market is a worthy aim, the authors contend that widening access and participation to higher education should not be narrowly focused only on employability but indeed can produce much wider societal benefits, which impact positively on health and well-being and civic society (Field 2012; Marmot 2015; UNESCO 2016; Learning and Work Institute 2017). Recent educational policy strategies (DELNI 2012, 2015, 2016) in promoting a lifelong learning ethos, place considerable emphasis on attracting learners who are already in the workforce (i.e. adults). To this end, the aim of *Further Education Means Success* (DELNI 2016) is to increase the role of further education in the delivery of intermediate higher education and to develop a single credit and qualifications framework, which would promote a clear and flexible progression route for learners. Additional funding was committed to increase part-time intermediate qualifications in FE colleges. Community engagement is also highlighted in the DELNI (2015: 22) strategy, stressing that FE and HE institutions (FEIs and HEIs) 'have an obligation ... to contribute to the social, cultural and economic life of the wider community'. Acknowledging the good work already carried out by FEIs and HEIs in Northern Ireland, the report suggests that, among other things, institutions should develop 'partnerships with voluntary organisations and the wider community' (2015: 22).

Current policies and procedures for widening access and participation and Accreditation of Prior Learning in FE colleges in Northern Ireland

As previously mentioned, the seven FE colleges in Northern Ireland each have their own WAP plans, which can be accessed via their college websites. However, in all but two there was less readily available information around APL opportunities. These plans and strategies reflect the Northern Ireland government's commitment to lifelong learning and the provision of improved progression routes to targeted groups who are traditionally under-represented in further and higher education.

The largest of the regional FE colleges, Belfast Metropolitan College (Belfast Met), claims to 'actively encourage ... students from disadvantaged backgrounds' to apply to the College, and commits to supporting them 'throughout their student journey'. Citing a desire to 'change perceptions and raise aspirations', they acknowledge that 'having a diverse student population impacts positively on everyone's learning and development' (Belfast Met 2021). Importantly, the College also proactively develops 'links with organisations who work directly with people who are facing barriers to their educational progression', as part of their wider community engagement strategy. Importantly, their website explicitly welcomes requests for application and enrolment support for disadvantaged learners, including: people experiencing economic hardship; those in or previously from a care setting; the homeless; individuals previously involved with the criminal justice system; people with a mental health illness; carers; and single or young parents. Belfast Met (2020) has specific guidance for applicants about its APL processes, defining APL as the 'informal/non-formal learning … you have done up to this point which has not already been formally assessed'. It also provides applicants with step-by-step guidance to navigate the APL application process. Of all the FE colleges, this was the most comprehensive and easily accessible information on APL. Moreover, this guidance also promoted the value of such experiential learning and provided an offer of support to help applicants complete their Portfolio of Evidence of Learning.

This same commitment to educational social justice is expressed in the WAP policies of Southern Regional College (SRC), which frames such policies as contributing to both 'social cohesion and economic development', as well as having 'a series of underpinning core values' which 'help define the widening access culture within the college'. For example, the College has a core value of 'Putting Learners First', which includes a commitment to 'accessible and informative student support services', 'an inclusive approach to widening access', and to advance the 'learning of those most marginalised in society' (SRC 2020).

Each of these regional FE colleges has its own uniquely complex catchment area, and each is compelled to devise a WAP strategy that best serves the educational, social and economic needs of that area. South Eastern Regional College (SERC), arguably more explicitly than the other FE colleges, highlights that its WAP strategy has been developed as per a 'detailed analysis of the needs of our community by quintile' – which highlighted pockets of significant deprivation within the catchment area; and, subsequently, prioritises 'addressing social inclusion by providing opportunities for those not in work, to obtain a professional or technical qualification allowing them to gain employment and escape the benefit cycle' (SERC 2020). Moreover, the SERC WAP strategy is based on a partnership between the College and the local Community Voluntary Sector (CVS), which seeks to 'provide well-supported programmes that give opportunities for those from deprived backgrounds to re-enter education, and undertake meaningful qualifications which lead to employment or progression to higher level courses' (SERC 2020). While SERC did not have specific pages or publications around APL, its WAP plan and admissions policies also include commitments to: 'provide appropriate support for those within the SERC catchment area who fall within the Access to Success target groups to progress in the long-term towards higher education'; and 'continue to promote suitable progression routes towards higher education'.

The acknowledgement of the duality between an area's social and economic imperatives, and the utility of partnership approaches between FE colleges and the CVS, are also evident in the WAP strategy of Northern Regional College (NRC), which encompasses a commitment to 'provide students with a life-changing, supportive and innovative experience, which will equip them with the skills to compete successfully in the global employment market and meet the needs of local industry and employers' (NRC 2018). In terms of community engagement, NRC 'has a strong community-facing focus and seeks to provide education and training opportunities for those who might not normally engage with the College'. NRC also has accessible information around APL which makes clear the value the College places on such learning; provides a helpful list of examples of APL and a step-by-step guide to the application process; and lists contact details where applicants can get help to complete the enrolment process (NRC 2018).

Arguably, the most detailed WAP plan among the regional FE colleges – particularly in terms of highlighting 'target groups' – is from South West College (SWC 2017), whose WAP strategy acknowledges and makes explicit reference to the 'particularly high level of education, skills and training deprivation' in the catchment area, and the long-standing issues of low participation in higher education among 'young Protestant males from areas of high deprivation', learners with disabilities, and adult learners who have been out of education for some time. Moreover, this WAP plan outlines the progress made in increasing participation levels among these social groups, and ambitious targets for continued increases in the future. In terms of readily available information around APL, SWC also has accessible guidance for applicants, which, helpfully, makes explicit reference to: 'prior learning gained through community-based learning'; and 'learners who may have exited a HE programme prior to completion or the receipt of credit' (SWC 2021).

The WAP plan of North West Regional College (NWRC) acknowledges the multiple economic and social challenges of its catchment area, such as the highest claimant count in Northern Ireland, the highest rates of economic inactivity amongst the working age population in Northern Ireland and the fact that 39% of its regulated enrolments[6] reside within Quintile 1[7] communities. In recognition of these challenges, NWC has in place a Careers Academy that provides a one-stop careers service to help under-represented groups access further and higher education and employment, and a designated WAP officer who engages with the local CVS to co-facilitate 'community roadshows' to target the hardest-to-reach learners (NWC 2020).

This brief review of WAP and APL strategies across the six regional FE colleges highlights some important messages in terms of informing potential students about learning opportunities they may not know exist. The WAP strategies outlined above all encompass significant cognisance of the social and economic realities of their catchment areas, and an equally significant commitment to ensure that the opportunity to access higher education is open to all sections of society. FE colleges play an important role in widening access to higher education and, in line with the prevailing government policy (DELNI

2015), there is strong evidence of engagement with local communities and schools, recognising the unique role that community-based access programmes can play. However, progression to higher education via APL is a lesser-known option and while some colleges provide excellent and accessible information on APL progression routes, the information is somewhat scant in others. If government is serious about encouraging more adults in the workforce to progress to higher education, there are clearly huge benefits for all to a wider recognition and uptake of APL for entry and advanced standing.[8]

Case study 1: Widening access through Foundation degrees – a partnership approach

Ulster University (hereafter the University) positions itself as Northern Ireland's civic university; it joined 30 other UK universities in 2019 to produce a Civic University Agreement (Ulster University 2019). Underpinning this agreement is a partnership approach to educational attainment, which requires providers to undertake widening access and participation activities with a view to enhancing their civic mission, including activities which 'work with further education colleges to create diverse pathways into higher education, including for people in work or with caring responsibilities' (OFS 2019: 3).

The University has placed at the heart of this partnership approach a unique arrangement based on the Foundation degree as the intermediate qualification of choice, and in line with DELNI (2016) policy. The Foundation degree is a qualification which responds to regional employment needs, enables access to higher education and offers a clear pathway for articulation to undergraduate honours degrees. It is the University's vehicle of choice for partnership with FE colleges, since it is characterised by its 'aim to contribute to widening participation and lifelong learning by encouraging participation by learners who may not previously have considered studying for a higher level qualification or prefer a more applied curriculum' (QAA 2020: 3). The University has transferred much of its intermediate-level provision in the form of validated Foundation degrees to the local FE colleges, specifically the six regional colleges and the College of Agriculture, Food and Rural Enterprise (CAFRE). This is in order to reflect regional requirements and support for the community, as befits a civic university. It is also a function of the landscape of tertiary education in Northern Ireland.

The range and scope of the University's Foundation degree provision is remarkable: working with the six FE colleges and CAFRE, as of September 2020, the University validated 100 Foundation degrees over 24 campuses across Northern Ireland. Foundation degrees sit at Level 5 of the national Framework for Higher Educational Qualifications (FHEQ), and the University's Qualifications and Credit Framework stipulates that the award should comprise a minimum of 240 credit points, usually at Levels 4 and 5, with at least 40 credits of work-based learning at Level 5. Clear and formalised articulation routes are identified for each Foundation degree at validation: 'approved provision is termed validated if developed by an institution and offered to its own students who are Associate Students of the University' (Ulster University 2020a: 12). This distinction is important: the college develops the curriculum, which the University validates; and the students are college students, who are accorded the status of Associate Students of the University, with limited associated benefits.

A snapshot of regional validated provision in 2019/20 illustrates the extent and importance of the provision. A total of 3,399 students were registered on Foundation degrees across the province, and in that year 1,468 were expected to graduate. The courses that attracted the highest enrolments were all full-time courses, apart from one part-time Counselling course (Table 6.1).

Table 6.1 Highest enrolling Foundation degrees, 2019/20

Foundation degree	Total enrolments 2019/20
FdEng Software Engineering, Belfast Metropolitan College	89
FdSc Counselling, Northern Regional College	70
FdSc Agriculture and Technology, CAFRE	59
FdSc Computing, South Eastern Regional College	53
FdSc Computing, South West College	50

Progression from the Foundation degree is based on an articulation model, where 'the associated Honours degree is completed in up to two further years of full-time study, or the equivalent part-time in a "2 + bridging + 1" model' (Ulster University 2020a: 7), where bridging can range from 0 to 120 credits depending on the curriculum match. Most full-time honours degrees have a mandatory placement year (60 credits at Level 5). The University permits exemption from placement for articulating students on the basis of the work-based learning module of 40 credits at Level 5.

As they integrate academic and work-based learning, the main aim of Foundation degrees is to secure relevant employment, by addressing key skills shortages: they 'are intended to equip learners with the skills and knowledge relevant to employment, so satisfying the needs of employees and employers' (QAA 2020: 3). Hence, in a given year, the expectation is that at least half of a graduating cohort will secure employment, and half will articulate to university. In September 2020, 487 students articulated to honours degrees from Foundation degrees, which was a better result than had been expected in the midst of the COVID-19 pandemic.

Most students articulated to courses in Computing, Engineering and the Built Environment. The honours degree courses or subject areas that attracted the highest numbers are set out in Table 6.2.

Table 6.2 Most popular articulation routes, September 2020

Articulation route (full-time and part-time combined)	Total articulating to year 2/ final year
Software Engineering/Computing Science	88
Civil Engineering	33
Health and Wellbeing	33
Business Studies	32
Sports Studies/Coaching and Performance	29
International Travel and Tourism	27
Leisure and Events Management	17

When it was introduced initially, the Foundation degree largely displaced existing HND/HNC provision, and colleges were encouraged by the DfE to switch awards. However, HND provision continues to be offered since employers more readily understand it, despite DfE investment in targeted advertising campaigns, and it often therefore competes with the Foundation degree for enrolments. The use of the Foundation degree as the knowledge component of Higher Level Apprenticeships (HLAs) has also been problematic; in Northern Ireland, the apprenticeship concludes on the award of the Foundation degree (there is no other end-point assessment), which is also when colleges can claim final payments. This leads to considerable pressure in some sectors to compress the length of study for the award; however, as apprentices are taught on day release, this limits the number of contact hours available in a week and puts considerable pressure on such students who may end up studying over the entire calendar year.

This divergence from practice elsewhere arose from the more flexible approach adopted by Northern Ireland's devolved administration. While Apprenticeship Standards implemented in England define requirements for both occupational competence and independent End Point Assessment (QAA 2019: 14), Northern Ireland's Apprenticeship Frameworks focused on the design of a *single* award/qualification for apprenticeship occupations in line with policy commitment 2 of the Northern Ireland Strategy on Apprenticeships (DELNI 2014: 27). This was driven by feedback from small businesses, which reported confusion over multiple components and complicated qualifications associated with existing apprenticeships. Like many aspects of life in Northern Ireland, implementation and review of the strategy was affected by the three-year suspension of the devolved administration from 2017.

Employee engagement was intended to be at the heart of the Foundation degree (QAA 2020: 5), with input into design, review and even assessment. In Northern Ireland, however, provision has been largely driven by the FE colleges' identification of market demand. This has led to cases where almost 100%

of some cohorts articulate to the linked university course, rather than securing employment. Colleges also express concern in relation to sourcing work-based learning placements for their students, another consequence of insufficient employer input into the design process. There may also be a regional requirement to offer a similar curriculum on all campuses, leading to small intakes (the expectation is 15 per class minimum).

From the students' perspective, smaller classes and closer individual tuition in the FE colleges are clear advantages. Entry requirements are also lower for Foundation degrees: typically, applicants should have the equivalent of two A Levels, while honours degree courses require at least three A Levels. Even with lower entry requirements, a full-time student can complete a Foundation degree and top-up in the same amount of time it takes to complete an honours degree with mandatory placement (four years). The MaSN cap places a particular constraint on this activity. The University incentivises progression and credit transfer by attracting better-qualified students into year 1, balancing that with taking large numbers of articulating students into year 2, and satisfying the MaSN cap by aligning Foundation degree offers with A Level offers through a published equivalence table. This can be challenging for Foundation degree students, as a pass may not be enough to secure a full-time place on a linked top-up course, but it is usually sufficient for part-time places. Costs are similar, too, with most full-time Foundation degrees and honours degree courses charging £4,395 per annum in 2020: with lower entry grades, students can complete a Foundation degree and top-up in the same amount of time as it would take to complete an honours degree, and for the same cost.

The extent of collaborative validated provision, and specifically the Foundation degree, which permits seamless articulation to linked honours degrees, demonstrates in a major way that Ulster University is committed to widening access and participation beyond the immediate scope of its own degree-level provision and is enabling other parts of the education sector to provide alternative routes of access to the University.

Case study 2: APL pathway to BSc Hons Community Development

As mentioned earlier, there is considerable policy drive for institutions to recognise APL as a means of entry to further and higher education programmes. Ulster University's (2020b) APL policy provides applicants who have not achieved the required qualifications with a mechanism to demonstrate their learning, via alternative certification and/or experience, normally demonstrated through a portfolio of evidence. Widening access and increasing the participation of disadvantaged or marginalised groups in higher education is closely aligned to the professional values of the Community Development team at Ulster University (Hawthorne-Steele et al. 2015). To this end, the team developed an APL pathway to facilitate advanced standing of experienced community workers onto Level 5 of the part-time BSc Hons Community Development. In order to support participants to complete APL portfolios, the team developed a short (20-credit Level 4) course that focused on models of experiential learning, critical reflection, non-formal and informal learning, and key areas of the National Occupational Standards in Community Development Work (ESB 2015). The APL pathway is founded on Freire's (2014) pedagogy of hope, viewing education as a social justice issue, which has the possibility of transforming communities.

Over the years, the team have gathered considerable qualitative data from participants on their experience of engaging withn the APL pathway (Cownie et al. 2014; Moreland and Cownie 2019). A common theme is the fear experienced by participants as they commence their journey back into education. One participant stated:

> ... when I started the new course [the BSc Hons Community Development], some of the same feelings and emotions of fear arose, and I had some new ones including excitement, self-satisfaction and relief. (Graduate Student)

Participants also voiced their fears in submitting work for accreditation: 'I became quite nervous about emailing the finished piece to the tutors'. As noted above, many participants have poor experiences of formal education. Based upon negative injunctions given to them, such as being told they are 'stupid', 'a hopeless case', 'cannot string two words together', or 'will never make anything of your life', many have scripted themselves as failures. Submitting written work as part of the APL short course also alerts staff to those students who may require additional support. Whilst some participants may be advised to take preliminary qualifications first, if they require essential skills literacy, in our experience most learners are highly capable of academic study at higher level. Indeed, over the 16+ years in which this pathway has been offered, over 80% successfully complete the APL programme, progressing onto the BSc Hons Community Development. However, over this time the team have identified a high proportion of participants with undiagnosed dyslexia or other related learning difficulties. It has become apparent that the low self-esteem of these participants is often largely due to the negative labelling during their school years. With a correct diagnosis and support structures in place, many of these learners graduate with first class or 2:1 classifications. With earlier diagnosis and support now in place in schools, we anticipate that this problem should eventually be eradicated.

On the other hand, the power of positive peer and tutor support is well demonstrated by the following participants:

> On reflection of the feedback on my first essay, this was a confidence booster as I did not have much faith in my ability to write an essay at all. (APL Student)

> Peers are vital for our sanity as well as our understanding. The realisation that you are not the only one who is finding something difficult or to bounce ideas off is essential. (APL Student)

I think that a great deal of effort is made to include the class in the participatory process. For me a very empowering and liberating experience was taking part with peers. (UP Student)

This exemplifies the importance of creating a shared learning environment where knowledge is not held in the hands of the tutor but rather learners' knowledge and experience is valued (Mezirow 1991). The role of critical reflection in this process is clearly articulated by one participant, who stated that: 'Experiential learning is learning through the reflection of doing. So, for experience to teach us anything we must be prepared to acknowledge our own successes and failures'. The same participant added:

We must challenge our actions and processes to glean as much learning as possible from past or ongoing events and we must be prepared to critique ourselves, something that must be learned as it does not come naturally to the majority of us. (APL Student)

Many of the participants of APL who successfully completed the BSc Hons Community Development have commented that completing the APL pathway was the turning point in their lives, which gave them the opportunity to gain access to higher education:

Without the chance to APL as my pathway to the degree, I would never have dreamt it possible to go to university, let alone complete a degree and get such a fantastic job that I have now working within community development. (Graduate Student)

The APL pathway continues to be an important feature within the team's widening access strategy and indeed, in 2016, they obtained the AONTAS Adult Learner STAR Award.[9] More recently, the team added the Unblocking Potential (UP) short course as a further option within this pathway, which provides a first step back into education for adults with few or no qualifications. Accredited by Ulster University, this programme is divided in two parts, enabling participants to gain 10 credits at Level 3, before progressing to the second part, to gain 10 credits at Level 4. The team designed this in recognition of an increasing number of prospective APL applicants who would not meet the criteria to gain advanced standing into Level 5. The programme focuses on understanding and overcoming barriers to learning, raising self-confidence and developing study skills. Delivered in local communities (and more recently online, during the current pandemic) and with bursaries available through widening access monies, this creative innovation offers further opportunities for those who would never dream of being able to access third-level study. One graduate of the BSc Hons Community Development, who progressed via the UP programme, stated: '[t]he community course [UP] changed everything for me ... made me see that I wasn't stupid ... and could even think about applying for university' (Graduate Student). Successful completion of the UP programme coupled with some experience in the community/voluntary sector enables participants to gain direct entry to Level 4 of the BSc Hons Community Development. Participants have also utilised this programme to gain entry to other degree and further education programmes, and gain the skills and confidence to obtain employment.

The APL pathway outlined here accords validity and formal credit-bearing recognition to students' community-based experiential learning. It is premised upon building strong support networks, through collective learning and peer-study groups. At the heart of this programme is an attempt to demystify education, to lift the burden of failure which many participants have carried throughout their lives, and to affirm their capacity to learn. This is grounded in the assertion made by Freire (2014), that the power of education has the ability to release the truth in people, and so ignite a fire of hope embedded in praxis, to fan the flames for social change.

Conclusion

This chapter has outlined the key policy priorities in Northern Ireland concerning widening access and participation and provided two examples of ways in which FEIs and HEIs are attempting to address these priorities. The DELNI (2015) strategy is committed to ensuring that prospective students can easily access high-quality information on relevant further and higher education courses. Whilst significant work has been done on the publishing of standardised Key Information Sets, more could be done to promote APL as a means to access higher education. A Northern Ireland Government website providing information on different routes to higher education outlines the range of qualifications accepted by UK universities, and does include a reference to APL.[10] Whilst the information is useful in reinforcing the principle that there are many routes to progress through education, the guidance is deliberately vague, since acceptance onto any programme is predominantly decided by educational institutions and, more specifically, course directors, and is therefore largely dictated by market demand. The impact of market demand is also felt keenly by Foundation degree students, who must compete with university students as well as their peers for limited places on full-time final-year degree programmes.

The DELNI (2012: 16) strategy set out its vision that by 2020, 'Northern Ireland will be internationally recognised as a region where participation in higher education is accessible to all citizens based on academic potential and regardless of social background'. Whilst HEIs and FEIs have made some progress towards achieving this, pandemic notwithstanding, the publishing of standard Key Information Sets and use of university league tables stands in direct conflict with the target of widening access and increasing participation of non-traditional students. The recognition that 'widening participation extends beyond recruitment and selection and covers the entire student journey ...' (DELNI 2012: 46), coupled with the incentives to resource widening participation strategies, demonstrates clearly that encouraging non-traditional students into higher education and supporting them to succeed in their programmes is a risky business. If the Northern Ireland Executive is serious in its commitment to a more equal society and giving young people the best start in life (NIE 2016), it must ensure that adequate support is given to educational activities which have demonstrable positive outcomes for those who are '... MOST ABLE but LEAST LIKELY to participate ...' (DELNI 2012: 14).

Notes

1 APL is synonymous with the recognition of prior learning (RPL), more commonly used in Scotland, the Republic of Ireland and throughout Europe. We use the term APL in this chapter to encompass the accreditation of both credited (APCL) and experiential (APEL) learning.
2 www.studentfinanceni.co.uk
3 We use this term to encompass all students from backgrounds where university attendance is below the regional average. In Northern Ireland, this refers to people in the lowest socio-economic groups; those with disabilities, physical, mental and learning; young males, particularly young Protestant males from low participation areas; people from areas of multiple deprivation; and older learners, specifically learners in employment (DELNI 2012: 45).
4 For details, see https://www.ons.gov.uk/methodology/classificationsandstandards/otherclassifications/thenationalstatisticssocioeconomicclassificationnssecrebasedonsoc2010.
5 As outlined by the Regulated Qualifications Framework (UK Government undated).
6 Regulated qualifications developed by awarding organisations are recognised by the Council for the Curriculum, Examinations & Assessment (CCEA), once they meet the regulatory requirement. Approved qualifications are eligible for public funding through DfE. For further information, see Ofqual, CEA, QAA (2019).
7 According to the Northern Ireland Multiple Deprivation Measure, Quintile 1 is the most deprived.
8 Advanced standing allows applicants with sufficient experiential or certificated learning to be exempt from part of a programme and enter onto the programme at an advanced stage of learning.
9 Annual awards of AONTAS (the National Adult Learning Organisation in Ireland) recognising the positive impact adult and community education has on communities across Ireland.
10 https://www.nidirect.gov.uk/articles/routes-higher-education.

References

Belfast Met (2020) *Higher Education: Accreditation of prior experiential learning (APEL) process.* Available at: https://www.belfastmet.ac.uk/siteFiles/resources/docs/AccreditationofPriorExperientialLearning-HigherEducation.pdf (accessed 10 February 2021).
Belfast Met (2021) *Student Wellbeing.* Available at: https://www.belfastmet.ac.uk/Studentwellbeing/ (accessed 12 February 2021).

Cownie, E., Hawthorne-Steele, I. and Moreland, R. (2014) *The Degree of Transforming Community Spaces: Principles to praxis*. Coleraine: Ulster University.

Department for Employment and Learning (DELNI) (2012) *Access to Success*. Available at: https://www.economy-ni.gov.uk/sites/default/files/publications/del/Access%20to%20Success-An%20integrated%20regional%20strategy%20for%20widening%20participation%20in%20HE_0.pdf (accessed 10 February 2021).

Department for Employment and Learning (DELNI) (2014) *Securing Our Success: The Northern Ireland Strategy on Apprenticeships*. Available at: https://www.economy-ni.gov.uk/sites/default/files/publications/del/Securing%20our%20Success%20The%20NI%20Strategy%20on%20Apprenticeships.pdf (accessed 22 February 2021).

Department for Employment and Learning (DELNI) (2015) *Graduating to Success*. Available at: https://www.economyni.gov.uk/sites/default/files/publications/del/Graduating%20to%20Success-Higher%20Education%20Strategy.pdf (accessed 9 February 2021).

Department for Employment and Learning (DELNI) (2016) *Further Education Means Success: The Northern Ireland Strategy for Further Education*. Available at: https://www.economy-ni.gov.uk/sites/default/files/publications/economy/FE-Strategy%20-FE-Means-success.pdf (accessed 10 February 2021).

ESB (2015) *Community Development National Occupational Standards*. Available at: http://www.esbendorsement.org.uk/index.php/nos (accessed 12 February 2021).

Field, J. (2012) Is lifelong learning making a difference? Research-based evidence on the impact of adult learning, in D. Aspin, J. Chapman, K. Evans and R. Bagnall (eds.) *Second International Handbook of Lifelong Learning*, Dordrecht: Springer.

Freire, P. (2014) *Pedagogy of Hope: Reliving Pedagogy of the Oppressed*. London: Bloomsbury (first published 1994).

Hawthorne-Steele, I., Moreland, R. and Rooney, E. (2015) Transforming communities through academic activism: An emancipatory, praxis-led approach, *Studies in Social Justice*, 9 (2): 197–214.

Learning and Work Institute (2017) *Healthy, Wealthy and Wise: The impact of adult learning across the UK*. Leicester: Learning and Work Institute. Available at: https://learningandwork.org.uk/resources/research-and-reports/healthy-wealthy-and-wise-the-impact-of-adult-learning-across-the-uk/ (accessed 15 February 2021).

Marmot, M. (2015) *The Health Gap: The Challenge of an Unequal World*. London: Bloomsbury.

Mezirow, J. (1991) *Transformative Dimensions of Adult Learning*. San Francisco, CA: Jossey-Bass.

Moreland, R. and Cownie, E. (2019) Reclaiming university adult education: A Freirian approach to widening participation and tackling educational inequality, *The Adult Learner: The Irish Journal of Adult and Community Education*, 2019: 57–79.

NICATS (1999) *Report of the Northern Ireland Credit Accumulation and Transfer System (NICATS) Project*. Available at: https://www.bolton.ac.uk/Quality/PDA/ModuleAndProgrammeDesign/Documents/NICATS.pdf (accessed 8 February 2021).

Northern Ireland Executive (NIE) (2016) *Draft Programme for Government Framework 2016–21*. Available at: https://www.northernireland.gov.uk/sites/default/files/consultations/newnigov/draft-pfg-framework-2016-21.pdf (accessed 8 February 2021).

Northern Ireland Executive (NIE) (2021) *Programme for Government: Draft Outcomes Framework*. Available at: http://www.niassembly.gov.uk/globalassets/documents/raise/publications/2017-2022/2021/executive-office/2021.pdf (accessed 8 February 2021).

Northern Regional College (NRC) (2018) *Widening Access and Participation Plan 2018/19–2020/21*. Available at: https://www.nrc.ac.uk/site-search/results/search&keywords=widening+access+/ (accessed 12 February 2021).

North West Regional College (NWC) (2020) *Widening Access and Participation Plan 2020–2021.* Available at: http://www.nwrc.ac.uk/widening-access-and-participation-plan-2020-21/ (accessed 10 February 2021).

OECD (2020) *OECD Skills Strategy Northern Ireland (United Kingdom): Assessment and recommendations* (OECD Skills Studies). Paris: OECD Publishing.

Office for Students (OFS) (2019) *Civic University Agreements: Exploring synergies with Office for Students access and participation regulation and funding.* Office for Students Civic University Commission conference, 19 July 2019.

Ofqual, CEA, QAA (2019*) Referencing the Qualifications Frameworks of England and Northern Ireland to the European Qualifications Framework.* Available at: https://ccea.org.uk/downloads/docs/regulation-asset/Qualifications%20Regulation/Referencing%20the%20Qualifications%20Frameworks%20of%20England%20and%20Northern%20Ireland%20to%20the%20European%20Qualifications%20Framework.pdf (accessed 10 April 2021).

Quality Assurance Agency (QAA) (2019) *Characteristics Statement: Higher education in apprenticeships.* Gloucester: QAA.

Quality Assurance Agency (QAA) (2020) *Characteristics Statement: Foundation degree,* 4th edn. Gloucester: QAA.

South Eastern Regional College (SERC) (2020) *Widening Access and Participation Plan 2020/21–2022/23.* Available at: https://www.serc.ac.uk/public-information/policies-and-procedures (accessed 7 February 2021).

South West College (SWC) (2021) *Accreditation of Prior Experiential Learning (APL).* Available at: https://www.swc.ac.uk/learn/higher-education/accreditation-of-prior-experiential-learning (accessed 8 February 2021).

South West College (SWC) (2017) *Widening Access and Participation Plan 2017/18–2019/20.* Available at: https://www.swc.ac.uk/swc/media/Documents/Support/Higher%20Education/WAPP-201718-201920.pdf?ext=.pdf (accessed 7 February 2021).

Southern Regional College (SRC) (2020) *Widening Access and Participation Plan, 2020/21–2022/23.* Available at: https://www.src.ac.uk/the-college/policies (accessed 7 February 2021).

UK Government (undated) *What Qualification Levels Mean.* Available at: https://www.gov.uk/what-different-qualification-levels-mean/list-of-qualification-levels (accessed 10 April 201).

Ulster University (2019) *Ulster University among 30 universities to sign new 'Civic University Agreement' to reaffirm local role.* Available at: https://upp-foundation.org/wp-content/uploads/2019/07/CUC-conference-Access-and-Participation-and-Civic-University-Agreements-.pdf (accessed 12 January 2021).

Ulster University (2020a) *Partnership Handbook.* Available at: https://www.ulster.ac.uk/__data/assets/pdf_file/0006/307824/Partnership-Handbook.pdf (accessed 7 January 2021).

Ulster University (2020b) *Accreditation of Prior Learning (APL) Policy* (first published 2006). Coleraine: Ulster University.

UNESCO (2016) *Third Global Report on Adult Learning and Education* (GRALE 3). UNESCO Institute for Lifelong Learning. Available at: https://unesdoc.unesco.org/ark:/48223/pf0000245913 (accessed 15 February 2021).

7 The role of credit in the Scottish Credit and Qualifications Framework

Sheila Dunn

Introduction

2021 marks 20 years since the launch of the Scottish Credit and Qualifications Framework (SCQF, or the Framework). During those 20 years the Framework has developed, grown and adapted to the changing educational landscape in Scotland, whilst its purpose, aims and principles have remained largely unchanged and the concept of credit and its transferability has remained fundamental to its success. Indeed, the title of the SCQF was carefully thought about at its conception, with the word 'credit' very deliberately coming before the word 'qualifications' to indicate that credit was key in developing routes for progression, minimising the duplication of learning and maximising credit transfer and the recognition of prior learning.

This chapter will explore the importance of the inclusion and use of credit within the SCQF, the links with credit transfer and the recognition of prior learning, as well as providing a brief overview of the SCQF itself.

The SCQF

The SCQF is a framework for lifelong learning and is designed to enable the inclusion of a wide range of qualifications and learning programmes[1] of differing types and sizes underpinned by a robust system of quality assurance. There are many routes and pathways to follow in education and training in Scotland and the SCQF reflects this by promoting a parity of esteem across all qualifications (academic, vocational, general, formal, non-formal and sector specific), allowing individual learners to move up, down and across the Framework as their learning and work/career progresses.

The SCQF is designed to allow maximum flexibility for learners to progress through their learning journey, irrespective of the nature of the learning they undertake and the sector(s) in which they undertake that learning. The purpose of the SCQF, put simply, is to make the Scottish system of qualifications easier to understand and use for everyone. Its aims are to:

- support lifelong learning
- clarify entry and exit points for qualifications at all levels
- show learners and others potential routes for progression and credit transfer
- show the level and credit (size) of the different types of Scottish qualifications and learning programmes
- enable credit transfer to be made between qualifications so as to assist learners to build on previous achievement
- promote the use of recognition of prior learning.

The governance of the SCQF is different from many other national qualifications frameworks (NQFs) around the world in that it is not owned by government or any one sector or organisation but managed by the SCQF Partnership (SCQFP), a company limited by guarantee and a registered charity. The SCQFP Board comprises four partner organisations: the College Development Network (CDN); Quality Assurance Agency for Higher Education (QAA); Scottish Qualifications Authority (SQA); and Universities Scotland. Membership of the Board consists of one senior representative from each of the partner organisations and an independent chairperson. There are also two spaces for co-opted members, one for the chair of the SCQF Quality Committee and one representing the interests of employers. In addition, the Scottish Government has observer status. The SCQFP model reflects Scotland's long tradition of partnership working across educational organisations and sectors, and the SCQF Board partners share a common goal in seeing the use of the Framework successfully embedded across Scotland. The SCQF Partnership itself consists of a small executive team responsible for ensuring the quality and integrity of the SCQF and promoting the benefits of using the Framework to stakeholders across Scotland and beyond.[2]

Unlike many other NQFs around the world and indeed in the UK, the SCQF is a voluntary framework and there is no legislation associated with it (although it encompasses the frameworks of Scottish Qualifications Authority (SQA) and of the Framework for Qualifications of Higher Education Systems in Scotland (FQHEIS), which bring their own forms of regulation managed respectively by SQA and QAA Scotland). Therefore, there is no requirement for any organisation to put its qualifications and learning programmes onto the SCQF and as a result it is key to the success of the SCQF that it is seen as a useful tool, a trusted resource and one which is beneficial for organisations to engage with. It also means that it is important that the SCQF is simple to understand and flexible enough to allow all types of organisations to engage with it, whilst at the same time retaining a robust underpinning quality assurance model[3] to ensure trust in the system.

The SCQF therefore brings together the main formal Scottish academic and vocational qualifications systems into one single, unified framework with the Framework for Qualifications of Higher Education Institutions in Scotland (FQHEIS) and those owned by the SQA embedded within the SCQF, as noted above. This means that all higher education institutions (HEIs) and the SQA are expected to use the SCQF definitions of level and credit to describe their qualifications and learning programmes. As a result, the Framework includes all types of learning, including all mainstream qualifications in Scotland (school qualifications, vocational programmes and higher education) as illustrated by the SCQF diagram[4] (SCQF Partnership 2017).

In addition, the Framework is designed so that other qualifications and learning programmes sitting outside that mainstream offer can be included and, whilst not visually shown on the SCQF diagram, there are now over 11,500 qualifications and learning programmes (SCQF Partnership 2020) in total on the Framework with almost a 1,000 of these from outside the mainstream system (SCQF Partnership 2019a), owned by employers, community learning organisations, professional bodies and voluntary organisations to name but a few. In total, over 300 (SCQF Partnership 2020) organisations have engaged with the SCQF by going through the process to include their qualifications and learning programmes onto the SCQF.

SCQF levels and credit points

The SCQF has 12 levels to allow the unique features of Scottish qualifications to be included. Thus, school learners are able to undertake a range of qualifications from Levels 1 to 7, with Nationals at Levels 1–5 and then Highers and Advanced Highers at Levels 6 and 7, with the Highers at Level 6 providing the main access to university and the Advanced Highers being on the same level as traditional first-year university, which if undertaken at school can provide a competitive edge to applications or some credit transfer. The structure of Scottish undergraduate degrees is different from those in the rest of the UK up to honours, where the frameworks across the UK align.

The levels are described by a set of descriptors which are applicable to all sectors and types of programmes. Each level is described using five characteristics (SCQF Partnership 2021):

• Knowledge and Understanding
• Practice: Applied Knowledge and Understanding
• Generic Cognitive Skills
• Communication, ICT and Numeracy
• Autonomy, Accountability and Working with Others.

SCQF credit points are used to indicate the volume of learning expected to be undertaken by a typical learner in order to successfully achieve the learning outcome. The amount of time taken by an individual learner in reality may be different but that does not affect the number of credit points awarded. The credit value is attached to the units/modules and the qualifications and learning programmes and this does not change if a learner spends more or less time to successfully achieve the learning outcomes. Neither does the credit value change for a unit or module if the unit/module is then incorporated into another programme, even if the significance of the unit/module is different in the new programme.

One SCQF credit point, representing a notional 10 hours of learning, is the smallest piece of learning recognised on the Framework. There is no upper limit on the volume of credit. Notional learning hours include all of the learning activities required to achieve the learning outcomes of a qualification/ learning programme, such as:

- face-to-face contact
- self-study time
- practical work
- online learning
- the time to plan, study for and undertake assessments.

The mix of these activities will be different depending on, for example, the type of programme, the intended target audience and mode of delivery and there are no specific rules or guidelines within the SCQF principles regarding the makeup of this mix for any specific qualifications or learning programmes included within the Framework. This is in order to provide the greatest flexibility and to ensure that all types of qualifications and learning programmes can potentially be credit rated and included on the Framework. This approach also allows qualification and programme owners, and indeed awarding bodies[5] and education sectors, to have their own additional rules on this mix and still be able to meet the criteria for inclusion of qualifications and programmes on the SCQF.

All qualifications and learning programmes on the SCQF must be allocated a level and a credit value (with the exception of research degrees which are only given a level). The process of allocating SCQF level and credit is referred to as *credit rating*. This process is a formal, quality-assured process and is carried out by those with experience and knowledge of the subject areas, the sector concerned, the SCQF and the SCQF level descriptors. These individuals must make a professional judgement on both the best fit of level and on how many hours it would take a typical learner to achieve the learning outcomes, thus calculating the SCQF credit points.

There are no rules as to the number of credit points required at any particular level on the SCQF, so it is possible to have large pieces of learning at low levels on the Framework and very small pieces of specialised learning at the higher levels. This allows for the widest possible range of learning to be included on the Framework and for the Framework to accommodate the different types of learning an individual may undertake in their learner journey.

The 'design rules' relating to levels and credits for certain types of qualifications and learning programmes are left in the charge of the programme owner, awarding body or sector, thus providing complete flexibility and allowing the Framework to work across all sectors. This feature of the SCQF makes it different from many other qualifications frameworks around the world where there are restrictions in the size, the type and sometimes the sectors that can be included in the framework or at a particular level laid down by the framework owner or regulator.

SCQF criteria and principles

In order to maintain this flexibility of approach, it is very important that it is underpinned by robust quality assurance to ensure the trust in the Framework by all stakeholders and users. All qualifications/learning programmes must meet four criteria to be included on the SCQF. The criteria are that all qualifications and learning programmes must be:

- written in learning outcomes[6]
- a minimum of ten notional learning hours (one SCQF credit point)
- formally assessed[7]
- quality assured.

The process of credit rating is a devolved one – that is, it is not carried out by the central body, the SCQF Partnership. The process is carried out by organisations called credit rating bodies (CRBs), which have been given the authority to carry out credit rating for the SCQF. In 2021 there were over 50 such bodies, including universities, colleges, the SQA and a small number of other organisations, operating within a robust quality assurance model overseen by the SCQF Partnership and the SCQF Quality Committee.[8] Each CRB will design its credit rating system to meet the 25 SCQF principles contained within the SCQF Handbook but also to fit in with its own internal design, development, approval and review processes, thus resulting in slightly different systems in different CRBs. It should be noted, however, that all credit rating processes must incorporate the use of the SCQF level descriptors. In addition, the SCQF Handbook states that the process should also involve the use of other reference points such as other relevant qualification or learning programme descriptors, higher education subject benchmark information (QAA 2020), SQA specifications and other appropriate sources of information and guidance (SCQF Partnership 2015).

There are external quality assurance mechanisms to ensure that the systems designed by CRBs are in line with the SCQF principles and operating effectively, and the SCQF Handbook makes it very clear in the first principle for CRBs that, 'Credit Rating Bodies (CRBs) and the SCQF Partnership have equal responsibility for ensuring the quality and integrity of the Scottish Credit and Qualifications Framework' (SCQF Partnership 2015: 2).

The SCQF Quality Committee has oversight of all issues concerning the ongoing maintenance and assurance of the Framework and reports to the SCQF Board. Approval of any new CRB must be ratified by both the SCQF Quality Committee and the Board. The Quality Committee consists of experts in quality assurance of credit, qualifications and frameworks from a range of sectors, awarding bodies and other quality assurance bodies.

In the early years of the SCQF, CRBs were limited to HEIs and the SQA. The list was then expanded to include all of Scotland's colleges. In 2009, after a pilot, this role was extended to other organisations which are able to demonstrate they can meet the criteria within the published SCQF Quality Assurance Model[9] and go through a successful approval process. The SCQFP oversees this devolved system, operates the SCQF Quality Assurance Model and supports all CRBs through capacity-building activities, advice and guidance.

The extension of CRBs to include such organisations as the Scottish Police College – Tulliallan, the Scottish Fire and Rescue Service, and the Chartered Banker Institute further helps to promote the parity of qualifications and learning programmes that may be obtained outside the mainstream education system, and allows the holders of those credit-rated qualifications and learning programmes the ability to use the credit gained to access other programmes of study or future employment.

SCQF, recognition of prior learning and credit transfer – benefits and challenges

Not all national qualification frameworks use credit or have credit transfer as a fundamental part of. Bjornavold and Coles commented in 2010 that 'Credit transfer is an important part of the way some frameworks facilitate portability. By ensuring units are admitted to a framework these can be combined in different ways to allow the building of a qualification which is suited to the learners' future needs' (Bjornavold and Coles 2010: 21).

The development of the SCQF was built on a history of using credit in Scotland which had started with the SCOTCAT scheme in 1991, used as the credit system for higher education in Scotland. The concept of one credit equalling ten hours of study time was established within that scheme. It was then adopted as the value for one SCQF credit point with the definition slightly refined to the notional learning time for a typical learner to achieve the learning outcomes of a qualification or learning programme.

In 2009, SQA started to feature SCQF levels and credit points on the Scottish Qualifications Certificate, which all school leavers in Scotland who successfully complete their school qualifications receive, as well as college students achieving SQA qualifications such as Higher National Certificates and Diplomas. The certificate includes the SCQF level and credit gained for each unit and qualification and also includes a summary totalling all the SCQF credit a learner has gained at each SCQF level.

Credit recognition plays a fundamental part in Scottish education and the movement of learners from school to college to university to work is underpinned by a general understanding and use of the SCQF and its credit transfer system across Scotland.

SCQF credit points are the building blocks for credit recognition and transfer. They provide a way to quantify the amount of learning achieved and they indicate the typical amount of time taken to complete a unit/module or a qualification or learning programme. Along with the allocation of the SCQF level, SCQF credit points can, for example, help learners gain:

- access to different stages of education
- entry to a programme
- exemptions from units/modules
- exemptions from full years of study (advanced standing).

Examples of these include a learner gaining direct entry onto the third year of a degree programme with a vocational qualification; the ability of a learner to provide evidence of an alternative entry qualification to those normally accepted by a provider/institution; and a learner gaining exemption from some of the modules contained within a programme, reducing the time taken to complete a qualification. The SCQF credit points along with the SCQF level descriptors also allow employers and education providers to compare different qualifications and the amount of learning that has been achieved, or requires to be achieved, thus potentially being able to promote alternative entry requirements, entry points and to develop a range of alternative pathways to gaining qualifications for learners.

The aims of the SCQF specifically reference recognition of prior learning (RPL) as they: 'support the [Scottish Government's] aims of fair work and social justice by ensuring that it provides tools and resources which can recognise prior learning, support progression and improve social inclusion' (SCQF Partnership 2019b: 6). This aim is also reflected in the SCQFP strategic plan 2019/22 with one of the stated strategic priorities being: 'Promoting recognition of prior learning – to ensure unnecessary repetition of learning and equality for all learners' (SCQF Partnership 2019b: 15). This aim and priority are underpinned by a section of the SCQF Handbook dedicated to RPL comprising a set of seven principles relating to the process of RPL and credit transfer with accompanying guidance. The Handbook notes that '… credit awarded through RPL should be regarded in the same way as credit awarded through other learning and assessment processes' (SCQF Partnership 2015: 29), with principle 22 also stating 'SCQF Credit Points awarded as a result of RPL for informal or non-formal learning are of the same value as credit gained through formal learning' (SCQF Partnership 2015: 3), thus promoting the parity of esteem of credit no matter where and how it is achieved. The Handbook goes on to stress the need for the process of RPL and credit transfer to be underpinned by a robust process, stating that 'Regardless of how credit is awarded, a learner needs to provide evidence of his/her learning and the evidence needs to be assessed and quality assured by qualified practitioners' (SCQF Partnership 2015: 30).

However, credit transfer and the recognition of prior learning does not simply happen on the identification of the volume of credit alone. There are many other aspects that institutions and providers have to take into consideration, such as subject match, level and the validity and currency of evidence provided. An RPL claim for credit usually involves a comparison of the individual's learning (or qualification in the case of credit transfer) with the aims and learning outcomes of the qualification or learning programme to which either entry or exemption is being sought. This means that providers and institutions need clear processes for RPL and credit transfer and these need to be clearly outlined and promoted to learners.

The SCQF launched its first RPL Toolkit in 2010 and has refined and developed this further with an online version in 2019.[10] This toolkit is designed to provide guidance for learners, education providers and employers on the process of RPL. From a learner seeking to have their experiential learning recognised or wanting to use formal credit rated qualifications to access further learning, to the education provider supporting a learner to make an application for RPL, to information for employers on how RPL can bring benefits to the workplace, the toolkit provides generic signposting information about steps in the processes depending on starting points and desired end outcomes.

The online toolkit notes a number of benefits for learners from RPL, the two key ones relating to credit being:

- *Gain credit towards a qualification to shorten the normal period of study by providing evidence of your knowledge, skills and understanding needed.*

- *RPL may be used to demonstrate learning that could be considered as comparable to standard entrance requirements for admission on a programme of study.*

However, the toolkit also notes the equally important benefits of RPL as a way to:

- *Increase your self-esteem and improve confidence by recognising your achievements and transferable skills and plan how to build upon this to meet your personal goals.*

- *Plan for new career opportunities or learner pathways by recognising learning achieved that can be mapped to jobs or training whilst acknowledging your own personal strengths and weaknesses.*

An extract from the 2019 SCQF European Qualifications Framework[11] Referencing report illustrates a very particular use of credit transfer in Scotland:

> *Articulation[12] is one of the most commonly used routes of credit transfer. It enables learners who hold SQA's Higher National Certificate (HNC) and Diploma (HND) qualifications to transfer directly into the second or third year of a degree programme. This transfer of full credit is known as gaining advanced standing. The acceptance of the full credit for transfer from HNCs and HNDs to degree programmes will depend on a number of considerations including the matches of subject matter between the HNC/D and the target degree programmes. Decisions on the amount of credit that can be accepted for transfer rests with the receiving HEI institution.*
>
> *Articulation routes are well established. HNC and HND qualifications, which sit at SCQF Levels 7 and 8 respectively, are higher education short-cycle programmes intended to develop advanced level knowledge and skills for industry. They are considered to be stages within the First Cycle of tertiary level qualifications in the Bologna/European Higher Education Area Framework.*
>
> *In 2013–14 49% of all learners completing HNC/D qualifications articulated into the second or third year of degree programmes. However, as mentioned above, the number of credit points which can be transferred from one qualification to another is determined by the receiving institution, and many learners have discovered that they cannot transfer the full credit value of their HNC/HND to their corresponding degree programme.*
>
> *The issue of full credit transfer is being addressed by the Scottish Funding Council in their strategy for widening access to higher education, through the mechanism of Outcome Agreements. By including requirements for articulation in the funding agreements with the individual institutions, the SFC aims to increase the number of learners articulating into degree programmes with advanced standing, to 75% of HNC/D students by 2025.* (SCQFP 2019a: 52)

There is acknowledgement across Scotland, however, that there is still a significant amount of progress to be made with RPL and credit transfer to ensure that all learners get full recognition for learning they have already undertaken and are not required to repeat learning already achieved. Processes should be clearer and easier for learners to navigate. The achievement of credit should be used to support mobility across the full range of learner journeys recognising that learners do not always follow a linear route. Whilst there are many examples of RPL and credit transfer successfully taking place (especially in articulation from further to higher education),[13] it is recognised that systems do not always align as effectively as they could and that for an individual trying to access a programme with a set of previous achievements which may not follow a tried-and-tested pathway, this can still be a tricky process to engage with. This topic has featured in a number of key reports.

In 2016, the Commission for Widening Access (COWA) published its final report, *A Blueprint for Fairness* (Scottish Government 2016). A number of the recommendations of this report addressed the need for mechanisms to be developed to remove duplication of learning and to provide recognition of learning undertaken through access and bridging programmes.[14] The report also recognised the distance that had been travelled in creating a range of articulation agreements between colleges and universities but that there was still some way to go.

Recommendation 4 in particular stated that 'Universities, colleges, local authorities, schools, the SFC funded access programmes and early years' providers should work together to deliver a coordinated approach to access which removes duplication and provides a coherent and comprehensive offer to learners' (Scottish Government 2016: 25). This should entail:

> the development of mechanisms by which access programmes undertaken at one institution, or in one part of the country, can be recognised by other institutions, while also serving institutional and local needs. Credit rating programmes on the Scottish Credit and Qualification Framework (SCQF) should be considered where appropriate. (Scottish Government 2016: 25)

A recently published report by the National Articulation Forum recommended that the Scottish Funding Council (SFC) should revise this current definition and to '[e]mphasise that articulation is about giving credit for previous study so that the same SCQF level in the same subject area is not repeated, opening up the potential for new and innovative approaches (such as transferring credit from any pre-university experience) that support the objective of articulation' (Universities Scotland 2020: 6).

The initial vision of a single definition of credit which would be signed up to by all sectors was realised and this has contributed to the mutual trust that has been built up over the years across sectors allowing for the development of processes for credit transfer and RPL. However, the existence of a credit and qualifications framework, a single definition of credit and the promotion of the use of credit is not enough to deliver a truly unified and consistent approach to credit transfer and RPL. It also needs:

- a set of committed partners keen to promote the use of the framework and the recognition of all forms of prior learning to its fullest extent;
- dedicated organisations willing to operate as credit rating bodies supporting the Framework and setting up quality assured, robust processes for RPL and credit transfer;
- a shared vision and understanding of the benefits of credit recognition and transfer not just to individuals but to the economy as a whole when the cost of repeating learning already achieved is reduced;
- a joined up approach not just in the processes for RPL and credit recognition but in the other parts of the system which can affect the success of credit recognition, such as funding, curriculum delivery patterns and learner support guidance.

This was recognised by Bjornavold and Coles in 2010 when they commented that:

> *A comprehensive NQF addressing the fragmented character of qualifications systems can not be realised without clear and credible coordination ... [and that] ... Creating support for a comprehensive NQF therefore requires the definition and implementation of national management mechanisms representing something more than partial interests of providers and users.* (Bjornavold and Coles 2010: 34)

SCQF credit continues to play a fundamental part in learner progression providing a common currency on which the processes of RPL and credit transfer can be based. However, the success of those processes and the use of credit depends on many other factors, as outlined in this chapter, and SCQF credit goes hand in hand with the SCQF level descriptors underpinned by the SCQF principles and those robust quality assurance systems and processes in place for the Framework. All of that also goes in conjunction with the strong processes put in place by the range of partners and stakeholders, including credit rating bodies, right across the educational landscape in Scotland in order to recognise qualifications on the SCQF and to deliver RPL and credit transfer.

In 2001, it was noted in *An Introduction to the Scottish Credit and Qualifications Framework* that 'in the future, provided it comes within an appropriate quality assurance system, and is subject to reliable and valid means of assessment, any short programme, module, unit or work based learning has the potential for incorporation into the framework' (SCQF 2001: 3).

The SCQFP continues to work to ensure that the SCQF and credit play a fundamental part in the recognition of learning and the development of the widest possible range of learner journeys[15] and this can still be seen in the SCQFP's current *Strategic Objectives 2019–2022* in its list of current drivers for future work:

> *Maintaining quality and integrity is key to preserving confidence in Scottish qualifications and we will continue to work with credit rating bodies to ensure quality and integrity whilst supporting them in recognising more learning on the Framework to help create more comprehensive learner journeys.* (SCQF Partnership 2019b: 14)

At the end of 2002, the *National Plan for the Implementation of the Framework* noted that, 'Today, there is a greater recognition and understanding of the importance of learning for all than there has ever been. There has also never been a time when, across the world, so many people are engaging in and enjoying the benefits of learning' (SCQF 2002: 5). The Plan notes that '[t]his means there is now an enormous potential for creating, and making available, a rich range of opportunities and resources for learning' (2002: 5).

At the time of writing in 2021, this quote is just as pertinent today as the world faces a period when people are being required to engage even more with learning via a range of new and different methods and when the need to have available the widest possible range of opportunities to allow individuals to upskill, reskill and get recognition for all of their achievements will be increasingly more important to allow those individuals to progress in their learning journeys.

Notes

1 'In the SCQF Handbook the term "qualifications and learning programmes" is used as a common phrase to describe the various terms used for programmes, qualifications, courses, units and modules that are used in the different sectors involved in lifelong learning in Scotland' (SCQF Partnership 2015: 6).
2 The SCQF can help *individuals* ... gain formal recognition for their learning and skills; understand the level of their learning; improve confidence and self-esteem; help them to plan and progress their chosen learning pathway; avoid duplication of learning; compare their qualifications to others in the UK, Europe and beyond.

   The SCQF can help *employers* ... understand both academic and vocational qualifications and the level of employees' skills; inform effective recruitment; support job evaluations and workforce development; gain recognition for in-house training; understand the level of their training; provide their employees with clear development pathways; compare their training to others in the UK, Europe and beyond.

   The SCQF can help *institutions and organisations* ... develop alternative pathways for learners; provide formal recognition and credit for learners; understand qualifications from other parts of the UK, Europe and beyond; understand qualifications from other sectors; develop programmes through the use of level descriptors.
3 SCQF *level descriptors* describe in broad terms what a learner should be able to do or demonstrate at a particular level. The complexity of learning and the level of demand increases from Level 1 through to Level 12.

   SCQF *credit points* are a way of describing and comparing the amount of learning that has been achieved or is required to achieve the learning outcomes of a programme or qualification. One SCQF credit point equals 10 notional learning hours.

   Notional learning hours is the time required for a typical learner to achieve the learning outcomes. It includes all learning activities required for the achievement of the learning outcomes including the assessment.
4 Available at: https://scqf.org.uk/media/0pdfnrnn/scqf-diagram-2017-a6-web.pdf (accessed 12 January 2021).
5 In this chapter, the term 'awarding body' means any organisation whose remit is the development of qualifications and the quality assurance of assessment and certification.
6 Learning outcomes are statements of what a learner knows, understands and is able to do, defined in terms of knowledge, skills and competence, on completion of a learning process.
7 Formal assessment measures and records an individual's achievement – the assessment of learning. Assessment may involve observation of practical skills, product evaluation or questioning, or a combination of some or all of the three, and will be quality assured.
8 For the list of current CRBs, see the SCQF website: www.scqf.org.uk.
9 The QAM is available at: https://scqf.org.uk/media/xmqdiwea/qam-complete-final-2020-1.pdf (accessed 1 February 2021).

10 The RPL Tool is available at: https://scqf.org.uk/guide-to-rpl/rpl-tool/ (accessed 27 January 2021).
11 The EQF is a common European reference framework (meta qualifications framework), consisting of 8 levels, which acts as a translation tool for other national qualifications frameworks.
12 Articulation is defined by the Scottish Funding Council as a student gaining entry into the second year of a degree with a Higher National Certificate (HNC) gained at college, or into the third year with a Higher National Diploma (HND) gained at college.
13 The SCQF website has a range of learner case studies demonstrating how individuals have used the SCQF and credit to further their own learner journeys. Available at: https://scqf.org.uk/case-studies/ (accessed 27 January 2021).
14 The COWA report defines bridging programmes as 'academically based programmes which enable disadvantaged learners to supplement their attainment by engaging with university curricula. Examples include academically rigorous summer schools, gateway programmes and top-up schemes'. For Access to Higher Education programmes, see Chapters 3 and 6 of this book.
15 The SCQF website has a range of learner case studies demonstrating how individuals have used the SCQF and credit to further their own learner journeys. Available at: https://scqf.org.uk/case-studies/ (accessed 27 January 2021).

References

Bjornavold, J. and Coles, M. (2010) *Added Value of National Qualifications Frameworks in Implementing the EQF*. EQF Framework Series: Note 2. Luxembourg: Publications Office of the European Union. Available at: http://www.ehea.info/media.ehea.info/file/Qualifications_frameworks/02/7/note2_en_597027.pdf (accessed 26 January 2021).
Quality Assurance Agency (QAA) (2020) *Subject Benchmark Statements*. Available at: https://www.qaa.ac.uk/quality-code/subject-benchmark-statements (accessed 2 April 2021).
Scottish Credit and Qualifications Framework (SCQF) (2001) *An Introduction to the Scottish Credit and Qualifications Framework*. Glasgow: SCQF.
Scottish Credit and Qualifications Framework (SCQF) (2002) *SCQF National Plan for the Implementation of the Framework*. Glasgow: SCQF.
Scottish Government (2016) *A Blueprint for Fairness: The final report of the Commission on Widening Access*. Edinburgh: Scottish Government. Available at: https://www.gov.scot/publications/blueprint-fairness-final-report-commission-widening-access/ (accessed 18 January 2021).
SCQF Partnership (2015) *SCQF Handbook*. Available at: https://scqf.org.uk/media/svxnjdts/scqf_handbook_web_final_2015.pdf (accessed 13 January 2021).
SCQF Partnership (2017) *The Scottish Credit and Qualifications Framework*. Available at: https://scqf.org.uk/media/0pdfnrnn/scqf-diagram-2017-a6-web.pdf (accessed 2 April 2021).
SCQF Partnership (2019a) *Referencing the Scottish Credit & Qualifications Framework (SCQF) to the European Qualifications Framework (EQF)*. Available at: https://scqf.org.uk/media/wrzox2oi/eqf-re-referencing-report-final-may-2019.pdf (accessed 10 January 2021).

SCQF Partnership (2019b) *SCQF Partnership: Our strategic objectives 2019–2022.* Available at: https://scqf.org.uk/media/hmaoj53d/strategic-plan-2019-22-final.pdf (accessed 27 January 2021).

SCQF Partnership (2020) *The SCQF: Leading the way in Scotland's Learning: Annual Impact Report 19/20.* Available at: https://scqf.org.uk/media/gfynhmp5/scqfp-annual-impact-report-final-web-single-page-nov-2020.pdf (accessed 13 January 2021).

SCQF Partnership (2021) *SCQF Levels.* Available at: https://scqf.org.uk/about-the-framework/ (accessed 2 April 2021).

Universities Scotland (2020) *National Articulation Forum Final Report 2020.* Available at: https://www.universities-scotland.ac.uk/wp-content/uploads/2020/08/Final-Report-of-National-Articulation-Forum-2020-1.pdf (accessed 13 January 2021).

8 Credit and curriculum in Wales, devolution, Bologna and Brexit: An eclectic journey

Bob Morgan

Introduction

Any discussion of education policy and structures in Wales starts with devolution. It is often said that devolution is not an event but a process. This has certainly been the case in Wales. What started with the Government of Wales Act 1998, saw three others in 2006, 2014 and 2017. There have also been important reports such as those of the Richard Commission (2004), the Holtham Commission (2010) and the Silk Commission (2014). Up until Brexit, devolution was the largest experiment that the UK had chosen to perform on itself. Brexit itself has also had important implications for the education system in Wales, in particular on the higher education sector through the Bologna Process. This chapter provides a commentary on both.

The devolution process in Wales has developed from an initial conferred powers model, giving only minor secondary legislative authority, to a reserved powers model with full primary law-making powers in the devolved areas. The idea is to see policies evolve that are more closely aligned with the needs and preferences of the Welsh nation. Rhodri Morgan (2002), the then first minister of Wales (Prif Weinidog Cymru), in a speech to the National Centre for Public Policy in Swansea, spoke of putting 'clear red water' between Wales and England in terms of public service policy development. Education, being a devolved issue, has been at the heart of this process, though whether or not the sector has seen lasting improvements is a matter of some debate.

Important as devolution has been, one should not forget that education policy in Wales before devolution was not entirely tied to what went on in England (Daugherty 2000). It is true that education provision in Wales was made via legislation mainly concerned with England, though ministerial responsibility did lie with the Secretary of State for Wales and administrative responsibility with the Welsh Office. As Daugherty (2000: 1) pointed out, '... the 1988 Act would have to take account of the fact that Wales, while not a nation state, would expect a National Curriculum for its state-funded schools to take account of the distinctiveness of the Welsh nation, its language and its culture within the United Kingdom'.

As we shall see, Brexit has had major implications for the higher education sector in Wales and indeed for the UK as a whole through its effect on the ability to create and sustain networks, both formal and informal. Networks serve as structures for policy development, student and staff exchanges, joint research and collaborative workings such as joint curricula and awards. The development of such networks relies on trust and the development of strong social capital. Brexit has damaged the ability to build both. In the words of Marginson (2017: 8), '[f]or higher education, one UK sector where the relationship with Europe has been unambiguously positive – a win–win for both European countries and the United Kingdom – the consequences will be every bit as destabilising as it was predicted before the vote'.

The situation in Wales, then, regarding education in the devolution era is complicated. It is characterised by a bewildering host of initiatives and policies, as for the first time the Welsh Government was able to pull directly on the levers of powers to reform structures, curriculum, assessment, pedagogy and accountability. The narrative describing the development of policy is thus of necessity painted with a broad brushstroke. There appears to have been a determination to differentiate Wales from the English trajectory, particularly in the schools. As we shall see, however, higher education was much more difficult to control and influence as institutions jealously guarded their autonomy. Crucially, though, they were all too aware that they compete in an extremely competitive domestic UK and international market. A determined attempt to reconfigure the sector was only partially successful. A different path of student finance was forged but had to be quickly rolled back as the harsh realities of finance and the Barnett formula[1] cut in. Higher education was also part of the European Higher Education Area and the Bologna Process with its attendant bureaucratic structure. As we shall see, this presented both constraints and opportunities.

The Welsh context

Wales is a small country, comprising about 5% of the UK population. As far as education is concerned, there are 1,130 primary schools, 7 middle schools, 205 secondary schools and 39 special schools. One of its most distinctive features is the role of the Welsh language, with 428 of its primary schools, 5 of its middle schools and 49 of its secondary schools teaching through the medium of Welsh (OECD 2017). As we shall see, the school and college sector was an area in which there was a real attempt to put clear red water between Wales and England.

As far as higher education is concerned, the Welsh Government has over the years attempted to initiate change. During his tenure as education minister, Leighton Andrews often warned that universities must adapt or die. There was thus a determined attempt to reconfigure the sector. The perceived problem was that there were too many small institutions, many of which lacked the critical mass to compete effectively. The proposed model was consolidation into no more than six institutions, and this did provoke a response.

The University of Wales Newport merged with the University of Glamorgan to become the University of South Wales. The original proposal was also to include the University of Wales Institute Cardiff (UWIC) but this was successfully resisted by the governing body, and instead it became Cardiff Metropolitan University, demonstrating the difficulty of reforming autonomous institutions that were determined to resist. Voluntary reform did take place elsewhere, however, with Lampeter University, Swansea Metropolitan and Trinity Carmarthen merging to become University of Wales Trinity Saint David.

One interesting aspect of the higher education sector, and one which really differentiated it from England, was in student financial support. In 2012, the Welsh Assembly Government introduced a tuition fee grant. This really did put 'clear red water' between Wales and England. This was a non-means-tested,

Table 8.1   The devolution journey

Year	Event/publication
1999	First sitting National Assembly
2001	Publication of *The Learning Country* Secondary school league tables abolished
2003	Launch of Credit and Qualifications Network for Wales
2002–5	SATs for pupils aged 7, 11 and 14 phased out
2003–7	Welsh Baccalaureate rolled out
2004–5	Foundation Phase published
2008	Publication of School Effectiveness Programme
2010	2009 PISA results published
2011	20-point plan unveiled
2012	New school banding system introduced Review of qualifications for 14–19-year-olds
2013	National Reading and Numeracy Tests introduced
2014	*Qualified for Life* published *Improving Schools in Wales* published
2015	*Successful Futures* and *Teaching Tomorrow's Teachers* published Qualifications Wales becomes operational as independent regulator
2017	*Education in Wales: Our national mission* published
2020	Curriculum for Wales unveiled

Source: Adapted from Evans (2021).

non-repayable grant available to Welsh and EU students to cover the cost of increasing tuition fees. But the cost of this scheme proved unsustainable and the whole issue of student funding was reviewed by Professor Ian Diamond (Diamond 2016). The result was that the fee grant was replaced in September 2018, with a shift towards funding for living cost expenses. Welsh students also maintained access to the student loan scheme.

Just how complicated education policy in Wales is can be gleaned from tables 8.1 and 8.2, which list the plethora of policy initiatives that have occurred since devolution. For many, this is simply policy overload. In a survey by WISERD (2016: 9) on teachers' views of the education sector in Wales, perhaps the most telling comment was '… having to jump through hoops to satisfy various initiatives. I have been teaching 30yrs, I know what works for me, leave me alone + let me teach!!!'.

Evans (2021) has perhaps provided the most analytical and comprehensive coverage of educational policy development in Wales. He divides the devolution period since 1999 into three distinct phases. These are shown in Table 8.2.

During the first phase we can actually see the emergence of Morgan's 'clear red water' between Wales and England. The Welsh Government ended Standard

Table 8.2 Phases of education policy in Wales

Phase	Characteristics	Ministers involved
Phase One (1999–2010) Devolution and a licence to innovate	Comprehensive reform agenda, divergence from England, rowing back from accountability, trust in teachers, innovative policy development	Rosemary Butler: May 1999–October 2000 Jane Davidson: October 2000–June 2007 Jane Hutt: July 2007–December 2009 Leighton Andrews: December 2009–June 2013
Phase Two (2010–2015)	Renewed focus on standards, reintroduction of national testing and school categorisation, stronger emphasis on international comparators, call for data	Leighton Andrews: December 2009–June 2013 Huw Lewis: June 2013–May 2016
Three (2015–2021) Curriculum for Wales and culture of collaboration	Whole system reform, move to self-evaluation, policy co-construction, collaboration involving a range of partners, teacher autonomy	Kirsty Williams May 2016–

Source: Adapted from Evans (2021).

Attainment Tests (SATs) at Key Stages 1, 2 and 3. The publication of school-level pupil performance, used to generate school league tables, also ended. This was part of a desire to shift responsibility and accountability onto schools. The first phase also saw a concentration on developing innovations in the curriculum. Three initiatives stand out. At the primary level came the introduction of Flying Start and the Foundation Phase, and at the secondary level the Welsh Baccalaureate was introduced. The latter was phased in between 2003 and 2007 and revised in 2015.

The Welsh Government, then, has been determined to use the full scope of its devolved powers to free itself from the English orbit and develop a Welsh Way. Thus, whereas in England we have seen a concentrated focus on school types and parental choice, in Wales we see no academies or free schools and few foundation schools exempt from local authority control. Wales is wedded to the community-based comprehensive school model. The interesting question of course is whether this constant churning is destabilising, making it difficult to establish the necessary stability for coherent policy delivery. What follows is a selective narrative of the major development from this kaleidoscope.

The starting point of all this churn had been the publication of *The Learning Country* (National Assembly for Wales 2001). On reading it one is struck by its grandiose language. Jones and Roderick (2003: 225) stated that it did '... represent a radical departure ... providing Wales with an education system based on different social principles which amounts to a statement about the nature of Welsh society'. Egan (2017: 3) claims that it

> ... created the essential features of the education system we have in Wales today including our own schools' inspectorate, qualifications body, a largely state-provided school system and the continuing role of local education author-ities. It also reflected the values inherent in a predominantly state-provided, bilingual and comprehensive school system.

The Credit and Qualifications Network

National qualification frameworks are formal structures used to define qualifi-cation systems. They emerged as important policy instruments in the 1990s. In the UK, responsibility for education lies with four jurisdictions, and there are differences between them. The Credit and Qualifications for Wales (CQFW) was formally adopted in 2002 and launched in 2003. Its aim is to develop and implement common principles and standards to measure, award and compare learning achievements of students from the age of 14. It was initially managed by the Welsh Government through three strategic partnerships:

- ACCAC (Qualifications, Curriculum and Assessment Authority for Wales)
- ELWa (Education Learning Wales)
- HEFCW (Higher Education Funding Council for Wales).

In 2006, the Welsh Government transferred the functions of ELWa and ACCAC to the Welsh Assembly, and so CQFW became a partnership between the Welsh Assembly Government and HEFCW. CQFW is underpinned by five key goals:

1 Enabling all to develop and maintain essential skills
2 Encouraging lifelong learning for all
3 Exploiting knowledge in business and educational institutions
4 Encouraging development of businesses and workers to gain new skills
5 Helping peoples within their communities to develop new skills.

Creating a qualifications network, though, is not easy. Bergan (2007, 2009), for example, has identified five components in the make-up of qualifications: level, workload, quality, profile and learning outcomes. CQFW approaches these difficulties by using the concept of eight High Level Principles: credit, learning time, recognised standards, level, title, purpose, learning outcomes and assessment.

The CWFW uses the three-pillar approach:

1 Higher education
2 Regulated qualifications, viz. GCSEs, GCE (A/AS level) and the Welsh Baccalaureate
3 Quality-assured lifelong learning.

The fan diagram shown in Figure 8.1 illustrates the levels and examples of qualifications and learning provisions within CQFW and is used widely by stakeholders.

Figure 8.1 CQFW fan diagram

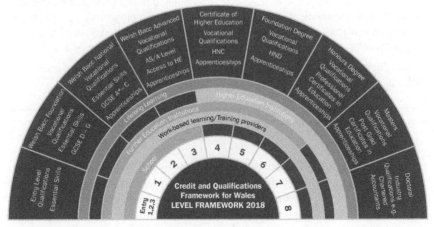

Source: Welsh Government (2019: 6).

An important development came in 2015 with the setting up of Qualification Wales, an independent statutory body that was given the duty of regulating for non-degree qualifications in Wales, including vocational qualifications. It has two principal aims:

- ensuring that qualifications and the Welsh qualification system are fit for purpose
- promoting public confidence in qualifications and the Welsh qualification system.

Qualification Wales has come under particular scrutiny recently because of its handling of the examination crisis due to the COVID-19 pandemic during the summer of 2020.

In 2014, the Department of Education and Skills of the Welsh Government commissioned a qualitative review of the performance of CQFW by Arad Research (Welsh Government 2014a). The research consulted a large number of stakeholders and concluded that CQFW performed a useful function, though there were issues regarding its role, profile governance and implementation. Table 8.3 gives a summary of its reported strengths and weaknesses.

Table 8.3 CQFW reported strengths and weaknesses

Strengths	Weaknesses
Allows for greater recognition of prior and informal learning through the QUALL pillar[2]	Lack of uptake and embedding across sectors
Facilitates the recognition of non-mainstream provision	Learners and employers more focused on full-time qualification
Use of credits makes it easier to articulate and communicate achievement across sectors, levels and geographic areas	The implied parity of all qualifications and seamless progression routes does not exist in reality because of poor articulation between the pillars
Avoids duplication and addresses issue of learner drop out	Lack of user-friendliness and poor overall levels of stakeholder understanding and engagement

Source: Adapted from Welsh Government (2014a).

Another interesting aspect of CQFW is the relationship between the two most important providers within CQFW, that is, the higher education institutions (HEIs) and the further education institutions (FEIs). Over the last ten years there has been a determined effort to rationalise the structure of the further education sector in order to achieve economies of scale and synergies. A report by the Welsh Government (2015) wanted to encourage this process by establishing a more holistic and regional approach to post-16 education in Wales, supported by stronger regional planning.

There has certainly been progress in this area, achieved mainly through mergers and partnerships with universities. Thus, we have seen Merthyr College and Coleg Sir Gar become constituent colleges of the University of South Wales and Trinity Saint David respectively. Coleg Cymoedd (College of the Valleys) was created by the merger of Coleg Morgannwg, Aberdare and Ystrad Mynych. As far as financing is concerned, the main model followed is franchise. Under this model the HEI retains responsibility for student numbers, curriculum, quality provision and student experience. Table 8.4 shows the latest figures for higher education enrolments in further education colleges in Wales.

Table 8.4 Higher education enrolments in further education colleges in Wales, 2019/20

	Full-time enrolment	Part-time enrolment	Higher apprenticeships	Total
Bridgend College	255	459	—	714
Coleg Cambria	242	205	54	501
Cardiff & Vale College	324	237	60	621
Coleg y Cymoedd	127	248	81	456
Gower College Swansea	180	140	60	380
Coleg Gwent	638	292	—	930
Grŵp Llandrillo Menai	557	679	29	1265
The College Merthyr Tydfil	253	67	—	320
NPTC Group	403	185	—	588
Pembrokeshire College	43	85	41	169
Coleg Sir Gâr	466	397	128	991
Total	3488	2994	453	6935

Source: Colegau Cymru (2020: 2).

Another important development came in 2012/13 with the introduction of the £9,000 tuition fee. This proved to be a catalyst for a move away from a grant-based, per credit system of higher education funding to a more student fee-based regime. The vestiges of the per credit regime remain, however, particularly for part-time undergraduate provision.

The per credit funding regime allocation is based upon funding cells (HEFCW 2019). A funding cell refers to:

- Level: undergraduate (not franchised out); undergraduate (franchised out)
- Mode: part-time; and
- Academic subject category.

The CQFW is mapped to levels within the European Qualifications Framework (EQF). This is a common reference framework designed to make qualifications across different countries both within Europe and beyond. It was set up in 2008 and revised in 2017. It is an eight-level learning outcomes-based framework for all types of qualifications. It serves as a translation tool between different national qualification frameworks. The interesting question here of course is where does this leave the UK post-Brexit? As it stands, the UK is still part of the Bologna Process. The decision to leave the ERASMUS scheme, however, may be indicative of a difficult relationship going forward.

As far as the nature of qualifications in Wales is concerned, there has been a recent important development. This has been the introduction of a new curriculum at secondary level. Reports by the OECD (2014, 2017) had shocked the Welsh educational establishment. After the 2014 report, the Welsh Government took the opportunity to revise and review its whole strategy, and the result was the report *Qualified for Life* (Welsh Government 2014b). This was a five-year plan for education for 3–19-year-olds. It was built around four strategic objectives:

- An excellent professional workforce with strong pedagogy based on an understanding of what works.
- A curriculum which is engaging and attractive to children and young people and which develops within them an independent ability to apply knowledge and skills.
- The qualifications young people achieve are nationally and internationally respected and act as a credible passport to their future learning and employment.
- Leaders of education at every level working together in a self-improving system, providing mutual support and challenge to raise standards in all schools.

It was also decided to invite Professor Graham Donaldson to review Wales' curriculum and assessment arrangements. The result was the publication of *Successful Futures* (Donaldson 2015), the recommendations of which were accepted by the minister of education, Huw Lewis. Wales had now entered Phase 3. In the words of Evans (2021),

> [b]y accepting in full Donaldson's recommendations, Lewis had effectively marked the beginning of a new era in policy development ... that would define Wales' education system from mid-2015 to the present day.

Evans noted that the OECD (2020) defined the new curriculum 'as the "cornerstone" of the country's efforts to move from a performance-driven education system to one more clearly focussed on the learner', and predicted that 'the new curriculum would herald a softening in neoliberal ideology and a more collegiate approach to policy development'. As Evans indicated, 'Lewis (2015) himself noted that "the sustained and active participation of educational practitioners and the wider community" would be essential to the curriculum's successful implementation'.

Successful Futures is a large and detailed report with 68 recommendations, including in particular the plans for a new Welsh curriculum to be adopted in 2022. The new curriculum is quite a radical change. Students will no longer learn in lessons broken down by traditional subject boundaries. Instead, the new curriculum is divided into Areas of Learning and Experience (Evans 2015):

- Expressive arts
- Health and wellbeing
- Humanities (including RE, which should remain compulsory to age 16)
- Languages, literacy and communication (including Welsh, which should remain compulsory to age 16, and modern foreign languages)
- Mathematics and numeracy
- Science and technology.

English and Welsh will remain statutory compulsory subjects, as will religious studies and relationship and sexuality education.

Let us now move on to consider the higher education sector.

Higher education, ECTS, Bologna and Brexit

Higher education institutions are autonomous organisations and therefore the Welsh Government's ability to put 'clear red water' between Welsh institutions and the English model is somewhat limited. Thus, the definitive reference point for all UK higher education providers is the *UK Quality Code for Higher Education*, the latest edition was published by the Quality Assurance Agency in 2018. Wales does have its own Quality Assessment Framework set out by HEFCW (2020), but with mechanisms to ensure close relevant alignment with the *UK Quality Code* through close working with HEFCW, Estyn (the education and training inspectorate for Wales), Colleges Wales, Universities Wales and QAA Cymru.

The contours of the governance of the higher education sector in the UK are well known, and will not be repeated here. With Brexit, however, a rather more interesting line of approach is to interrogate the way that the higher education sector and its institutions in Wales, and indeed the UK, have interacted with those in Europe, and to speculate how this might change in the future. This is an important topic. Johnson and Wolf (2009) noted the significant impact of globalisation on higher education. Increasing interdependency in the world economy makes it essential that transparency of cross-national equivalency is to the fore.

The Bologna Process was designed to create a European Higher Education Area (EHEA). The process was formally started in 1999 with the signing of the Bologna Declaration (1999). The ultimate aim was to establish by 2010 a coherent, compatible and competitive EHEA, attractive for European and non-European students. This had followed on from the Sorbonne Declaration, signed in May 1998 by the UK, France, Germany and Italy, which called for the removal of barriers within the higher education sector, and development of a common framework for teaching and learning.

The difficult issue now was how to make this operational across a Europe with its diversity of structures, regulations, quality processes and institutions. The response was to create a general, bureaucratic, sector-wide European mechanism (Morgan and Lydon 2009).

The initial way forward was through a six-point action plan:

1 The adoption of a system of easily readable and comparable degrees through the use of learning outcomes and level descriptors
2 The creation of a system based on two cycles roughly translating into Bachelor's and Master's (this was later increased to three cycles)
3 The establishment of a system of credits allowing for transfer and accumulation
4 The encouragement of staff mobility
5 Development of European co-operation in quality assurance
6 The introduction of a European dimension in higher education.

These were later supplemented by four others:

• An emphasis on lifelong learning
• Promoting the attractiveness of the EHEA
• Emphasis on institutions and students as equal partners
• An EHEA and European Research area – two pillars of the knowledge-based society.

Creating a bureaucratic structure ensuring cross-national equivalency was not easy for the reasons Bergan (2007, 2009) pointed out earlier. Nevertheless, a bureaucratic structure emerged:

• The European Credit Transfer and Accumulation System (ECTS) eased the problems of transferring and accumulating credits between countries and institutions.
• The Dublin Descriptors (Joint Quality Initiative 2004) set out in general terms the levels of credits that would have to be achieved in Bologna cycles 1 and 2.
• The emergence of learning outcomes in both curriculum design and module descriptors. This aspect was important and indeed controversial. The approach was seen by many as constricting the learning process, leading to

a target-led structure. However, as far as Bologna was concerned, it was a necessary part of the bureaucratic furniture. They could be related to external reference points such as the Dublin Descriptors, and crucially used in articulation as networks of universities emerged and developed (Morgan and Lydon 2009).

* The development of trusted and comparable quality assurance systems.

Agreement in terms of the number of ECTS credits needed to achieve qualifications under the Bologna Process had been relatively easy, with for example the bachelor's degree having a value of 180 ECTS credits, normally achieved by studying 60 ECTS credits per year. What proved more difficult was the time value and intensity of an ECTS credit. For most of mainland Europe, one ECTS credit was measured as equal to between 25 to 30 study hours. The Welsh (and UK) metric, however, fell outside this range with one ECTS credit being the equivalent of 20 hours of study. A particular difficulty arose with the one-year British-taught master's degree, compared to the normal two-year programmes elsewhere. The perception amongst many Bologna signatories was that these British master's were perceived as lightweight. Squaring this circle would involve defining a credit in terms of equity of standards and expectations of study. The use of learning outcomes was crucial to this.

This European, sector-wide activity on bureaucratic credit and curriculum structures and comparable quality assurance systems played a large part in the Welsh higher education sector. As we have seen, the Credit and Qualification Framework for Wales (Welsh Government 2017), for example, maps into the European Qualifications Framework. However, the construction of such structures could only go so far in building a true European Education Area.

What really drove the creation of the Single Education Area across Europe in so many areas (well-accepted quality assurance systems, student and staff exchanges, joint curricula and awards, research and recognition of achievement) relied on developments at a much more micro level. The evolution of higher education had taken different routes across the states of Europe, both in terms of the development of institutions delivering higher education and qualifications offered. Bologna now provided a common framework structure, but the crucial development had to come at the institutional and indeed at the course and module level through the building of trust and reciprocity.

Building trust, however, is not easy. Institutions needed to have confidence that credits accumulated in one country were consistent in terms of quality and standards with those gained in others. It is here that ERASMUS played a crucial part. In its early years, the financing arrangements involved the construction of networks of universities under what were termed ICPs (Inter-university Cooperation Programmes). This led to the construction of what Morgan and Lydon (2009: 70) termed 'clusters of trust'. What drives partnership development is mutual benefit and common interests underpinned by strong personal relationships that build the necessary trust (Mattessich and Monsey 1992; Huxham 1996; Vangen and Huxham 2003), rather than the development of cycles, credit metrics and programme descriptors.

One interesting feature as far as Wales is concerned in building these trust networks was the opportunity that arose from regional networking, for example through the Four Motor Regions initiative established in 1988. Originally a four-region network of European regions, Catalonia, Rhône-Alpes, Baden Württemberg and Lombardy, it was later expanded to include as associate members Wales, Flanders, Quebec and Malopolska. South Wales always had close relationships with south Germany, in particular with Baden Württemberg. Cardiff, Swansea, Newport and Pontypridd, for example, were twinned with Stuttgart, Mannheim, Ravensburg and Heidenheim respectively.

The University of South Wales (USW) took advantage of this geographical linkage by developing deep trust relationships with a number of universities in Baden Württemberg, using ECTS to create additional bachelor programmes in business management and engineering. One initiative demonstrating how Bologna stimulated cross-country educational innovation is particularly interesting. The Duale Hochschule Baden Württemberg (DHBW), a federal institution headquartered in Stuttgart, developed a particular model known as co-operative education. This involves deep-rooted partnerships with organisations in both the private and public sectors (Gohringe 2002; Schenkenhofer and Wilhelm 2019). The model goes beyond what is generally known as work-based learning into what is more correctly termed work-integrated learning (WIL). Students must have a contract of employment with an approved partner, and then undertake semesters of intense academic study alternating with a structured placement period with the partner. There is thus high integration of theory and practice. USW created a number of business programmes allowing students from the DHBW to import 120 home ECTS credits. They then undertake the final 60 ECTS credit phase in Wales, 30 ECTS credits of normal formal academic study followed by a WIL-validated module of 30 ECTS credits validated and supervised by USW, allowing the student to graduate with the USW bachelor's.

Creating this structure involved high levels of trust and understanding by the participant academic faculty of the curriculum, in particular the differing learning, teaching and assessment approaches. The understanding of the differing pedagogic approaches came through close working that built confidence about the outcomes and standards. This could not be achieved simply by articulation of level and module descriptors.

This model of integrating credit-based work experience into undergraduate degree structures in Welsh universities had been suggested by Morgan (2003) in a paper arguing that devolution had presented a real opportunity for demonstrating the efficacy of higher education in playing a central role in regional economic development. It would, however, have necessitated a different approach to university funding as it then was to give greater emphasis to the outreach model as opposed to the elite model. The CCFW does in part recognise this through credit rating in the lifelong learning pillar.

But what of the future as the implications of Brexit start to unwind? Brexit is certain to alter the landscape of higher education, influencing the relationships that the UK has as a whole built with EU countries as a member, and also those that individual universities have built with European institutions. Potentially adverse consequences include the UK losing access to EU research funding, mobility programmes and collaborations; and losing EU staff and students, with potentially significant implications for the quality and quantity of research outputs and more broadly for the financial viability and reputation of UK HEIs (Courtois and Veiga 2020).

One definite loss has been the deliberate decision to leave ERASMUS+ and replace it with a new programme, the Turing Scheme, seen by most commentators as grossly inferior. An excellent comparison of the two schemes is provided by Jones (2021), who is often referred to as the father of ERASMUS. In an important recent development, however, the Welsh government has announced a new international exchange programme very much based on ERASMUS+. Here we can see that 'clear red water' hinted at by Rhodri Morgan. Running initially from 2022 to 2026, it has a budget of £65 million. The fundamental principle of the programme will be reciprocity. Where necessary, the programme will fund costs related to the inward mobility of learners, teachers and young people from partner organisations abroad. It is hoped that this will enable existing partnerships that have been built up under ERASMUS+ to continue and help to create new ones, raising Wales' international profile as well as offering opportunities to those who benefit directly. Cardiff University will be responsible for developing the details of the scheme. Students will still be eligible to apply for the Turing Programme.

Conclusion

Rhodri Morgan in his famous 'clear red water' speech clarified that he wished to use devolution to forge a future for Wales that was plainly different from that of England. Wales would now put behind it the oft-quoted entry into the *Encyclopaedia Britannica*, 'For Wales see England'. Well, perhaps. The COVID-19 crisis has certainly increased the profile of devolution and made people on both sides of the border more aware of the powers of the devolved nations, which can now chart their own courses.

Education, of course, can play an important part in nation-building. This can be seen in an innovation in the early days of devolution to insert a break in the interconnected education systems of Wales and England. The Curriculum Cymreig (ACCAC 2003) encouraged the teaching of a Welsh dimension to Welsh children. Its aim is to promote an understanding in children of the distinctive quality of living and learning in Wales and to further their sense of belonging to their local community and country. As the devolution journey has proceeded, certainly the gaps between Wales and England have widened, with for example the introduction of the Foundation Phase in the primary sector and the new curriculum in the secondary sector being rolled out and due to begin in 2022.

Fundamental change in the governance of post-16 education is also underway. CQFW is a kaleidoscope of providers, ranging from sixth-forms, to

FEIs and HEIs, work-based learning, and adult and community education. The core governance architecture has been the Welsh Government, HEFCW, local authorities and Estyn. The Welsh Government (2016) published a report by Professor Hazelkorn investigating the governance of post-compulsory education, with particular reference to HEFCW. It recommended the establishment of a Commission for Tertiary Education and Research. It will be responsible for overseeing the post-16 sector, including HEIs and FEIs, apprenticeships, sixth-forms and Welsh Government research.

As far as higher education is concerned, a major complication will be Brexit. The major policy issue of the Welsh Government over which it has some control has been reconfiguration and the size of the sector. Bologna and membership of the European Higher Education Area presents a different set of problems. ECTS was crucial, as it introduced a common currency as far as the credit framework was concerned, together with the three level cycles and their associated descriptors. As we have seen, however, the building of this bureaucratic structure was only a start, as trust and reciprocity had to be built to construct appropriate circles of trust. Such circles are now under severe strain as the consequences of Brexit roll out.

Notes

1 'The Barnett formula is used by the UK Treasury to calculate the annual block grants for the Scottish government, Welsh government and Northern Ireland executive. It therefore determines the overall funding available for public services such as healthcare and education in the devolved nations' (Institute for Government 2020: 1).
2 Quality Assured Lifelong Learning (QALL), Social Care Wales. Available at: https://socialcare.wales/learning-and-development/quality-assured-lifelong-learning-qall.

References

ACCAC (Awdurdod Cymwysterau, Cwricwlwm ac Asesu Cymru) (2003) *Developing the Curriculum Cymreig.* Cardiff: Welsh Assembly Government.
Bergan, S. (2007) *Qualifications: Introduction to a Concept.* Higher Education Series #6. Strasbourg: Council of Europe.
Bergan, S. (2009) Academic recognition: Status and challenges, *Assessment in Education: Principles, Policy and Practice,* 16 (1): 39–53.
Bologna Declaration (1999) *The European Higher Education Area.* Available at: https://www.eurashe.eu/library/modernising-phe/Bologna_1999_Bologna-Declaration.pdf (accessed 29 May 2021).
Colegau Cymru (2020) *Higher Education in Further Education Institutions Briefing: Challenges and opportunities in difficult times.* Available at: https://www.colleges.wales/en/category/publications (accessed 29 May 2021).
Courtois, A. and Veiga, A. (2020) Brexit and higher education in Europe: The role of ideas in shaping internationalisation strategies in times of uncertainty, *Higher Education,* 79: 811–27.

Daugherty, R. (2000) *The National Curriculum in Wales: Early policy development 1987–1989*. Paper presented to the British Educational Research Association Conference, Cardiff University, 7–10 September.

Diamond, I. (2016) *Review of Higher Education Funding and Student Finance Arrangements*. Cardiff: Welsh Government.

Donaldson, G. (2015) *Successful Futures*. Cardiff: Welsh Government. Available at: https://gov.wales/sites/default/files/publications/2018-03/successful-futures.pdf (accessed 29 May 2021).

Egan, D. (2017) *After PISA: A way forward for education in Wales*. Merthyr Tydfil: Bevan Foundation.

Evans, G. (2015) Revealed: The radical education overhaul which will dramatically change the way our children are taught, *WalesOnline*, 25 February. Available at: https://www.walesonline.co.uk/news/wales-news/revealed-radical-education-overhaul-dramatically-8713170 (accessed 29 May 2021).

Evans, G. (2021) Back to the future: Reflections on three phases of education policy reform in Wales and their implications for teachers, *Journal of Educational Change*. Available at: https://link.springer.com/content/pdf/10.1007/s10833-021-09422-6.pdf (accessed 3 May 2021).

Gohringe, A. (2002) University of Cooperative Education – Karlsruhe: The dual system of higher education in Germany, *Asia-Pacific Journal of Cooperative Education*, 3 (2): 53–58.

Higher Education Funding Council for Wales (HEFCW) (2019) *Circular: Funding allocations 2020/21*. Available at: https://www.hefcw.ac.uk/wp-content/uploads/2020/08/W20-20HE-HEFCW-Funding-allocations-2020_21.pdf (accessed 30 May 2021).

Higher Education Funding Council for Wales (HEFCW) (2020) *Quality Assessment Framework for Wales*. Cardiff: Welsh Government. Available at: https://www.hefcw.ac.uk/wp-content/uploads/2020/08/W20-10HE-Annex-C-QAF-April-2020-English-2.pdf (accessed 29 May 2021).

Holtham, G. (2010) *Fairness and Accountability: A new funding settlement for Wales*. Cardiff: Welsh Government. Available at: https://gov.wales/sites/default/files/publications/2018-10/fairness-and-accountability.pdf (accessed 3 May 2021).

Huxham, C. (1996) *Creating Collaborative Advantage*. London: Sage.

Institute for Government (2020) *Barnett Formula*. Available at: https://www.instituteforgovernment.org.uk/printpdf/10118 (accessed 15 April 2021).

Johnson, M. and Wolf, A. (2009) Qualifications and mobility in a globalising world: Why equivalency matters, *Assessment in Education: Principles, Policy and Practice*, 16 (1): 3–11.

Joint Quality Initiative (2004) *Shared 'Dublin' Descriptors for Short Cycle, First Cycle, Second Cycle and Third Cycle Awards*. Available at: https://www.uni-due.de/imperia/md/content/bologna/dublin_descriptors.pdf (accessed 29 May 2021).

Jones, G.E. and Roderick, G.W. (2003) *A History of Education in Wales*. Cardiff: University of Wales Press.

Jones, H.K. (2021) *Turing One-way Street No Match for ERASMUS Highway*. Edinburgh: European Movement in Scotland. Available at: https://www.euromovescotland.org.uk/turing-one-way-street-no-match-for-erasmus-highway/ (accessed 29 May 2021).

Marginson, S. (2017) Brexit: Challenges for universities in hard times, *International Higher Education*, 88: 8–10.

Mattessich, P.W. and Monsey, B.R. (1992) *Collaboration: What Makes it Work?: A review of research literature on factors influencing successful collaboration*, St. Paul, MN: Amherst H. Wilder Foundation.

Morgan, B. (2003) Higher education and regional development in Wales: An opportunity for demonstrating the efficacy of devolution in economic development, *Regional Studies*, 36 (1): 65–73.

Morgan, B. and Lydon, J. (2009) Bologna: Some thoughts on its effect on the internationalisation of higher education, *Journal of Applied Research in Higher Education*, 1 (1): 64–72.

Morgan, R. (2002) Clear red water: Rhodri Morgan's speech to the National Centre for Public Policy Swansea, *Socialist Health Association*, 11 December. Available at: https://www.sochealth.co.uk/the-socialist-health-association/sha-country-and-branch-organisation/sha-wales/clear-red-water/ (accessed 14 April 2021).

National Assembly for Wales (2001) *The Learning Country: A paving document*. Cardiff: Welsh Government.

OECD (2014) *Improving Schools in Wales: An OECD perspective*. Paris: OECD. Available at: http://www.oecd.org/unitedkingdom/Improving-schools-in-Wales.pdf (accessed 29 May 2021).

OECD (2017) *The Welsh Education Reform Journey: A rapid policy assessment*. Paris: OECD. Available at: http://www.oecd.org/education/The-Welsh-Education-Reform-Journey-FINAL.pdf (accessed 29 May 2021).

OECD (2020) *Achieving the New Curriculum for Wales: OECD education policy perspectives*. Paris: OECD. Available at: https://www.oecd-ilibrary.org/docserver/37ba25ee-en.pdf?expires=1622287745&id=id&accname=guest&checksum=5C8E0819ED-6234044BAFDABD95ED2AC3 (accessed 29 May 2021).

Quality Assurance Agency (QAA) (2018) *The UK Quality Code for Higher Education*. Gloucester: QAA. Available at: https://www.qaa.ac.uk/quality-code (accessed 29 May 2021).

Richard, I. (2004) *Commission on the powers and electoral arrangements of the National Assembly of Wales*. Cardiff: Welsh Assembly Government. Available at: https://image.guardian.co.uk/sys-files/Politics/documents/2004/03/31/richard_commission.pdf (accessed 18 May 2021).

Schenkenhofer, J. and Wilhelm, D. (2019) Fuelling Germany's Mittelstand with complementary human capital: The case of the Cooperative State University Baden Württemberg, *European Journal of Higher Education*, 10 (4): 1–21.

Silk, P. (2014) *Empowerment and Responsibility: Legislative powers to strengthen Wales*. Cardiff: Commission on Devolution in Wales.

Vangen, S. and Huxham, C. (2003) Nurturing collaborative relations: Building trust in interorganisational collaboration, *Journal of Applied Behavioural Science*, 39 (1): 5–31.

Wales Institute of Social and Economic Research, Data and Methods (WISERD) (2016) *Is there a 'Crisis' in Welsh Education?* Cardiff: Welsh Government. Available at: https://www.cymmrodorion.org/wp-content/uploads/2017/07/Is-There-a-%E2%80%98Crisis%E2%80%99-in-Welsh-Education.pdf (accessed 29 May 2021).

Welsh Government (2012) *Review of Qualifications for 14 to 19-Year-Olds in Wales*. Cardiff: Welsh Government. Available at: https://gov.wales/sites/default/files/publications/2018-02/review-of-qualifications-for-14-to-19-year-olds-in-wales-final-report-and-recommendations_0.pdf (accessed 29 May 2021).

Welsh Government (2014a) *The Credit and Qualifications Framework for Wales: A qualitative review of its impact.* Cardiff: Welsh Government. Available at: https://gov.wales/sites/default/files/statistics-and-research/2019-07/140717-credit-qualifications-framework-qualitative-review-impact-en.pdf (accessed 29 May 2021).

Welsh Government (2014b) *Qualified for Life.* Cardiff: Welsh Government. Available at: https://dera.ioe.ac.uk/21054/1/141001-qualified-for-life-en_Redacted.pdf (accessed 29 May 2021).

Welsh Government (2015) *Review of Higher Education in Further Education Institutions.* Cardiff: Welsh Government. Available at: https://gov.wales/sites/default/files/publications/2018-02/review-of-higher-education-in-further-education-institutions.pdf (accessed 29 May 2021).

Welsh Government (2016) *Towards 2030: A framework for building a world-class post-compulsory education system for Wales. Review of the oversight of post-compulsory education in Wales, with special reference to the future role and function of the Higher Education Funding Council for Wales.* Cardiff: Welsh Government. Available at: https://gov.wales/sites/default/files/publications/2018-02/towards-2030-a-framework-for-building-a-world-class-post-compulsory-education-system-for-wales.pdf (accessed 29 May 2021).

Welsh Government (2017) *Credit and Qualifications Framework for Wales (CQFW).* Cardiff: Welsh Government. Available at: https://gov.wales/sites/default/files/publications/2018-03/cqfw-brochure.pdf (accessed 29 May 2021).

Welsh Government (2019) *Credit and Qualifications Framework for Wales (CQFW).* Cardiff: Welsh Government. Available at: https://gov.wales/sites/default/files/publications/2019-01/cqfw-brochure.pdf (accessed 25 June 2021).

Part 3

Credit and learner mobility

9

The use of credit in institutional collaboration: The example of the Midlands Enterprise Universities' Credit Compass Initiative

Anne Danby

Introduction

Student mobility is one of the areas where credit practice comes alive. Having a broadly equivalent currency of learning allows students to study flexibly and in accord with the dynamics of their lives. Credit gives a structure to the consideration of the stage of the programme of learning to which students should be given entry in relation to subject content and level of learning. In the vast majority of cases, the receiving higher education provider (HEP) uses a process known as recognition or accreditation of prior learning (RPL/APL). Through this review of awarded credits or qualifications and experiential learning, the receiving HEP can decide whether the applicant can enter at an advanced stage of the programme, or whether there is learning, usually in the form of whole modules, that they will not need to repeat. Although this process is in theory simple, student transfer between courses and institutions is not as common as might be expected. Dent et al. (2017) found that students felt that processes, information, advice and support should be more straightforward and high profile, and that HEPs should regard student mobility as a form of student support rather than viewing it as a recruitment process. All this has significant implications for the future careers of the students involved, and for the continuation metrics for institutions.

The ability to apply learning from one course in order to access another was an expectation of the 2013 QAA *Quality Code* (Chapter B6: Assessment of Students and the Recognition of Prior Learning), reflecting established practice over many years. Flexibility of study, student choice and lifelong learning are themes that come in and out of fashion: they featured in the Augar Review of post-18 education and funding (DfE 2019), commissioned by Theresa May. This stated commitment to lifelong learning was reiterated by Boris Johnson in September 2020 when he said, 'And so today I want to set out how this government will offer a Lifetime Skills Guarantee to help people train and retrain – at any stage in their lives – and enable us not just to come through this crisis, but to come back stronger, and build back better' (Johnson 2020). It also featured in the Queen's Speech in May 2021: 'Legislation will support a lifetime skills guarantee to enable flexible access to high-quality education and training throughout people's lives' (HRH Queen Elizabeth II 2021). While a lot of this initiative is focused on skills, there is a higher education role. The Cabinet Office Implementation Unit is looking again at credit transfer across HEPs, including possible bespoke collaborative arrangements between providers.

From its inception in January 2018, the Office for Students (OfS) was establishing itself as the sector's regulator. In February 2018, the OfS issued its Regulatory Framework for Higher Education in England, setting out the conditions of registration for HEPs. It clearly emphasised the importance of student choice, and the responsibility of HEPs to provide clear information: 'to support students to make the right higher education choices for them. Students sometimes wish to transfer from one course or provider to another. Research suggests that students do not see the ability to transfer as a market mechanism, and that there is relatively little latent demand for transfer' (OfS 2018: 25–26). Even though only a small number of students may need or want to change course, OfS notes that '[m]any providers have formal transfer systems in place but many students are unaware of the transfer opportunities available. The OfS will work to ensure that in practice students are able to transfer within and between providers wherever it best meets their needs and aspirations' (OfS 2018: 26).

It is notable that there has been a relatively recent change in one of the key measures of institutional success which supports HEPs to make transfer easier. Continuation was historically only positive if a student remained within the same provider. The introduction of the Teaching Excellence Framework in 2016 brought in a range of updated metrics to enable students to compare institutions and make a choice informed by more than student satisfaction and numbers of good honours degrees. Continuation is now classed as positive if the student has remained in higher education, regardless of whether they have transferred between institutions. This has reduced one of the barriers to universities promoting student mobility.

Capturing the zeitgeist of this phase in higher education, in March 2018 the Vice Chancellors' Board of the Midlands Enterprise Universities (MEU) group decided to look into the potential for setting up an MEU academic credit alliance between the six members at the time: Birmingham City University, Coventry University, University of Derby, University of Lincoln, Nottingham Trent University and University of Wolverhampton. The Midlands Enterprise Universities work together on priorities for the region, with the aim of producing job-ready graduates to support the Midlands Engine for Growth. The aim of the credit alliance was to facilitate easier movement of students between the member universities. The alliance would support student access to courses, and would be referenced in the Student Protection Plans[1] required by the 2017 Higher Education and Research Act. At the launch of the Midlands Credit Compass in October 2019, the chair of the MEU, Professor Kathryn Mitchell (University of Derby), explained that all the member universities were committed to social mobility and lifelong learning. Despite the habitual competition for students, they had therefore taken the decision to work collaboratively so that students can be successful. It is to be noted that the change to how continuation was measured smoothed the way in part, as facilitating transfer to another HEP would maintain continuation metrics for the source university.

Consultation and scoping

A working group composed of representatives of each of the six member universities met regularly to initially scope what a credit alliance might look like, and then to refine the proposal. The working group changed over time in terms of scope and representatives, and I was involved in the initial meetings. In the meetings there was a detailed discussion on whether an MEU Credit Transfer Alliance would be of benefit, what should be in scope and what should be left for future consideration.

The first meeting established the terms of reference, specifically:

- The aim of the MEU Credit Alliance is to enable students to transfer easily from one university to another, should this be necessary
- Support student access to programmes
- Should be referenced in Student Protection Plans
- Focus on undergraduate provision initially
- Assumes all MEU partners accept each other's credit
- Strongly desired by the MEU VCs.

Consultation was carried out with key people across both academic and professional services within each university, to enable the group to capture all the aspects that should be considered. This consultation formed part of the scoping exercise to ensure that we were designing something that was of use, and that could be implemented effectively. The consultation was broadly welcomed across the board; there were common lines of enquiry around competition, range and implementation. As the concept was developed, the queries from the consultation and the deliberations of the working group were considered and, in some cases, investigated further to ensure a workable and effective outcome.

What scenarios should the framework cover?

The consultation indicated that a clear view should be reached on whether the credit alliance should apply just for course closures, or for routine student mobility. There were differences of opinion here depending on whether the focus was on institutional competition or the requirements of the Office for Students. The team identified two clear scenarios that the alliance could or should address.

The first was to provide a contingency offer for students of member HEPs in the face of a catastrophic institutional event, such as loss of a technical building, or suspension of an institution's Tier 4/student visa sponsor licence. This was dubbed the *Godzilla Plan*, and was to be invoked in emergencies, and referenced in institutional Student Protection Plans. (1) There was initial discussion about mapping curriculum between cognate programmes, but it was clear that this would entail a great deal of work, with annual updates to reflect curriculum changes, for a very small likelihood that it would be invoked. What was therefore developed was a set of steps that the MEU members would follow, if such an event occurred. A catastrophic events action plan was designed, and is in place in case of need.

The second scenario was to improve continuation rates by making transfer within the group membership smoother and more accessible. Sector-level information on students transferring between providers was available from the *Student Transfers: Experimental Statistics* report (OfS 2020), showing 3% per cent of undergraduate students had changed to a new institution one year after entry in the 2017/18 academic year, which gave a ballpark figure to base discussions upon. The figure encompassed both transfers to the next level of study, and re-starting studies, with and without the corresponding transfer of credits. The rate of transfer was shown to increase steadily over the period 2012/13 to 2017/18. To better support the development, a Higher Education Statistics Agency (HESA) data request was submitted to uncover more detail about student transfers into and out of MEU member universities in the recent past, transfers to and from non-MEU providers, and how many students fully left higher education when they left MEU institutions. The response to the request demonstrated that facilitating transfer between members was realistic and would give good benefits, both for students in terms of continuing their education, and for the HEPs in terms of continuation and recruitment.

Should we harmonise recognition of prior learning policies?

The implications for key metrics such as the National Student Survey (NSS), graduate destinations and good honours should be considered, especially if allowing entry to the final year. There was different practice between the members in allowing entry to the final year, and whether applicants could also claim RPL against modules within that year. On the theme of different RPL rules in different providers, there was the question of whether grades would be imported with the credit and, if so, how would equivalence be assured and classifications be truly representative? Perhaps the universities in the group would need to agree on a single RPL process. Harmonising regulations is a complex process, because it impacts on other activities, such as award classification calculations. The degree of variation can be illustrated with a comparison of RPL credit limits in each partner, not least because the number of credits per module varies (see Table 9.1).

Table 9.1 Maximum credit limit for prior learning

Award	Level	Uni 1	Uni 2	Uni 3	Uni 4	Uni 5	Uni 6
CertHE (120)	4	60	80	50% of the total credit for the level	75	80	60
DipHE (240)	4	120	120	50% per level	120	120	120
	5	60	40	50% per level	30	40	60
Foundation degree (240)	4	120	120	50% per level	120	120	120
	5	60	40	50% per level	30	40	60
Ordinary degree (300)	4	120	Fallback award only	50% per level	120	120	?
	5	90		50% per level	120	80	
Top-up (120 L6)	6	60	0	50% per level	0	0	60
Honours (360)	4	120	120	50% per level	120	120	120
	5	120	120	50% per level	120	120	120

Note: Maximum limits may be reduced by professional, statutory or regulatory bodies or by local regulatory requirements depending on the course and the award.

Current individual RPL practice takes into account different credit values of modules, usually by mapping learning outcomes and skills from previous study onto specific modules on the recipient programme. Where there is not a straight equivalent, applicants are asked to provide a narrative or personal mapping exercise to demonstrate where module learning outcomes and skills have been achieved in previous study and experience. Although this can be a time-consuming and complex process for the applicant, it is also a useful personal reflective activity, and enables the recipient institution to assure its standards. Conversely, aligning RPL processes and thresholds would involve aligning institutional credit frameworks, requiring large-scale re-validation of programmes and regulatory overhaul. There was unease about having institution-wide automatic entry arrangements, analogous in some ways to articulation/progression agreements, as the latter are scrutinised through a quality process for each coupling, and it would completely bypass academic judgement. This was judged to be too brave an approach. Therefore, it was considered that aligning RPL policies in the six member institutions was not going to show a significant benefit that would justify the institutional upheaval and risk involved.

Should curricula be aligned?

Extending from these considerations was the question of whether curricula would need to be aligned, including tracking curriculum modifications and accounting for pre-requisite study, or whether comprehensive mapping of cognate programmes in each institution would be required. This would enable clear messaging to students that completion of Level 4 in a programme at institution A would automatically ensure entry directly into Level 5 of the aligned programme at institution B. Some professional, statutory and regulatory bodies (PSRBs) have specific restrictions or requirements about how much credit must be studied within the programme at a particular provider. This was particularly likely to be true for technical and clinical bodies. However, accreditations are considered individually, and a national curriculum is not in place for programmes at different HEPs. Alignment to subject benchmark statements is an expectation, but that alignment can be flexed to provide a distinctive offer in each HEP. Indeed, unique or notable features of a programme are usually encouraged to drive market differentiation and attract students.

It was agreed to try to map a programme across the six member universities, to gauge the time and therefore financial investment required. This was a challenge from the start, as the aforementioned drive for distinctiveness in the market makes finding cognate programmes for all members challenging. BEng Hons Mechanical Engineering was chosen, as it was offered to all members and, due to PSRB accreditation, was likely to be fairly well aligned already. The research, mapping and write-up took a total of 67.5 hours. The mapping revealed that the closest direct module to module alignments amounted to a maximum of 60 credits out of a total of 360 for an honours degree. It should be noted that the mapping itself relied on the judgement of the person doing the mapping, and their familiarity with the subject. Clearly replicating this across all programmes at all institutions, and then updating annually, was found to be unfeasible due to the time and cost implications, and the reliability of this type of mapping. One interesting benefit of the trial was that module content mapping emerged as the best way to identify student transfer opportunities. Mapping learning outcomes was found to be the least valuable approach due to the variation in institutional conventions around how to frame outcomes. Mapping of module learning outcomes is still the most common methodology, as reported in Atlay and Turnbull (2017), and perhaps it is time to review that approach.

The Midlands Credit Compass

The scoping and development process stripped back the possible approaches down to the fundamentals. What remained were the key issues inhibiting student transfer between programmes in different universities, and these were what needed to be addressed. Students face barriers to mobility, often at a time when they are under the significant stresses that have driven the need to make a change. Awareness of the credit framework and its equivalence between institutions is not universal. Consequently, neither the option to transfer nor how to go about transferring is widely understood. This observation is supported by Dent et al. (2017), who found that 61% of students surveyed were not aware of their ability to transfer, while 73% did not know where to find advice and guidance. Institutions also reported that promotion of RPL and transfer were not consistently prominent (Atlay and Turnbull 2017). Clearly, visibility and simplicity were key priorities in the design of the credit alliance tool. We have seen that persuading students to remain on programme when they are not able to effectively engage is counter-productive, and may be a reason why some students leave higher education completely, rather than exploring transfer immediately or after a break. Having a smooth process to orient students towards member institutions who share similar values and missions would help some of those students to see opportunity rather than failure or an ending to their studies.

The Midlands Credit Compass (MCC) was therefore shaped around the key principle of providing high-quality guidance for students. MCC forms an accessible service where students can get advice from a named contact at the university to which they would like to move. This service establishes a valuable link between such students and their intended destination, and thus makes the idea of transfer less daunting. There are timelines established to ensure a swift progression through the process, and support for the application. This support is available for up to five years from leaving their programme, aligning with the recent government interest in lifelong learning (DfE 2019). It should be noted that although the development process focused to an extent on cognate programmes, this support is explicitly extended to students who want to change the subject of their programme as well as the institution. All of the member universities have the same information on their webpages and are proactive in promoting the Compass to students who indicate that they intend to leave their programme. This concerted and consistent approach is a real strength of the scheme, so students navigating a transfer or re-entering higher education experience joined up support and a coherent process. The working group noted that currently the transfer of credit relies on the individual practices and policies of providers and that students who decide to transfer usually have to work out all the nuances themselves. The collaboration of the group of universities improves the chances for students to continue their education and to be successful in their choice of career.

The Midlands Credit Compass was launched in October 2019 at an event attended by members of the MEU and guests from sector organisations, including the Office for Students. At the launch, Nicola Dandridge, chief executive of the OfS, said,

> *What I think is fantastic about the Midlands Credit Compass is the fact you've got this collaboration of universities and higher education providers coming together to see how they can work together to address this quite tricky issue of how we can support students who need to transfer.* (MCC 2019)

Professor Kathryn Mitchell, chair of MEU and vice-chancellor at the University of Derby, said,

> *The Midlands Credit Compass will improve opportunities for students to access quality advice and guidance and re-engage with higher education across the Midlands. It also demonstrates our joint commitment to putting students at the heart of the system, supporting student access, choice and flexibility.* (cited in Higgins 2019)

This initiative was developed in direct response to the new higher education environment under the Office for Students and the political interest in lifelong learning, social mobility and student choice. In doing so the MCC also addresses long-established barriers for students who do not wish to continue study at their current provider. The MCC significantly raises the awareness of the possibility of transfer for students at the member institutions, allowing them to take their skills and knowledge with them rather than having to start from scratch. The use of credit through existing RPL processes is vital to giving students the best chance of success, while making the move a realistic option. The enhanced support and advice and the provision of named contacts at the receiving university make the whole process smoother and more welcoming. As the Midlands Credit Compass has been in existence for just under two years at the time of writing, its impact is yet to be realised. However, it represents a significant step forward for a group of universities and their students, in the true spirit of student mobility.

Note

1 These plans 'must be tailored to the specific circumstances of an individual provider. It must include the provider's assessment of the risks to the continuation of study of the provider's students, the likelihood that those risks will crystallise, and the severity of the impact on students should the risks crystallise' (OfS 2018: 100).

References

Atlay, M. and Turnbull, W. (2017) *Aspects of Credit Practice in English and Welsh Universities*. Oxford: UK Credit Forum.

Dent, S., Mather, H., Nightingale, J. et al. (2017) *Should I Stay or Should I Go?: Student demand for credit transfer and recommendations for policy and practice.* Sheffield: The University of Sheffield. Available at: https://www.sheffield.ac.uk/polopoly_fs/1.748940!/file/Should-I-Stay-or-Should-I-Go-full-report.pdf (accessed 4 February 2021).

Department for Education (DfE) (2019) *Review of Post-18 Education and Funding.* Available at: https://assets.publishing.service.gov.uk/government/uploads/system/uploads/attachment_data/file/805127/Review_of_post_18_education_and_funding.pdf (accessed 4 February 2021).

HRH Queen Elizabeth II (2021) *Her Majesty's most gracious speech to both Houses of Parliament* [speech], 11 May. Available at: https://www.gov.uk/government/speeches/queens-speech-2021 (accessed 18 May 2021).

Johnson, B. (2020) *Lifetime skills guarantee* [speech], 29 September. Available at: https://www.gov.uk/government/speeches/pms-skills-speech-29-september-2020 (accessed 18 May 2021).

Office for Students (OfS) (2018) *Securing Student Success: Regulatory framework for higher education in England.* Available at: https://www.officeforstudents.org.uk/media/1406/ofs2018_01.pdf (accessed 12 November 2020).

Office for Students (OfS) (2020) *Student Transfers: Experimental statistics on students changing course from 2012–13 to 2017–18.* Available at: https://www.officeforstudents.org.uk/media/a498bec0-69f9-4dc9-a87a-6627dadb7512/student-transfers-experimental-stats-report.pdf (accessed 19 June 2021).

Pollard, E., Hadjivassiliou, K., Swift, S. et al. (2017) *Credit Transfer in Higher Education: A review of the literature.* London: Department for Education. Available at: https://assets.publishing.service.gov.uk/government/uploads/system/uploads/attachment_data/file/595633/Credit_transfer_in_Higher_Education.pdf (accessed 18 May 2021).

Quality Assurance Agency (QAA) (2013) *UK Quality Code for Higher Education: Chapter B6: Assessment of students and the recognition of prior learning.* Gloucester: QAA.

10

Brexit: its impact on learner mobility and recognition of qualifications from the perspective of learners and providers of education and training programmes

Volker Gehmlich

Overview

On 1 January 2021, the United Kingdom finally left the European Union (EU),[1] Single Market and Customs Union, thereby voluntarily losing its rights and benefits as a Member State of the EU. In the previous year, the EU and the UK had negotiated the terms of an agreement for a future relationship, in line with the result of the referendum held in Britain on 23 June 2016 in which a majority voted to leave. The day before Christmas Eve 2020, just before the transitionary period ended on 31 December of that year, the UK and the EU agreed in principle on the details of the UK's withdrawal from the EU, which is commonly referred to as 'Brexit'. The process of ratification of the draft agreement has started, according to the EU members' national rules and regulations.

What does this mean?

As the UK is no longer part of international arrangements of the EU, the free movement of persons, goods and services has come to an end; the UK from now on is a third-party country in EU terminology. In a press release on 31 December 2020, the EU stipulated that henceforth UK citizens *inter alia* no longer had the freedom to study in the EU, service providers such as education and training organisations would no longer benefit from the country-of-origin principle, and the mutual recognition of professional qualifications would come to an end. As a consequence, for example, UK students require a visa to study in the EU; doctors, nurses, dentists, pharmacists, vets, engineers and architects with British qualifications must have these recognised in each of the Member States in which they wish to practise; and offshore training providers and higher education institutions (HEIs) will have to adjust to the national laws of each EU country in which they want to operate. EU students in the UK will be liable for the much higher fees for international students. It will also be much more complicated to undertake study placements in business organisations in the UK for EU students or in the EU for UK students. EU graduates will find it much more difficult to work in the UK and vice versa because regulations such as entitlement to social security benefits need to align. Indirect effects will emerge over time, some of which are to be expected, but others no doubt will take many by surprise.

Why all the fuss?

When the result of the referendum was announced, many people across Europe did not really understand what it amounted to. Ambiguity started with the use of the term 'Brexit', coined at the time of the referendum. Its use is misleading:

- First, 'exit' does not refer to Britain or Great Britain alone, as the acronym 'Brexit' would lead you to believe, but includes Northern Ireland as well; in other words, the United Kingdom as a whole – including its four devolved educational systems – left the EU.
- And Brexit not only impacted the EU Single Market and Customs Union but also the European Atomic Energy Community and all other EU policies.

Disappointingly, some positive signs during the negotiations did not materialise. Although the UK will continue to cooperate on some EU research, it will have no involvement in any education and training programmes, including ERASMUS+.

In the UK, the Spirit of the Past appears to have returned with the EU Member States once more being referred to as 'The Continent' or 'Mainland Europe', terms widely used before the UK joined the EU, and possibly a hint to the vision of 'Splendid Isolation'. Though the words themselves are not a concern, they do seem to indicate a certain conscious or unconscious distancing. The important thing is what the Cooperation Agreement means in practice. At first glance, the negotiated terms appear to be a setback rather than a step forward from the viewpoint of a non-UK resident, but unknown opportunities may come knocking. Therefore, it is essential to look at the whole package to ensure that nothing has been overlooked.

Status quo at the beginning of 2021

This chapter will only address the parts of the Agreement that could have implications for learner mobility and the recognition of qualifications. It is not a deep analysis, as the original text was not available when this chapter was written. The following paragraphs try to indicate possible future changes arising from Brexit. The chapter, of course, can only describe how things might develop; there is no guarantee that they will, and other factors may emerge which render these ideas obsolete. The overriding principle should be that if there are losers, they should be supported; if there are potential opportunities, they should be exploited on both sides of the Channel.

The accord, the *Trade and Cooperation Agreement*, is often shortened to its first part, Trade Agreement. In this chapter, however, the focus will be on some of the factual details and likely impacts relating to the second part of the accord, the Cooperation Agreement, which concerns education and training in particular. The issues – learner mobility and recognition of qualifications – are addressed in Table 10.1: 'Mobility and EU programmes', the terms used in the *EU–UK Trade and Cooperation Agreement: A new relationship, with big changes* (European Commission 2020).

Table 10.1 Mobility and EU programmes

Consequences of the UK's decision to leave the EU, Single Market and Customs Union	Benefits of the EU–UK Trade and Cooperation Agreement
• An end to the recognition of professional qualifications • An end to the free movement of people: UK nationals no longer have the freedom to work, study, start a business or live in the EU	• Non-discrimination clause ensures equal treatment of EU citizens for short-term visas • Co-ordination of some social security benefits
The UK will no longer benefit from EU funding programmes, including: • education and training programmes, such as ERASMUS+ • NextGenerationEU, aimed at speeding up the EU's collective recovery from the COVID-19 pandemic	The UK can participate in five EU programmes open to third-party participation (subject to a financial contribution), including: • Horizon Europe (limited to research and innovation) • Euratom Research and Training programme

Threats or opportunities: A matter of perception

Perspectives of learners: Mobility

In terms of research, the British Government announced that the UK would continue its international collaboration between universities and would associate with Horizon, the EU programme for innovation and research, with the Euratom Research and Training programme, and three other research initiatives that are open to third-party participation, subject to a financial contribution. Although changes may occur as regards the amount of financial support and project management in its widest sense, it is anticipated that the situation will remain much as it was before. If mobility is involved, the UK will be treated as a third-party country from now on, unless special association arrangements can be made as they were for the Horizon projects.

EU mobility programme: ERASMUS

The UK is no longer able to participate in EU mobility programmes. Whereas the UK prime minister calmed the education and training sector in 2020 by stating that, for example, ERASMUS+ support would continue after Brexit, he was obviously referring to the outgoing grant period only. Those courses and individuals presently benefiting from ERASMUS+ will continue to be covered up to the end of the period of financial support, which has been extended because of COVID-19 to the end of March 2023. In the future, students, researchers and other academic staff can only participate in those EU programmes which are open to third-party countries, subject to a financial contribution. This might be interpreted as a financial advantage on the part of the UK.

Although ERASMUS is open to third-party countries in principle, the UK has not explicitly stated its wish to be associated with it any more, in contrast to its arrangements made for five research programmes. To compensate UK students for being excluded from ERASMUS+, the British Government announced its own mobility programme, Turing, which will also target students from disadvantaged backgrounds – who were not excluded from ERASMUS by the way – and will include any country in the world, not being limited to ERASMUS countries. There is a graduate route, by which graduates from outside the UK could be attracted to stay and work in the UK for up to two years after graduation with a post-study visa. As Turing's effectiveness will be evaluated in the light of the success of the ERASMUS programme, it seems appropriate to remind the reader of some of the benefits ERASMUS has provided to date for the EU and the UK.

In 1987, ERASMUS succeeded the Joint Study Programmes, created 10 years earlier, before there was even a Directorate for Education at the European Commission. In the 1970s, the main barriers to research study abroad were a lack of financial support and/or the non-recognition of study periods or qualifications gained abroad (see, for example, Gerstein 1974). In the years that followed, many EU initiatives were launched to find new opportunities for funding student grants and to break down barriers to academic recognition of student mobility. While ERASMUS fostered links between European HEIs to facilitate mobility, other programmes such as COMETT, for example, encouraged links between industry and universities for technology transfer and offered one strand for student and academic staff exchange. The widening of the programme in the following years encompassed the European Free Trade Association (EFTA), Austria, Finland, Iceland, Norway, Sweden (the UK had joined the EU in 1973), the Eastern European countries, Central Asia, the Western Balkans and the Mediterranean. At the same time as the enlargement programme, the deepening of all forms of co-operation was continued. Whereas the Joint Study Programmes depended on individual initiatives, the ERASMUS projects required contracts that committed whole institutions. For a limited time, ERASMUS became a strand of SOCRATES, a programme to encourage lifelong learning.

Many individual EU programmes in education and training merged step by step to finally become ERASMUS+ in 2014. All the achievements of the individual programmes were incorporated into the new structure. Today, financial support and academic recognition of study periods and work placements abroad are best practice. They have been the cornerstone of the present collaboration, comprising all forms and levels of education and vocational and professional training within a framework of lifelong learning based on well-established tools, such as qualification frameworks, quality assurance, and credit frameworks and systems, and put on a solid financial basis by grants from participating states distributed through the EU.

Currently, ERASMUS+ consists of three Key Actions plus two further ones: funding opportunities exist for the three Key Actions of Mobility, Cooperation and Policy, as well as for Sport and the Jean Monnet programme. Key Action 1 focuses on learner mobility, Key Action 2 fosters cooperation for innovation and good practice, whilst Key Action 3 supports policy reforms. The Jean Monnet programme encourages teaching, research study and debate on the EU, while the Sport Action promotes the development of the European Dimension in Sport. At first glance, Turing seems to focus on Action 1, possibly also Action 2 – but only in part. From now on, British students may receive a grant to study at any university in the world, in line with arrangements made by the British government. At the time of writing, it is yet to be determined whether institutions will be totally free to choose a partner anywhere, whether particular criteria will need to be fulfilled (laid down by whom?) and whether the national and/or regional government will directly or indirectly make pre-arrangements in particular countries when it comes to financial support.

Partnerships exist between UK and EU institutions, but will they survive Brexit? British students may be subsidised according to the Turing regulations, but it cannot be taken for granted that their EU counterparts will, unless national funds are to be made available. Would, for example, German students be prepared to pay the rather high study fees levied in the UK – compared with those of Germany – without compensation? If exchange became more difficult, would German institutions be interested to support mobility programmes with UK institutions? From the perspective of students, many things have changed since the beginning of the ERASMUS programmes: studying abroad is not as exclusive as it once was, since there are many more countries to select from; and many institutions run educational components in the English language, even when English is not the official language of the country.

The political reasoning not to participate was most likely dominated by financial issues, as the UK has a significant imbalance of incoming and outgoing students (including trainees) – more than 18,000 outgoing versus more than 30,000 incoming in 2018/19 (ERASMUS+ 2019). This is expected to change but at what price? The savings made in the short term could turn into a huge loss in the long term if the number of those wishing to go to the UK were to fall dramatically or if opportunity costs are taken into account. UK universities have been able to co-operate with any institution anywhere in the world. However, outside the ERASMUS+ countries, universities had to look for grants from sources other than the EU. This will be the case for universities of EU Member State countries if they wish either to continue or to begin to cooperate with UK institutions in the future. It is likely that countries such as Germany will support student mobility with national resources. The German Academic Exchange Service (DAAD) will have national funds at its disposal, but it will have to apply strict quality criteria in a very selective process, not the least because of the high fees levied in the UK. Some may still choose to go to the UK but many young people will lose the opportunity to study in another country; there will be a return to the years before 1973, before the UK joined the EU. How does this fit with the philosophy of openness, inclusion, learning to understand others, of coping with differing perspectives and approaches, challenging national and organisational cultures?

Perspective of learners: Recognition

Lisbon Convention

Cross-border academic recognition is in principle based on The Convention on the Recognition of Qualifications concerning Higher Education in the European Region, commonly known as the Lisbon Recognition Convention. It was developed by the Council of Europe and UNESCO and ratified by the UK in 1997. It became a global convention in November 2019. According to the Convention, recognition can only be refused if the qualification of the home country differs substantially from that of the host, which has to be proved by the authorities in the host country. Brexit will not change this. However, it has to be realised that this Convention aims to make recognition easier in a context in which each national authority determines what it will or will not recognise.

The ENIC-NARIC Network

Two bodies are charged with monitoring and facilitating the implementation of the Convention in the European Region, namely the Committee of the Convention, and the European Network of National Information Centres on Academic Mobility and Recognition (ENIC Network). ENIC was created in 1994 by the Council of Europe and UNESCO to develop policy and practice for the recognition of qualifications. It cooperates closely with NARIC, the network of National Academic Recognition Information Centres, which was founded by the European Union in 1984, and comprises all EU Member States, the countries of the European Economic Area (EEA), countries in Eastern Europe and Turkey. Its brief is to compare academic qualifications as part of the Bologna Process – that is, in the European Higher Education Area (EHEA)[2] – in terms of the wider ENIC Network. To become a member of the ENIC Network, a country has to set up a national centre, supported jointly by the Council of Europe and UNESCO by providing a Secretariat. While the main function of ENIC is to offer advice on recognition to its target groups – students, graduates, HEIs, employees and employers, and other stakeholders – NARIC focuses on facilitating academic recognition of qualifications and study periods in the Member States and on informing and advising on national systems and offering assistance to facilitate mobility. When it comes to comparing academic qualifications, the national centres play an essential supportive role in the Bologna Process.

The Bologna Process has fostered the development of cooperative activities such as the *European Recognition Manual* (European Commission, Lifelong Learning Programme 2016). The second edition, published in 2016, details the essentials necessary for academic recognition of qualifications or parts thereof. As the EU supports this and other NARIC projects, the UK might not directly benefit financially.

Recognition embraces, among other things, the following characteristics of a qualification: level, workload, quality, profile and learning outcomes. The key features of each of these elements are scrutinised according to templates, best practice and tools, such as qualifications frameworks, European standards and guidelines, and the *ECTS User's Guide* (European Commission 2015), all of which have been developed through projects financially supported by the EU. From now on, the UK will have no direct impact on any of the instruments developed, their conclusions and recommendations, or the design of new initiatives.

The ENIC-NARIC Network is the lynch pin concerning the UK's interests. In the future, there could be financial consequences for UK learners, academic staff and institutions of education and training who might have been potential beneficiaries. Representatives of the UK can only participate in and benefit financially from the EU if the matter in hand is dealt with at the level of both ENIC and NARIC. This is a loss on both sides: UK representatives have made a significant contribution to the development of guidelines and roadmaps, which have become the backbone of the EHEA. Within the framework of the Bologna Process, more or less all the key features of academic recognition have been developed or implemented. The EU does not own the Process. However, the EU is a full member and gives substantial direct and indirect support to its various activities. The Council of Europe and UNESCO are consultative partners.

In conclusion, Brexit will not have a direct impact on the NARIC Network but may have an indirect effect through the UK's membership of ENIC; in this way, the UK will still have a voice as far as issues of recognition are concerned. In financial terms, however, no grants will be given to the UK directly unless special arrangements are made.

ECTS

One tool for recognition is the European Credit Accumulation and Transfer System (ECTS), which is applied today in various forms and is now compatible with most of the credit systems in the world. ECTS thus allows for recognition of both degree and credit mobility and is also linked, either directly or indirectly, to qualifications frameworks within the EHEA and beyond. ECTS has become emblematic of university student mobility but it is no longer limited to higher education mobility and now encompasses recognition of learner mobility generally. This is underlined by the fact that later European systems, such as the European Credit System for Vocational Education and Training (ECVET), an outcome of the Copenhagen Process, took over key features of ECTS and adjusted them to the specifications of the vocational sector. In principle, ECTS and ECVET credits are interchangeable. However, the extent of recognition depends, for example, on the autonomy of the receiving institution (see European Commission, Lifelong Learning Programme 2016). To better understand a potential setback to the recognition of academic achievements across the UK and EU after Brexit, it may be useful to look at the history of ECTS.

ECTS started as a pilot system under the ERASMUS umbrella in 1989. At first, it was intended to be a transfer system to facilitate recognition of parts of the studies of students participating in ERASMUS. Institutions of higher education agreed to define terms such as 'credit' and 'grade', and such instruments as Student Application Forms, Learning Agreements, Transcripts and Records of Achievement were developed and implemented. As the pilot project was so successful, underlining the need for further development, ERASMUS commissioned a feasibility study to determine whether the system could be developed as an accumulation system for student achievements at universities at home and abroad. Furthermore, work experience could be credited and fully recognised. A requirement was that students were enrolled on comparable (i.e. not significantly different) study programmes (see the Council of Europe's Lisbon Convention). The feasibility study confirmed that ECTS was suited to become an accumulation system. The abbreviation ECTS was retained as it had become a trademark.

Groups of ECTS Governors were selected and financially supported by the EU to train university staff on-site and to run workshops and conferences to explain how the system worked. The Bologna Declaration with its Process from 1998 onwards pushed ECTS significantly, and the credit system was used not only for the transfer of study achievements during studies abroad, but as an all-round general recognition tool. Other qualifications acquired in educational settings, work-placements or prior learning activities were expressed in credits and documented in the Diploma Supplement, initiated by the Council of Europe and UNESCO. ECTS Governors oversaw the design and testing of grading systems to decrease any potential disadvantages faced by mobile students. These efforts were welcomed by the Bologna Conference in Yerevan, Armenia, in 2015, when the *ECTS User's Guide* (European Commission 2015) became the guide for recognition within the EHEA, and was even partly inserted into national laws. The Guide is a roadmap for lifelong learning, whether formal, non-formal or informal, and is closely linked to the labour market by supporting tools such as the Work Placement Certificate, the Diploma Supplement and Europass, which was partly initiated by the Council of Europe and UNESCO. Therefore, these endeavours have improved recognition and have significantly helped to increase the transparency of education and training – at least in Europe.

UK representatives contributed their experience in Scotland and Britain prior to the beginning of ECTS; the rest of Europe learned from their experience. Where credit systems had previously evolved, they often focused on the time a student had to spend attending classes. Sometimes credits were coupled with the number of hours per week or hours in class. The idea of notional learning time (NLT), a close link between volume of work and learning outcomes, came from UK partners but it took about six years to become the agreed basis for ECTS credit arrangements. Admittedly, old habits die hard, and therefore it is sometimes still a hidden practice to calculate the number of credits depending on the time spent. By and large, however, NLT also works as a quality assurance and accreditation system to check the correct application of ECTS' Key Features. It is inconceivable that Brexit will change that philosophy.[3]

Most likely, Brexit will not have any impact, as British institutions will continue to look for learning outcome equivalencies when it comes to recognition of qualifications or parts thereof. Constructive alignment has become a significant characteristic in the design of study programmes, implying that the agreement is determined by pedagogical beliefs rather than political imposition. The name may change, as might the number of credits allocated to a learning year, indicating slight national deviations, but the philosophy behind ECTS seems to be watertight, as the system rests on mutual trust, while accepting national variations. The level of co-operation will determine the extent to which recognition is permitted, as it has previously within the EHEA. Additionally, the development of national qualifications frameworks helps to recognise qualifications and to facilitate their portability. These frameworks act as a catalyst, particularly in relation to the European Qualifications Framework for Lifelong learning and the European Framework for Higher Education Qualifications (Europass online), which describe the qualification cycles (Bologna Working Group 2005). The national frameworks have to be referenced to the European frameworks in order to achieve a qualitative approach to credit. Today, frameworks exist for sectors, disciplines and for vocational education and training (VET) within a country or even across Europe. The UK *Subject Benchmarks Statements* (QAA 2020) were a forerunner of these frameworks. The EU supported the Turing Educational Structures in Europe project to facilitate a common understanding of education. It cannot be discounted, however, that because of Brexit co-operation as such will be more difficult, in particular the need for students and other learners to get a visa and – most likely – having to face other bureaucratic obstacles.

Professional qualifications

Qualifications frameworks are overarching; they are defined by learning outcomes accumulated at the end of qualification levels, and reflect a learner's knowledge, skills and competence. As the learning outcomes comprise lifelong and life-wide learning, they characterise an open and continuous system of qualifications. In a business environment, some professions require additional attributes for a person to be recognised and be allowed to operate in a defined profession, such as medicine or law.

Brexit has had a major impact on education and training for professional qualifications in terms of the mobility of labour. Professional qualifications of an EU Member State used to be more or less automatically recognised by the other Member States. Nurses, for example, who held a UK qualification could look for employment anywhere in the EU. But no regulated profession will be accepted automatically in the EU following Brexit. UK citizens holding a qualification from a UK institution or organisation will need the authorities in the EU country in which they wish to work or set up a business to recognise it. Holders of UK professional qualifications will be viewed in the same way as a professional from a third-party country. Doctors, architects, etc. will be able to submit their academic qualifications but these – though they may be recognised in line with the Recognition Convention – will not be sufficient for them to become active in their professional field. It can be assumed that red tape will reduce labour mobility. In 2019, the UK Government published *Amendments to the Principal Regulations Coming into Force Before Exit Day*. The amendments are described as guidance for bodies that regulate professional qualifications. At the time of writing, it is too early to comment on details of the likely impact of Brexit on mobility in the professions. However, political considerations may lead to some variations in practice, especially as responsibility for education in the UK is devolved to each of the four nations.

Perspective of providers

Co-operation arrangements

Organisations representing HEIs in the EU and UK highlighted their positive hopes when the deal was published. The European University Association (EUA), representing more than 800 HEIs across the continent, underlined the ambition of its members to continue working closely with UK institutions. In an official statement, published in its newsletter, the EUA's Secretary General stated on 30 December 2020: '[t]he deal brings much needed certainty for cooperation between universities across Europe and their UK partners'. The Secretary General added:

> ... *[t]he fruits of this cooperation will bear testimony to the fact that knowledge should not know borders. The new insights that we will create about the universe and our societies will foster progress as well as help us in meeting the grand challenges that we are facing together.* (Crowfoot 2020)

Similarly, the Director of Universities UK International underlined in the joint statement that, 'UUKi welcomes the deal and is keen to ensure that UK universities will be able to maintain their close ties with their European partners'. The Director further stated:

> ... *[w]e look forward to continuing our research collaborations in Horizon Europe. While we are deeply disappointed that no agreement was reached on Erasmus+, we look forward to working with EU partners through the UK's newly announced Turing Scheme, which will continue to support student exchange.* (Stern 2020)

To underline this train of thought, an article published in daily newspapers by the German Press Agency (dpa 2021) stated that Lower Saxony, one of the 16 federal states of Germany, was struggling to maintain co-operation between HEIs in the UK and Germany. Birgit Honé, Lower Saxony's Minister for European Affairs, was saddened by the UK's exodus from ERASMUS: '*Es ist ein Anachronismus, wenn jungen Menschen in einer Zeit, in der die Welt zusammenwächst, beim internationalen Austausch Steine in den Weg gelegt werden*' ('It is an anachronism when at a time the world is growing together, spokes are put in the wheel as regards international youth exchange' – my translation.) It was stated that the Ministers of European Affairs and of Education and Science would both support ongoing and even enlarged co-operation. To highlight this point, in September 2020 a co-operation agreement was signed between the representatives of HEIs in Scotland and Lower Saxony to support jointly financed projects. As a direct result of this agreement, an infrastructure for joint research was established. Hopefully, similar initiatives will be taken for enhancing learner mobility.

Based on the reaction across Europe, it may be assumed that co-operation will continue, at least from the point of view of HEIs and academic staff. Financial or bureaucratic issues, though, might hamper established activities, fuelling students' anxieties and concerns about whether mobility will be possible at all, whether it will become more complicated and/or more expensive, and whether their degree or vocational/professional qualification will be recognised. It is highly uncertain for students from the UK who wish to study in an EU Member State from 1 August 2021 whether their academic achievements will be recognised, as they were under ERASMUS, even assuming that financial needs will be covered by a Turing grant. Have the times been set back? Are we going to talk again about free movers?

The Rule of Origin for goods and services

The Rule of Origin is one of the key features of today´s foundation to support producers of goods and services to conduct their business across borders in a fair way. The Rule is managed and monitored by the World Trade Organization (WTO), which was established in 1955 as successor of the 1948 General Agreements on Tariffs and Trade (GATT). The WTO operates as the organisational framework in which the World Customs Organization (WCO) develops tools to ensure fair trade. As long as Britain was a member of the EU, it had preferential status, and trade within the internal market was free of tariffs. When the transitional Brexit period came to an end, UK producers of goods and services ceased to benefit from any preferential status, unless exceptions are made for particular goods and services as part of the agreement with the EU. The present agreement lists some examples for goods in particular but there is no reference to education and training institutions and their services. Several examples can be conceived of for which the Rule of Origin of the WTO may play a role. It all depends on the type of the service. If the good or service is categorised as private, it will be regulated by the tariffs and trade of the WTO and the WCO. Language schools or offshore campuses of UK institutions, for example, will be treated like any other institution outside the UK, which means that all financial or regulatory preferences will no longer be granted, and they will be considered in the same way as any private business organisation.

Question marks hang over the joint design of study programmes and the like by EU and UK institutions. They will probably be regarded as public services or charitable institutions so that the Rule of Origin will not be applied. However, the recognition of such degrees and their potential impact on the labour market might well change the picture. Similarly, articulation agreements, double and joint degrees are likely to be defined as public or merit services. However, this definition may depend on the purpose of the co-operation.

Conclusion

Notwithstanding the Brexit agreements, it is hoped that the statements and announcements made by institutions and organisations quoted above are not only good intentions but will come into being, and will be monitored and developed further, not for just a few students but for all learners from Europe and beyond. Mobility as an option should be maintained and facilitated; education and training should be made fully accessible in the European Higher Education Area. Recognition of qualifications is of key importance to achieve a culture of overall trust and continuous quality enhancement. National cultures and their approaches to learning and teaching will continue – within an overall qualifications and quality framework underpinned by mutual understanding. In the European Area, all members should operate on a level playing field.

One way to ensure a level playing field is to balance the numbers of students moving between institutions. Parity can be achieved by taking into account other activities, such as staff exchanges, guest lecturing, monitoring of students, assessment of dissertations and work placements. Institutions could check whether it is possible to vary the timeframe of exchanges to ease financial stress. It is to be hoped that institutions will be very creative in this respect.

As the UK is to remain a part of some research programmes, research will not be affected by Brexit to the same extent as mainstream educational and vocational/professional programmes and their learners across Europe.

Notes

1   Although the EU as it is known today did not exist before 1992, the term is used throughout the text for readability.
2   The creation of the EHEA was the objective of the Bologna Declaration. The UK was a co-initiator of the Declaration, which was signed by the European Ministers of Higher Education in 1999.
3   The ECTS Key Features encompass definitions of ECTS credits, learning outcomes, workload, allocation of credits, awarding credits, the accumulation of credits and the transfer of credits (European Commission n.d.).

References

Bologna Working Group (2005) *A Framework for Qualifications of the European Higher Education Area.* Bologna Working Group Report on Qualifications Frameworks. Copenhagen: Danish Ministry of Science, Technology and Innovation.

Council of Europe (1997) *Convention on the Recognition of Qualifications concerning Higher Education in the European Region.* Strasbourg: Council of Europe. Available at: https://www.coe.int/en/web/conventions/full-list/-/conventions/treaty/165 (accessed 4 March 2021).

Crowfoot, A. (2020) *European University Association and Universities UK International's common statement on the EU–UK agreement.* Available at: https://www.eua.eu/news/619:european-university-association-and-universities-uk-international's-common-statement-on-the-eu-uk-agreement.html (accessed 12 January 2021).

dpa (2021) Land hält an Uni-Austausch mit Briten fest, *Neue Osnabrücker Zeitung*, 10 January, p. 7.

ERASMUS+ (2019) *Erasmus+ in Numbers.* Available at: https://ec.europa.eu/assets/eac/factsheets/factsheet-uk-2019_en.html (accessed 11 January 2021).

Europass (online) Available at: https://europa.eu/europass/en/european-qualifications-framework-eqf (accessed 11 January 2021).

European Commission (2015) *ECTS Users' Guide.* Brussels: EU. Available at: https://ec.europa.eu/assets/eac/education/ects/users-guide/index_en.htm (accessed 4 March 2021).

European Commission (2020) *EU–UK Trade and Cooperation Agreement: A new relationship, with big changes.* Brussels: Publications Office of the European Union.

European Commission (n.d.) *ECTS Key Features.* Brussels: EU. Available at: https://ec.europa.eu/assets/eac/education/ects/users-guide/key-features_en.htm (accessed 4 March 2021).

European Commission, Lifelong Learning Programme (2016) *The European Recognition Manual for Higher Education Institutions: Practical guidelines for credential evaluators and admissions officers to provide fair and flexible recognition of foreign degrees and studies abroad,* 2nd edn. The Hague: EU. Available at: https://www.enic-naric.net/fileusers/European%20Recognition%20Manual%20Second%20Edition.pdf (accessed 4 January 2021).

Gerstein, H. (1974) *Ausländische Stipendiaten in der Bundesrepublik Deutschland: eine empirische Erhebung über Studiengang und Studienerfolg der DAAD-Jahresstipendiaten.* Bonn: DAAD.

Quality Assurance Agency (QAA) (2020) *Subject Benchmark Statements.* Gloucester: QAA. Available at: https://www.qaa.ac.uk/quality-code/subject-benchmark-statements (accessed 5 January 2021).

Stern, V. (2020) *European University Association and Universities UK International's Common Statement on the EU–UK agreement.* Available at: https://www.eua.eu/news/619:european-university-association-and-universities-uk-international's-common-statement-on-the-eu-uk-agreement.html (accessed 12 January 2021).

UK Government (2019) *Amendments to the Principal Regulations Coming into Force Before Exit Day.* Available at: https://www.legislation.gov.uk/uksi/2019/312/schedule/1/part/1/made (accessed 7 March 2021).

11

Credit and recognition in a more interoperable global context: Implications for data privacy, certification and the recognition of prior learning

Beverley Oliver and James Keevy

Introduction

The constructs of credit and recognition have historically been closely interrelated. History shows that the path to policy coherence on credit and recognition has taken some time to coalesce. Current practice within higher education institutions (HEIs) shows that efficient and effective practice is patchy. New challenges to credit are already in train: credit arrangements are increasingly being scrutinised in a global context where data systems are becoming more interoperable, and the traditional divides between formal, non-formal and informal learning are less apparent. Formal qualifications have increasing competition from micro-credentials and other short-course awards, many increasingly provided by non-traditional providers such as Google, Facebook and Salesforce, focused on creating their own skilled talent pools. This chapter explores global perspectives on these conundrums, including whether credit has a future and the implications with regard to interoperability, data privacy, data ownership and control as more technological systems develop. We propose standards for national learning ecosystems, built for international exchange, that would ensure recognition is interoperable across sectors, borders and lifespans.

The concepts of credit and recognition

Credit and recognition could be framed as references to future and prior learning: credit enables education providers to assign a volume of learning to fit the requirements for the completion of formal qualifications. Prospective learners can look ahead and, almost like Olympic hurdlers, can see the credit (that is, the number of courses or assignments) yet to be successfully completed in order to graduate. Recognition, on the other hand, can be credit granted for prior learning (achieved through courses or experience). Originally conceived in the United States to ensure professors taught sufficient hours to receive a pension (Turnbull 2020), credit became a default measure of learning focused on seat time. Over time, credit systems have been adopted in many countries, although in some jurisdictions providers are not compelled to participate in the credit system, and the granting of recognition is safeguarded as part of an institution's autonomy. But the tentacles of credit systems are much deeper than requirements for learners: this has led to the 'unitisation' (sometimes called 'modularisation') of learning that is now hard-wired into educational provision. Learning is segmented into allocations of hours per semester (for example, in Australia a unit is calculated as between 120 and 150 hours of learning, and the equivalent of one-eighth of a typical annual full-time student load). Government funding is calculated by unit enrolments and completions. Internally, much flows from this: enterprise systems (student management, learning management, timetabling and financial systems) operate on a unit basis. Academic workload allocation systems (prevalent in many universities) are calculated based on hours of teaching in units. In other words, units (also called modules) are the basic measure around which learning is quantified, and work and finances are calculated.

In other words, credit and recognition act as a currency, and particularly for learners, because in its traditional form, credit to be earned equals fees to be paid and time to be spent. Credit is the underpinning currency which enables learners to flow through an education system. For example, the graduation horizon is the rate-determining step for learners to move from their current earning status (for many, this would be part-time work to support themselves during study) to professional practice (and the hope of ongoing meaningful paid work in their career of choice). The opportunity cost of study can be roughly equated to the time needed to achieve the credit yet to be acquired – thus the process of attaining credit impacts the quality of life of a learner and their dependents and other family members who may be supporting them, financially or otherwise. Likewise for providers: credit yet to be achieved is potential future revenue. Unscrupulous providers could be tempted to lengthen the credit required in their courses to ensure the revenue stream is maximised. Or they could be tempted to offer too much credit and thereby set the learner up for failure.

How are credit practices (and qualifications) already being challenged and disrupted globally?

In an open market, consumers can freely take their credit from one provider to another. In an open (and some would say, meritorious) educational system, learners should be able to, within reason and discipline boundaries, take credit earned and move to another course or to another provider. They should also be able to achieve credit based on their prior learning in the workplace, if relevant, thereby 'banking' learning credits for future use. Research shows that, even in the most open systems, providers are free to implement such exchangeable credit policies or not: the Higher Education Credit Framework for England (Credit Issues Development Group 2008) clarifies how much credit can be attached to each qualification, and the expected effort (notionally 10 hours per credit point); however, implementation is subject to providers' autonomy and academic judgement. This means that in practice, 'UK higher education does not have a national framework' (Turnbull 2020: 5); 'instead, each university is essentially re-inventing the wheel in adopting credit, determining their own contextualised definitions and practices' (2020: 6). A similar problem exists in Australia: even though there is a clear national policy as part of the Australian Qualifications Framework, the extent to which it is implemented is virtually unknown (Ithaca Group 2018; Phillips KPA 2019) in that there are very little useful or useable data to ascertain the amount of credit given, or indeed that amount of credit that learners would like to be able to receive towards a future qualification (Phillips KPA 2019). Even though the Higher Education Standards Framework is mandatory for all providers, some providers choose to give very little credit because they fear their reputation will be tarnished and they will appear less exclusive; others almost engage in bidding wars, undercutting each other to win the student at all costs. Interestingly, and unsurprisingly based on the limited data available, those requesting credit were more likely to be of a mature age (over 20 years) rather than those who had recently completed secondary school. Even so, no research was undertaken on the postgraduate learner, only the undergraduate cohort (Phillips KPA 2019).

The coming challenges

This introduction points to past and present and future practices; global commentary would suggest that these issues will only become more urgent in the future. These are early days, but commentators observe that the symbiotic worlds of work and post-school education will be massively disrupted post-COVID (Norton 2020; Productivity Commission 2020; World Economic Forum 2020), and even more than had previously been predicted (Schwab 2017; Bughin et al. 2018; Deloitte Access Economics 2019; Ernst and Young 2019). UNESCO's Institute for Lifelong Learning alerts us to the need to: recognise the holistic character of lifelong learning (medium to long term); diversify learning provision; develop a lifelong learner competency framework; and to integrate our existing recognition, validation and accreditation mechanisms (UNESCO Institute for Lifelong Learning 2020: 9).

While providers may continue to work autonomously and inefficiently with credit, several disruptive movements have occurred in the past decade. In the world of yesterday, formal qualifications were esteemed almost unquestioningly, credit towards those qualifications was a desirable outcome and the focus was almost exclusively on the first-time higher education learner (the vast majority of bachelor graduates do not return to complete postgraduate qualifications). It is well documented that learners are still hungry for credentials, but not necessarily formal qualifications because they are too expensive, too time-consuming and not necessarily value for time and money invested (Australian Bureau of Statistics 2016). And evidence from elsewhere suggests that those with bachelor qualifications are disinclined to pursue further full qualifications because of the fees and opportunity costs: a 2019 study conducted in Australia found that post-bachelor workers recognised the need to develop skills for current and future jobs. The majority (58%) believed that having a formal certification of their skills was valuable to current and future employers. Some 56% of respondents were not planning to undertake any further formal learning; however, approximately 71% of those not interested in formal learning would be more likely to consider it if their prior learning or experience were recognised, thereby reducing the amount of study required to obtain a certification (Deloitte 2019).

Recognition, by its nature, is more applicable as learners become more mature and experienced. When the majority of prospective learners are novices in the field of study, credit to be attained is a helpful guide and decision-making tool. It translates as the time and money and opportunity cost yet to be invested. But in a post-COVID world, and as industry 4.0 accelerates, our focus is increasingly not only on novice learners, but also on experienced adult learners who need to up-skill and re-skill to secure meaningful paid work (World Economic Forum 2018; Centre for New Economy and Society Insight 2019). For all learners, but particularly for those already in the workforce and with caring responsibilities, time taken for study is crucial time away from earning and providing for one's own and others' sustenance. Just as a formal education system is crucial to a nation's economic productivity, producing qualified professionals ready for practice, so too the credit and recognition practices of its providers act as levers to ensure that learners spend not too little nor too much time acquiring credit which could have been granted as recognition. Quality assurance agencies focus on ensuring regulation guides practice (NZQA 2017; TEQSA 2019; QAA 2020).

Such learners now sign up to other less traditional providers and seek micro-credentials that are shorter and more targeted, usually to find and secure meaningful paid work (Oliver 2019). For example, Coursera is one of the most popular platforms for those seeking micro-credentials – what started as a massive open online course (MOOC) platform offering free short courses from universities has evolved into a career-focused learning-for-earning marketplace. Some micro-credentials offered there lead to credit towards formal qualifications; most however, do not.

Coursera's Professional Certificates are marketed as career-focused, affordable (pay only after a seven-day free trial), on demand (start when you're ready, go at your pace) and hands on. The vast majority are provided by companies such as IBM, Google, SAS, Salesforce and Facebook rather than traditional educators such as universities. Some courses, such as Google IT Support, have attracted over 400,000 registrations (though completion data are not provided). The collective enrolment in these Coursera courses by September 2020 was well over a million, many times the size of the largest prestigious universities in most countries. There is very little talk of universities and credit in these offerings: learners report their satisfaction, and whether they received a career benefit (Oliver 2020).

So far, we have looked at the broader concept of recognition of learning as it applies to certification, progression and professional standing: 'The principles and processes through which the knowledge, skills and competences of a person are made visible, mediated and assessed for the purposes of certification, progression and professional standing' (Keevy and Chakroun 2015: 191). The mechanism/tool/technology for recognition is learning outcomes (results of what a learner knows, understands and is able to do upon completion of a learning process). Through digitalisation and automation this could be done more seamlessly in the future, and increasingly use more artificial intelligence (AI). One of the major gaps here is the dearth of common taxonomies, specifically for the hierarchies within the different domains. Knowledge is the expectation, where the (revised) Bloom taxonomy is well developed and understood (Anderson et al. 2001; Lokhoff et al. 2010). The purposes of recognition are threefold: recognition for access to a formal qualification; recognition for credit as part of a formal qualification; and recognition for non-formal purposes, e.g. work-based training, social club, and so on. The proxies for/of recognition include various forms of certification: qualifications, part-qualifications, training certificates and (more recently) badges and similar signifiers of achievement through micro-credentials. Many such micro-credentials have brand names which are gaining traction in the marketplace: examples include a Micro-Master's and a Micro-Bachelor's from edX, and nano degrees from Udacity. Ultimately, recognition of learning (in all its forms) enables a person to gather and accumulate a (self) sovereign identity. This portfolio of learning is likely to become a new form of a credential (a 'credential of credentials') which is more than a qualification, expanding the notion of a credential to something that is more encompassing, more digital, more personal. The future may bring this greater 'credential fluency', which will rely increasingly on the basic tenets and enablers of interoperability, data privacy and a common taxonomy.

These developments are driven by developments in technology in concert with labour market imperatives, and the automation of hiring practices (Gallagher 2016, 2018). In a rapidly changing workforce, employers seek ready access to talented workers with the right skills for their immediate needs. Tertiary education, up to now the key producer of formal qualifications and trade certificates, will need to adapt. As Torres (2020) indicates:

> *[t]he single biggest struggle that companies, large and small, have today is finding the right person with the right skills at the right time. A national ILR infrastructure will allow learners to match their skills and their attainment to roles and positions they are pursuing.* (2020: 47)

Furthermore,

> *it will allow employers to better understand the skills they require and develop a new view toward recruiting and managing talent. To achieve this vision, higher education will need to reimagine how it documents the achievements of traditional and non-traditional learners.* (2020: 47)

In order to recognise learning in a consistent and transparent manner, be it nationally, regionally or even internationally, a set of agreed principles is required. In more formal contexts, such mechanisms have been well developed over many years (Heffernan 1973). The higher education sector stands out as following a time-based approach that included 'credits' and 'credit hours' linked to the duration of studies, often with intricate calculations based on the curriculum choices, semesters, in-class time and practical components of a programme. Since the advent of qualifications frameworks and the increased use of learning outcomes in the late 1980s, the concept of credit was further expanded to signify a volume of learning that could be accumulated independent of the duration of a programme (Tuck 2007). This concept of notional hours reflected the number of study hours required for achieving the learning outcomes specified for a qualification or part-qualification. Notional hours and credits became interlinked, the most prevalent ratio being 10 notional hours equivalent to one credit in some jurisdictions, with a recognition that a wide range of learning-related time, such as preparatory work, laboratory work assignments and class time, could all be accumulated towards the completion of the programme. In most countries, 120 credits was used as a benchmark to signal one year of full-time studies. The transition to the new and more consistent interpretation of credit has become pervasive in recent times, although exceptions remain in some sectors and geographic regions.

The flexibility of the notional hour concept fitted well with the increased popularity of online learning programmes as open and distance learning and massive open online courses (MOOCs) became more prevalent at the end of the twentieth century. As a result, students were able to accumulate credits in smaller, more manageable sprints. Part-qualifications became a mainstay of more formal education and training systems, including the technical vocational education and training (TVET) sector, and perhaps to a lesser extent the schooling sector. This shift to a building-block approach was not without controversy, as some part-qualifications became so atomised that experts became increasingly sceptical of their value (Allais and Marock 2020). Rules were introduced to place part-qualifications into core, fundamental and elective categories to ensure that appropriate rules of combination could be applied to ensure that the combination of credits led to a full qualification that was coherent. The use of exit-level outcomes and specific outcomes further guided the process. Complex credit accumulation and transfer (CAT) systems were developed to ensure consistency, more so to accommodate the transfer of credits between qualifications, and also the recognition of prior learning (RPL).

The approaches to credit and recognition described above are now used in many countries, and increasingly also in regions and even continents. In some instances, countries are only starting to transition to qualifications frameworks and there seems to be a strong global push for this to continue as international development agencies continue to provide specific support in this area. As an OECD Working Paper points out,

> [a]s the size of the alternative credentials market grows, governments may consider establishing quality frameworks for these programmes, both to protect consumers who have invested their own money and to provide a sufficient assurance of quality to support accountable public spending. (Kato et al. 2020: 35)

This opens the potential for conflict between qualifications frameworks and greater quality assurance measures versus the need for agility in creating certifications for new and emerging skills. Kato et al. recognise that an:

> important advantage of alternative credential programmes lies in the speed and flexibility with which they can respond to the demands of both employers and students, and finding quality assurance arrangements that offer sufficient space for innovation and appropriate assurance of quality are, for most OECD countries, some way off. (2020: 35)

These developments are leading to a more transparent and globally agreed nomenclature to recognise learning, which, in turn, provides strong impetus to the recognition of qualifications across borders. International networks such as ENIC-NARIC – and, more recently, the Groningen Declaration Network (GDN) – have moved in tandem with these developments. Over the last four years, early work has even been underway on a set of world reference levels that intend to provide more neutral global guidance (Hart and Chakroun 2019). Unfortunately, there have also been many unintended consequences of these shifts and the continued pressure on countries to transform in this direction. As flagged in the 2020 OECD Working Paper (Kato et al. 2020), reduced agility is one such consequence, as the formalisation into rule-based systems means that non-formal and informal learning becomes rigidly excluded, requiring a formal RPL process to be recognised. Some critics (Allais and Marock 2020), even argue that such developments, including the move towards more agile and responsive systems that include micro-credentials, are part of an outdated logic of reform, particularly in developing countries, which, in their view, will not be successful. In our view, institution-building, as argued by Allais and Marock (2020), is just as important, but not an alternative to the new normative instruments being developed for improved recognition and credentialing across the globe.

A look into the future of credit – does credit have a future?

There are increasing signs that the world is ready to move beyond the current conceptualisation of qualifications frameworks and, by implication, credit and forms of recognition. The COVID-19 pandemic has accelerated the move to digitalisation and the delivery of online learning. The rapid uptake of digital credentials certifying learning means that never before have systems been able to access so many machine-readable signifiers of formal qualifications achievement. At the same time, we have seen a strong move towards digital badges and smaller bit-sized learning courses that can be found outside of the formal system of qualifications. Since 2012, when MOOCs went searching for a business model, graduates have been showing their micro-credential achievements (nano degrees and MicroMasters) as well as, or instead of, a degree testamur. The result is a level of confusion among employers, leading to large-scale efforts to help the market make sense of this new world of credentials. Credential Engine, a non-profit entity in the United States, has undertaken to create credential transparency, reveal the credential marketplace, increase credential literacy and empower everyone to make more informed decisions about credentials and their value by creating a centralised Credential Registry to house up-to-date information about all credentials, using a common description language. To date, Credential Engine has identified 967,734 unique credentials in the US across four types of credential providers: post-secondary educational institutions (degrees and certificates); massive open online course (MOOC) providers (certificates, micro-credentials and online degrees from foreign universities); non-academic providers (badges, course completion certificates, licences, certifications and apprenticeships); and secondary schools (diplomas from public and private schools) (Credential Engine 2021).

As flagged previously, the notion of a credential, as something more than a qualification, encompassing various types of formal and non-formal learning, is also gaining traction. In this emerging future, many argue, there is less need for overly complicated systems of qualifications frameworks, and more need for interoperable platforms that allow for learning to be accumulated in more flexible ways, much closer to the world of work (Gallagher 2016). In this future there will also be less, if any, need for RPL. Through the increased sophistication in the use of AI, chunks of learning could be correlated in real time, and the learner guided to fill gaps in a much more co-ordinated manner. In an extreme version of this future, individuals can even be guided to develop competencies that match jobs that do not yet exist. In this future wherein we re-imagine credit and recognition, there are at least three foundational constructs that need to be in place, and in most cases need to be more actively developed within the broader international education and training sector: interoperability, data privacy and common taxonomies. We briefly unpack each of these constructs below.

The first construct is interoperability, specifically semantic interoperability. As noted by Shiohira and Dale-Jones (2019: 22), drawing on Morales and Orrell

(2018): 'interoperability is the ability of discrete computer systems or software to exchange and make meaningful use of shared data or other resources'. Semantic interoperability provides a more focused interpretation of the construct, where the emphasis is on consistency of meaning, relations between items and, generally, the ability for metadata to be read more constantly and reliably by machines (Shiohira and Dale-Jones 2019). As new forms of credit and recognition evolve, semantic interoperability provides the foundation for greater flexibility and more digital approaches. Frameworks to better understand interoperability exist, albeit outside of the education and training sector. The Data Commons Framework (Goldstein et al. 2018) is a well-known example, but there are also others. We would encourage more work in this area from an educational perspective, specifically in relation to the way in which data is treated in an education context, but even beyond this, to knit together chunks of learning, be they formal, non-formal or informal, more seamlessly and more digitally. Such processes will need to be guided by interoperability frameworks as they become more automated and AI-based. Of course, this also means there are risks, notably around data privacy.

Secondly, ethical concerns about data privacy and ownership are important to recognise in the future context being painted here. Data breaches, such as the now infamous Cambridge Analytica data scandal in 2015/16, have become more commonplace in modern society, and accentuate the point that as citizens we now have less control over our own data than ever before. Third-party applications, both private and public, aggregate to massive data lakes, which are, paradoxically, centrally owned, lack portability and have limited interoperability (Dale-Jones and Keevy 2021). The growing move towards peer-to-peer exchange systems can in some ways be seen as the public reclaiming their data, with self-sovereign identity often used as an example of this trend (US Chamber of Commerce Foundation 2020). Just as with interoperability, we are of the view that data ownership needs to be better understood and developed within the education and training sector as a prerequisite for new forms of credit and recognition to be realised. There is no doubt that increased digitalisation presents significant challenges to regulators across the world. The question is whether the increased cross-border initiatives, also regionally and even continentally, can address some of the gaps in national legislation, including that of weak data privacy and ownership measures (AUC/OECD 2021).

The third construct is deceptively obvious, in that we propose that a common taxonomy is needed to measure and interpret learning. Through more formal qualifications and, in recent years, qualifications frameworks with a strong focus on the use of learning outcomes, a common language has steadily begun to develop – this includes the notions of credit and recognition, which are the focus of this chapter. The challenge is that except for a reasonably well-developed taxonomy for knowledges, there is only limited research into other domains, such as skills, competencies and even values, and the definitions of each and the differences between them (if any). More digital forms of recognition, with improved interoperability of datasets and more peer-to-peer systems, open the opportunity for such taxonomies to be developed in new ways using algorithms that to date have not been possible. While such developments could facilitate RPL processes (Kitto et al. 2020), it is possible that RPL may not even be needed in a future where recognition becomes so seamless that the traditional formal, non-formal and informal delineations no longer apply. Moves towards developing consensus on some of these constructs, such as the Beijing Consensus on AI and Education (UNESCO 2019) and also, from an African perspective, the African Continental Qualifications Framework (Keevy et al. 2021), are pointing in this direction, but will, in all likelihood, require many years to consolidate.

The development of the blockchain has the potential to increase trust in all types of machine-readable credentials, including micro-credentials, certifications and qualification transcripts (Grech and Camilleri 2017). Williams (2019) asserts that the convergence of three technologies is likely to force radical change in higher education: learning analytics, artificial intelligence and blockchain, whose applications could include the independent, secure credentialling of a range of students' educational and occupational activities and achievements.

What standards are required to ensure recognition is interoperable across sectors, borders and lifespans?

Such initiatives must be broad in scale rather than introduced by single institutions or sectors. There have been repeated calls for policy-makers to fund lifelong learning accounts to engage, among others, those displaced by the changing nature of work (Business Council of Australia 2018; Monash Commission 2018; DfE 2019). Such a strategy requires a common approach where electronically documented achievements can be authenticated and accessed anytime and anywhere (Chakroun and Keevy 2018). The Comprehensive Learner Record is similar: a digital asset that helps learners share a verifiable record of their accomplishments (skills, competencies, outcomes, assessments, courses, programmes, degrees and internships) (Educause 2019). Even more impressive is the interoperable learning record system currently under consideration in the United States (American Workforce Policy Advisory Board Data Transparency Working Group 2019). Our concern here is not to champion any particular national solution, but to outline the key elements of an ecosystem that might make such a system workable on a national scale. Unlike most current individual learner accounts, the ecosystem becomes a comprehensive portal where there are rewards and incentives for all key stakeholders: learners, employers and providers. Policy-makers own the system and can use levers such as tax incentives and regulatory requirements to ensure rewards reach all stakeholders (or not, if they remain outside the system) in order to ensure the flow of skilled workers to areas of demand in the emerging labour market.

Figure 11.1 shows the key elements of any such national ecosystem that would encompass four broad stakeholder groups (learners, employers, providers and policy-makers) across five domains, all essential and interconnected. The ecosystem pictured here goes beyond lifelong learner accounts, which, to date, and according to recent research (OECD 2019), have had mixed success.

Figure 11.1 The key elements of a national ecosystem that connects learning to work

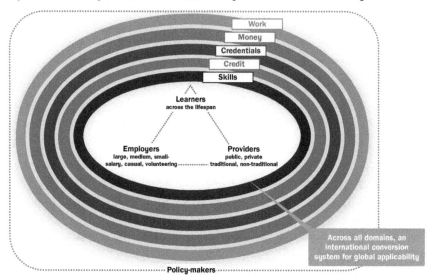

The bedrock of the proposed ecosystem is granular skills information, enunciating what learners at any stage of the lifespan have demonstrated and achieved, described in sufficient detail (level and field of education) to enable meaningful engagement by all parties. This is to counter the criticism of current formal qualification systems that produce high-level information about learners and degree achievements, but rarely more useful information about precise skills achievements. Using standard and agreed terminology and coding, such as the International Standard Classification of Education (UNESCO Institute for Statistics 2012) Fields of Education and Training, married with similar levels of education and training, would enable international exchange and greater portability.

Central to any such ecosystem are credentials and credit. Several countries have established lifelong learner accounts and credit banks. Examples include Korea (Kee 2015) and China (Xinying 2019). The concept entails allowing individual citizens, across the lifespan, to bank credit that can be used for re-skilling in the future as required. Some commentators recommend creating tax-advantaged Lifelong Learning and Training Accounts, to which workers can contribute funds, and use at any time during their careers to pay for education and training, portable from job to job (Fitzpayne and Pollack 2018). Aligned to this is the facility for learners to see their credentials – those they have already achieved (including formal qualifications, certifications, licences, micro-credentials and badges offered by any provider, public or private), as well as those that could be achieved as stepping stones to future work. Such future credentials could be accompanied by evidence that shows the learner their likelihood of success in achieving work (based on past graduate success). For many learners, finding work will be the principal incentive: this includes opportunities for paid work (to secure an income) and also volunteer work (for engagement with the community). Financial incentives underpin the system: funds could flow to learners, providers and employers who use the ecosystem, managed by policy-makers tightly attuned to the labour market (for employment-related credentials) and to the health system (for credentials that relate to mental and physical well-being).

Most importantly, any such national system would require an international conversion system that would enable ready translation across national borders. Although agreements may be underway or in place at the level of international bodies, somewhat surprisingly, such a conversion system for formal qualifications is barely visible to learners. The creation of global MOOC platforms has exposed degrees and micro-credentials available to learners offshore from the base campus of the providing institution: today, a learner in Brazil or Iceland can enrol in the MicroMasters offered by Curtin University in Western Australia. The credit they earn can be claimed and used in a formal Master's by that institution. But learners need to be able to recognise and understand the credit available to them in their own system. A rare example of this is learners at the FutureLearn platform being informed that achievement of a particular micro-credential earns them credit to the effect of one unit (one-eighth of a full-time equivalent study load) in the Australian system, or 15 UK credits, 4 US credits or 7.5 credits in the European Transfer Credit System. This is a trivial example; yet that such a simple translation exercise is a rare occurrence under-lines the larger challenge we are already facing.

Conclusion

As this chapter has shown, tomorrow's challenges are looming, and the higher education sector, working in concert with policy-makers and industry, must find pathways forward with some urgency. Adult learners and workers live and learn and earn in a global digital world. Now more than ever, post-COVID, where a day at the office actually might mean successful Zoom meetings from the living room, learners and workers can and will study anywhere with far greater convenience than a mere decade ago. The need to create sovereign systems to ensure credentials interact seamlessly with national labour markets is urgent; to ensure they have international connectors and translation systems is common sense. Fundamental to any such system is trust and value: trust that sovereign self-identity is guaranteed, that learning and earning is authentic and not simply a talent-matching algorithm, and that individuals have equitable access to formal and non-formal credentials that help them live authentically in their own communities.

References

Allais, S. and Marock, C. (2020) Educating for work in the time of Covid-19: Moving beyond simplistic ideas of supply and demand, *Southern African Review of Education*, 26 (1): 62–79.

American Workforce Policy Advisory Board Data Transparency Working Group (2019) *White Paper on Interoperable Learning Records*. Washington, DC: American Workforce Policy Advisory Board.

Anderson, L.W., Krathwohl, D.R., Airasian, P.W. et al. (eds.) (2001) *A Taxonomy for Learning, Teaching and Assessing*. New York: Addison Wesley Longman.

AUC/OECD (2021) *Africa's Development Dynamics 2021: Digital transformation for quality jobs*. Addis Ababa: AUC and Paris: OECD. Available at: https://www.oecd.org/development/africa-s-development-dynamics-2021-0a5c9314-en.htm (accessed 30 March 2021).

Australian Bureau of Statistics (ABS) (2016) *4235.0 – Qualifications and Work, Australia, 2015*. Canberra: ABS.

Bughin, J., Hazan, E., Lund, S. et al. (2018) *Skill Shift: Automation and the future of the workforce*. McKinsey Global Institute. Available at: https://www.mckinsey.com/featured-insights/future-of-work/skill-shift-automation-and-the-future-of-the-workforce (accessed 30 March 2021).

Business Council of Australia (BCA) (2018) *Future-proof: Australia's future post-secondary education and skills system*. Melbourne: BCA.

Centre for New Economy and Society Insight (2019) *Towards a Reskilling Revolution: Industry-led action for the future of work*. Geneva: World Economic Forum. Available at: http://www3.weforum.org/docs/WEF_Towards_a_Reskilling_Revolution.pdf (accessed 30 March 2021).

Chakroun, B. and Keevy, J. (2018) *Digital Credentialing: Implications for the recognition of learning across borders*. UNESCO. Available at: https://unesdoc.unesco.org/ark:/48223/pf0000264428?1=null&queryId=ae487b93-f039-4989-b0d8-a888aebf6e68 (accessed 30 March 2021).

Credential Engine (2021) *Counting U.S. Postsecondary and Secondary Credentials*. Washington, DC: Credential Engine. Available at: https://credentialengine.org/wp-content/uploads/2021/02/Counting-Credentials-2021.pdf (accessed 30 March 2021).

Credit Issues Development Group (2008) *Higher Education Credit Framework for England: Guidance on academic credit arrangements in higher education in England*. Gloucester: Quality Assurance Agency for Higher Education.

Dale-Jones, B. and Keevy, J. (2021) Digital credentials: Discussions on fluency, data privacy and the recognition of learning in higher education beyond COVID-19, in M. Venter and S. Hattingh (eds.) *Learning for a Better Future: Perspectives on Higher Education, Cities, Business & Civil Society*, pp. 193–209. Cape Town: AOSIS.

Deloitte (2019) *Where to Next? Beyond the skills gap: Higher education for a changing world*. Melbourne: Deloitte.

Deloitte Access Economics (2019) *The Path to Prosperity: Why the future of work is human*. Deloitte. Available at: https://www2.deloitte.com/us/en/insights/focus/technology-and-the-future-of-work/building-the-lucky-country.html (accessed 30 March 2021).

Department for Education (DfE) (2019) *Independent Panel Report to the Review of Post-18 Education and Funding* (the Augar Report). London: DfE.

Educause (2019) *7 Things You Should Know about the Comprehensive Learner Record*. Available at: https://library.educause.edu/-/media/files/library/2019/1/eli7164.pdf (accessed 31 March 2021).

Ernst and Young (2019) *Future of Work*. Available at: https://www.ey.com/en_au/future-of-work (accessed 10 May 2021).

Fitzpayne, A. and Pollack, E. (2018) *Lifelong Learning and Training Accounts: Helping workers adapt and succeed in a changing economy*. Washington, DC: Aspen Institute Future of Work Initiative. Available at: https://www.aspeninstitute.org/publications/lifelong-learning-and-training-accounts-2018/ (accessed 31 March 2021).

Gallagher, S.R. (2016) *The Future of University Credentials: New Developments at the Intersection of Higher Education and Hiring*. Cambridge, MA: Harvard Education Press.

Gallagher, S.R. (2018) *Educational Credentials Come of Age: A survey on the use and value of educational credentials in hiring*. Boston, MA: Northeastern University Center for the Future of Higher Education & Talent. Available at: https://www.northeastern.edu/cfhets/wp-content/uploads/2018/12/Educational_Credentials_Come_of_Age_2018.pdf (accessed 31 March 2021).

Goldstein, E., Gasser, U. and Budish, R. (2018) *Data Commons Version 1.0: A framework to build toward AI for good.*

Grech, A. and Camilleri, A.F. (2017) *Blockchain in Education*. Luxembourg: Publications Office of the European Union. Available at: https://doi.org/10.2760/60649.

Hart, J. and Chakroun, B. (2019) Developing world reference levels of learning outcomes: Potential and challenges, in *Global Inventory of Regional and National Qualifications Frameworks 2019. Vol. I: Thematic chapters*. Luxembourg: Publications Office of the European Union. Available at: https://www.cedefop.europa.eu/en/publications-and-resources/publications/2224-0 (accessed 31 March 2021).

Heffernan, J.M. (1973) The credibility of the credit hour: The history, use, and shortcomings of the credit system, *Journal of Higher Education*, 44 (1): 61–72.

Ithaca Group (2018) *Credit Pathways in VET and Higher Education*. Canberra: Department of Education and Training. Available at: https://www.dese.gov.au/uncategorised/resources/credit-pathways-vet-and-higher-education (accessed 1 April 2021).

Kato, S., Galan-Muros, V. and Weko, T. (2020) *The Emergence of Alternative Credentials*. OECD Education Working Papers No. 2016. Paris: OECD. Available at: https://www.oecd.org/officialdocuments/publicdisplaydocumentpdf/?cote=EDU/WKP(2020)4anddocLanguage=En (accessed 1 April 2021).

Kee, Y. (2015) Retrospect and prospect of the Academic Credit Bank System and its advancement of educational wellbeing in Korea, *International Journal of Continuing Education and Lifelong Learning*, 8 (1): 102–21.

Keevy, J. and Chakroun, B. (2015) *Level-setting and Recognition of Learning Outcomes: The use of level descriptors in the twenty-first century*. Paris: UNESCO.

Keevy, J., Castel-Branco, E., Bateman, A. et al. (2021) *Towards the African Continental Qualifications Framework: Mapping report*. Johannesburg: JET Education Services. Available at: https://www.knqa.go.ke/wp-content/uploads/2021/03/ACQF-EN_Mapping-Report_WEB-1.pdf.

Kitto, K., Sarathy, N., Gromov, A. et al. (2020) Towards skills-based curriculum analytics: Can we automate the recognition of prior learning?, in *Proceedings of the 10th International Conference on Learning Analytics and Knowledge (LAK '20)*, 23–27 March 2020, Frankfurt, Germany, pp. 171–80. Available at: https://opus.lib.uts.edu.au/handle/10453/141691 (accessed 1 April 2021).

Lokhoff, J., Wegewijs, B., Durkin, K et al. (eds.) (2010) *A Tuning Guide to Formulating Degree Programme Profiles Including Programme Competences and Programme Learning Outcomes*. Bilbao: Publicaciones de la Universidad de Deusto. Available at: http://tuningacademy.org/wp-content/uploads/2014/02/A-Guide-to-Formulating-DPP_EN.pdf (accessed 1 April 2021).

Monash Commission (2018) *Three Recommendations for Renewal of Post-compulsory Education in Australia*. Melbourne: Monash University. Available at: https://www.monash.edu/__data/assets/pdf_file/0010/1762507/19P-0131-The-Monash-Commission-24p-final.pdf (accessed 1 April 2021).

Morales, L. and Orrell, T. (2018) *Data Interoperability: A practitioner's guide to linking up data in the development sector*. Collaborative on SDG Data Interoperability.

New Zealand Qualifications Authority (NZQA) (2017) *Recognising Learning for Credit: Guidelines for the recognition and award of credit for learning*. Wellington: NZQA. Available at: https://www.nzqa.govt.nz/assets/qualifications-and-standards/CRT-RPL-guidelines-Oct-20.pdf (accessed 1 April 2021).

Norton, A. (2020) Universities need to learn the early lessons of lifelong learning, *Times Higher Education*, 6 January. Available at: https://www.timeshighereducation.com/opinion/universities-need-learn-early-lessons-lifelong-learning (accessed 1 April 2021).

OECD (2019) *Individual Learning Accounts: Panacea or Pandora's Box?*. Paris: OECD Publishing.

Oliver, B. (2019) *Making Micro-credentials Work for Learners, Employers and Providers*. Melbourne: Deakin University.

Oliver, B. (2020) *Coursera Professional Certificates and Google Career Certificates: A snapshot analysis*. Melbourne: Edubrief.

Phillips KPA (2019) *Academic Credit Arrangements (Credit Recognition): Final report*. Canberra: Department of Education. Available at: https://www.dese.gov.au/uncategorised/resources/academic-credit-arrangements-credit-recognition (accessed 1 April 2021).

Productivity Commission (2020) *National Agreement for Skills and Workforce Development Review: Productivity Commission study report*. Canberra: Productivity Commission. Available at: https://www.pc.gov.au/inquiries/completed/skills-workforce-agreement/report/skills-workforce-agreement.pdf. (accessed 1 April 2021).

Quality Assurance Agency (QAA) (2020) *Higher Education Credit Framework for England: Guidance on academic credit arrangements in higher education in England*, 2nd edn. Gloucester: QAA.

Schwab, K. (2017) *The Fourth Industrial Revolution*. Geneva: Portfolio Penguin.

Shiohira, K. and Dale-Jones, B. (2020) *Interoperable Data Ecosystems: An international review to inform a South African innovation*. Johannesburg: JET Education Services.

Tertiary Education Quality and Standards Agency (TEQSA) (2019) *Credit and Recognition of Prior Learning*, Guidance Note. Melbourne: TEQSA. Available at: https://

www.teqsa.gov.au/for-providers/resources/guidance-note-credit-and-recognition-prior-learning (accessed 1 April 2021).

Torres, R. (2020) The changing nature of student records: The interoperable learner record, *EDUCAUSE Review*, 2: 46–47. Available at: https://er.educause.edu/-/media/files/articles/2020/5/er20_21w.pdf?la=enandhash=CC6EEA8E0CA04557DFF65C8D-19C99CC268D993DD (accessed 1 April 2021).

Tuck, R. (2007) *An Introductory Guide to National Qualifications Frameworks: Conceptual and practical issues for policy makers*. Geneva: ILO. Available at: https://www.ilo.org/skills/pubs/WCMS_103623/lang--en/index.htm (accessed 1 April 2021).

Turnbull, W. (2020) *A Brief History of Credit in UK Higher Education: Laying Siege to the Ivory Tower*. Bingley: Emerald Publishing.

UNESCO (2019) *First Ever Consensus on Artificial Intelligence and Education*. Paris: UNESCO.

UNESCO Institute for Lifelong Learning (UIL) (2020) *Embracing a Culture of Lifelong Learning*. Hamburg: UIL. Available at: https://uil.unesco.org/lifelong-learning/embracing-culture-lifelong-learning (accessed 1 April 2021).

UNESCO Institute for Statistics (2012) *International Standard Classification of Education: ISCED 2011*. Montreal: UNESCO Institute for Statistics.

US Chamber of Commerce Foundation (2020) *Applying Self-sovereign Identity Principles to Interoperable Learning Records*. Washington, DC: U.S. Chamber of Commerce Foundation. Available at: https://www.uschamberfoundation.org/sites/default/files/media-uploads/Applying%20SSI%20Principles%20to%20ILRs%20Report.pdf (accessed 1 April 2021).

Williams, P. (2019) Does competency-based education with blockchain signal a new mission for universities?, *Journal of Higher Education Policy and Management*, 41 (1): 104–117.

World Economic Forum (WEF) (2018) *The Future of Jobs Report 2018*. Geneva: WEF. Available at: http://www3.weforum.org/docs/WEF_Future_of_Jobs_2018.pdf (accessed 1 April 2021).

World Economic Forum (WEF) (2020) *COVID-19 Risks Outlook: A preliminary mapping and its implications*. Geneva: WEF. Available at: https://www.weforum.org/reports/covid-19-risks-outlook-a-preliminary-mapping-and-its-implications (accessed 1 April 2021).

Xinying, Z. (2019) Beijing launches academic credit bank, *China Daily*, 10 November. Available at: https://www.chinadaily.com.cn/china/201711/10/content_34370454.htm (accessed 1 April 2021).

Conclusions and reflections on credit past, present and future

Wayne Turnbull and Harvey Woolf

For the reader who has diligently read every word of this book there is, we are afraid, no crock of gold hidden at the end of the rainbow. Yet the journey through credit's varied landscape in – and also beyond – the UK higher education sector that has been depicted in the various chapters of this book should be instructive and, for any optimists still standing after Brexit/COVID, encouraging. We have discussed the challenges of managing flexible higher education provision, considered implications of partnership working and examined the further/higher education interface. Our geographical adventures through and beyond these British Isles have revealed diversity in credit policy and practice, employing both theoretical and practical foci. In the wider world, innovative opportunities for learner mobility compete with the challenges posed by the post-Brexit withdrawal of the UK from the ERASMUS exchange programme.

In her foreword to this book, Professor Sue Rigby posits existential questions about learning and parity. This is a good place to begin, positioning credit as an effective means of comparing apples with pears in the same fruit-bowl rather than as an imposition of an all-banana diet. Yet, to be effective and efficient, such comparisons require both consistency of equivalence (policy) and the mechanisms to facilitate learner mobility (practice). As our contributors attest, twenty-first-century UK credit policy is fragmented and the implementation of such policy depends very much upon local arrangements that rarely align with those of other institutions.

Our opening chapter reminds us of the rationale for credit, recalling the foundation of the Open University (OU) in response to the Robbins Report on higher education published in 1963. Lord Robbins noted that in the early 1960s in the UK, under 5% of young people entered university and that all but 3% of working-class boys and 1% of working-class girls were excluded from access to opportunities that would afford them the greatest advantage. Comparative data from the USA and continental countries whose economies were surpassing that of the UK showed much higher and wider patterns of participation within well-established and co-ordinated systems of higher education. Innovations such as the Universities Central Council on Admissions and the University Grants Committee were constituted to meet the principle enshrined in the Robbins Report that demand, rather than supply, should determine the size and shape of the UK university sector. Yet the universities did not favour such innovation and fought through their influential alumni to preserve their elite autonomy ('Westminster was a battleground' – *The Guardian* 2005). In response, the reformist Labour government, swept to power on the currents of the white heat of technology and innovation in 1964, created 30 new publicly funded polytechnics, the Council for National Academic Awards (CNAA) and the Open University (Turnbull 2020). Not only had the number of students in higher education in the UK doubled by 1970, but the sector was diversifying and beginning to focus on the needs of learners.

From their first student cohort, enrolling in 1971, the OU has embodied the principle of learner-centred higher education in the UK. Many of the innovative features of the OU model (including learner-determined choice of when and what to study, discrete learning packages and recognition of prior learning) rely upon a common currency of learning and upon the award of credit in respect of academic achievement. By establishing early formal credit transfer agreements with the CNAA, the concept and practices of credit bled from the OU into the polytechnic sector and began to flourish where fertile ground was found. We emphasise this point because we think that it is important to both learn from experience and to recognise the importance of the OU to learner-centred higher education in the UK.

We also note that half a century after the enrolment of the first OU cohort, therefore following 50 years of flexible learner-centred provision, the OU itself notes that learner mobility and credit systems have yet to become mainstreamed within the UK higher education sector. We sense the frustration experienced by a university that operates across all of the nations of the UK arising from the dissonance in credit policy that is exacerbated by political devolution and by autonomous institutional practice. The OU's ongoing experience of credit policy and practice being influenced, even determined, by perceptions of relative status between higher education institutions (HEIs) leaves us wondering whether we remain mired in the elitist snobbery of the Establishment that was so hostile to Robbins' proposed reforms.

Although focused on different topics, the chapters covering the armed forces and Access to Higher Education Diplomas both offer concrete examples of credit policy being translated into practice and providing alternative pathways into higher education. Both chapters also engage in a critical appraisal of the strengths and weaknesses of such approaches, offering candid appraisals of their successes and shortcomings. Here we find proof of concept via practical application of policy into practice, leading us a long way from existential debates about credit. The transformational capacity of higher education to change minds and lives is herein directly facilitated by credit, with a value ascribed to the prior learning and/or skills of adult learners; credit is shown to be the key to unlocking learner potential. The use of credit in establishing functional interfaces between further and higher education is also demonstrated in the chapters on Northern Ireland and Scotland. We note that in the same year that the Dearing Report (1997) was published (which called for a UK-wide higher education credit and awards framework), the Kennedy Report (1997) also advocated the adoption of a common system of credit for further education in the UK. They are in good company with bodies such as the Royal Society, the Confederation of British Industry and the Council for Industry in Higher Education in advocating a national credit framework. Yet as the chapter on variations in the award of credit explains, there are louder, influential and entrenched voices that persist in opposing the very notion.

We would urge anyone with sufficient interest to model the impact of variations in institutional regulation in the award of credit on real student profiles. Even between two institutions, the differences in the outcomes for a student whose profile is exposed to the rules of another institution may be revealing and would most likely be different if the student was recovering from failure in a first attempt at a module. The basis for the award of credit should not be regarded, or even be dismissed, as an administrative detail; it is of fundamental importance to learners. The lack of a level playing field will result in different outcomes for learners achieving the same degree of attainment, based upon nothing more than local idiosyncrasies in regulation and/or policy. We describe this situation as a progression lottery and we feel that it reflects poorly upon a sector that purports to place learners at the heart of the system.

As has been suggested in the opening chapter (in relation to the OU that operates in all of the nations of the UK), credit policy and practice in the four corners of the United Kingdom is far from harmonious. England's credit *guidance* has recently been re-packaged as *advice*, further diluting the non-regulatory basis of credit policy. This subtle change in emphasis illustrates the waxing and waning of Westminster's sporadic enthusiasm for credit, as elaborated upon in the chapter on England. It is noted in the chapter on Wales that initial efforts were made to distinguish devolved policy emerging from the Senedd from that of Westminster, but such efforts have made little headway in the higher education sector (notwithstanding a bold experiment with credit-based funding). Scotland offers the other nations of the UK a synchronised model of credit-based policy and practice based upon an integrated post-16 credit and qualifications framework (the SCQF). The chapter on the SCQF is candid in scoping both the successes and the limitations of the impact of credit north of the border. It demonstrates the capacity for a sector with sufficient political will to develop and deliver the kind of integrated credit framework that Dearing, Kennedy and almost anyone (except those faceless forces of opposition) has been demanding for the UK for years.

Of all the chapters exploring differences in credit policy and practice in the UK, we reflect most on the experience related within the Northern Ireland chapter. Although a part of the UK, the unique features of the province's history and political culture represent an altogether different set of challenges and opportunities for credit policy and practice. We leave it to others to discuss the merits of devolution in Scotland, Wales or even the English regions but we acknowledge the fundamental importance of devolution to securing an end to the Troubles; devolution and power-sharing are a matter of life and death in Northern Ireland. Credit, we learn, is a fundamental tool in Northern Ireland's long-term economic strategy to up-skill the population and raise the aspirations of a generation in whom hope is invested for a peaceful future. When colleges in Northern Ireland talk about putting learners first, we have no doubt that they mean it.

There is nothing quite like a graduation ceremony. Costumed, choreographed and composed, a graduation ceremony is a justified celebration of achievement, of dreams realised, of academic success in the higher education sector. Yet many higher education learner journeys do not reach that destination, but instead come to an abrupt halt along the way. In the UK, the official agency for the collection, analysis and dissemination of quantitative information about higher education reports that around 50,000 entrants to first-degree programmes in each academic year neither achieve their initial target award nor transfer to another (HESA 2021). Discounting students who left university within 50 days of their enrolment (who are excluded from the HESA dataset), 10% of the full-time student population and one-third of part-timers will be at best spectators of the ceremonial graduation parade enjoyed by their peers. In mining communities the extent of excavated spoils could not be ignored in the form of towering pit heaps that transformed the landscape, but in academic communities our lost students are allowed to fade silently into the ether never to be spoken of again.

But must it always be this way, or can we think again about alternative routes of progression and forms of recognition for students whose academic progress towards an initial target award is stalled? Many arguments are presented within this book in favour of credit and of the provision of a flexible higher education framework for learners. In the chapter on the Midlands Credit Compass, we encounter a safety net, a means of retaining learners within a supportive credit framework that facilitates their atypical progression pathways. Although this initiative has been developed in response to a legislative requirement for Student Protection Plans, we feel that the principle has wider application and potential for replication elsewhere.

Whilst dropping out of higher education is certainly not a new concept (nor necessarily a disaster: step forward Bill Gates, Steve Jobs and Mark Zuckerburg), the cost to higher education students of dropping out is both a new and an unwelcome phenomenon. Here we address the financial elephant in the room, which has somehow remained largely ignored elsewhere in this book. The cost of participation in higher education in the UK is high, with most providers charging £9,000 per year for tuition (plus substantial sums for accommodation). It does not require a formula-ridden spreadsheet to calculate the costs to students of non-progression in higher education. Approximately £500 million in tuition fees in the UK is wasted each year, an enduring debt for those learners exiting with neither an award nor any alternative progression route. There is therefore a quantifiable, immutable argument in favour of a credit-based national framework that facilitates flexible, atypical learner progression and values all learner attainment.

Commentators postulated different models of the twenty-first-century learner experience during the latter days of the previous millennium (HEQC 1994). Yet despite their speculation, the learner experience of today's student continues to fit the traditional mould of yesteryear. This does not imply that advances in student mobility and flexibility should be dismissed and we recognise the role of credit in enabling students to return to learning, to *top-up* qualifications and to study at multiple locations. However, we further recognise that the benefits of such mobility and flexibility are enjoyed only by a few, atypical students. Universities may seek to promote opportunities for student mobility/international engagement and government may wish to promote opportunities for student choice in a diversified market, yet the dominant paradigm remains geared towards the teenage entrant whose next three years will be spent in full-time study in a single location.

Yet even the *typical student* may encounter circumstances that require them to deviate from their initial pathway. A *safety net* of credit-related policies and practices offering support for such students would mitigate the risk of a costly and untimely exit from the programme of study that they commenced. Furthermore, any perception that credit is awarded to all, but only *needed* by the few rather than the many, is flawed. The relationship between credit, academic achievement and awards is intrinsic in the academic regulations of the majority of HEIs in the UK. The awarding of credit represents the verification of academic achievement for an element of an award (module, unit or level) that may lead to a qualification (initial target or alternate exit award) and/or may be utilised within another context. A formal summary of awarded credit (be that a transcript, HEAR or Diploma Supplement) is an authenticated record of academic achievement that is owned by the learner in perpetuity. For some learners who do not attain a validated qualification, their certified credit for successfully completing elements of their study will become their award.

Having explored aspects of credit policy and practice throughout (and within the nations of) the UK, we can begin to identify features of a credit framework for higher education that would serve the best interests of learners. From the chapters on the OU and variation in credit policy we learn that consistency in credit policy and practice would serve learners better than existing regional/institutional variations. From the experience of partnership with the armed forces we learn that perceived cultural barriers to learner mobility between settings can be overcome. From the access to higher education chapter we learn that credit can assist in quantifying the prior learning and wider experience attained by adults. From our overview of the UK we learn that the attainment of an integrated credit and qualifications framework (such as the SCQF) is not merely possible but is desirable and demonstrably beneficial to learners. We are also reminded that we are indeed fortunate to have the luxury of debating the finer points of credit policy and practice, rather than fearing that the fragile political consensus may fracture and drag one corner of the UK back into an all-too-familiar nightmare scenario. We have learned that credit has an important role in helping to secure peace in Northern Ireland and we cannot think of a more compelling case than that.

The title of the Robbins Report (1963) was somewhat prosaic: *Higher Education: Report of the Committee appointed by the Prime Minister under the chairmanship of Lord Robbins 1961–63*. The prime minister who appointed the Committee was Harold Macmillan, although the report was received by Home and implemented by Wilson. Macmillan was reputed to have responded to a question about the greatest challenges faced by statesmen with the reply, '*Events, dear boy, events ...*'. We have certainly suffered our fair share of *events* in recent years, with a consequent impact on (and with potential for the development of) credit policy and practice.

As discussed in the chapter on Brexit, the departure of the UK from the European Union and the separate but related decision to withdraw UK students from participation in the ERASMUS programme has perplexed many commentators and stakeholders throughout the continent. The implications for learners in the UK are evident, especially for the 16,000 UK students who engaged in the reciprocal arrangement each year (Erasmus 2017). The UK Government has announced a replacement for ERASMUS called the Turing Scheme,[1] which offers comparable maintenance grant funding to ERASMUS, but no tuition fee contribution (and neither does Turing accommodate staff exchanges). Unlike ERASMUS, the Turing Scheme is not limited to participation in institutions based in countries in the European Higher Education Area. It remains to be seen whether the Turing Scheme will maintain the spirit of the ERASMUS programme, promoting shared cultural experiences amongst learners – and their institutions.

The global pandemic has put other problems into perspective, as evidenced by the lurch into Lockdown and pivot to online learning in the UK higher education sector in 2020 and 2021. We take the view (and we believe that the view is widely shared) that online learning should facilitate and complement rather than replace classroom/lab-based interactions. However, we are also encouraged by the emerging evidence from the 2019/20 and 2010/21 academic years that learners are able and willing to participate in learning that is conducted remotely from the physical fabric of their university. This opens up a range of opportunities for the development and provision of learning that is not only remote from a university campus but that is divorced from any university campus. An *international student* is studying in a given place that is different from their home country, but a *universal student* may study anywhere (*sans frontières*).

Could a learner in the UK who wishes to study, for example, Business Management at Osnabrück University, do so without leaving the UK? If it is feasible to deliver and assess over a distance within the UK, could it be possible to deliver and assess material over distance from a different country or from a number of different countries? We envisage the legion of naysayers, competing to be heard over the mob, declaring loudly why such a thing is impossible. Yet if curricular content is designed to be delivered online, then the remaining obstacles are simply administrative and can be overcome by the effective use of credit. As discussed in our final chapter, advances in technology can assist in facilitating a new approach to flexible and mobile learning. Provided the learning is undertaken within a coherent regulatory and administrative framework, evidence of attained learning via the award of credit can be certified digitally. Such digital credit would not be merely portable, but ubiquitous.

Credit practice in the UK higher education sector has lagged behind innovations in digital technology, particularly in the access provided to students and graduates about their verified academic achievements (in online transcripts and/or Higher Education Achievement Reports). Here the principle underpinning credit, that students should be at the heart of the system, is translatable into the verification of achievement. It is the learner who owns their data and verifiable records of achievement should be supplied by their institutions. We believe that online verification and digital certification of achievement (whether of awards, credit or both) should be an essential attribute of the twenty-first-century higher education landscape. A certificate is decorative whereas a digital transcript or Higher Education Achievement Report can be tamper-proof, secure and 100% verifiable (at the click of a mouse). Credential fraud is big business and credit-based online verification of academic attainment is the remedy.

Yet, as discussed in the final chapter, in order to take full advantage of the opportunities afforded by digital technology in the years ahead, a common dataset should underpin the information presented within digitally rendered records of achievement. This will also facilitate a more granular presentation of information about the learner, which may be of use in applications for further study or employment. Over a decade ago, the Burgess Group (Burgess 2004) recommended that the honours classification system should be replaced over time by a detailed breakdown of student academic achievement in the Higher Education Achievement Report. The outcomes of the Burgess Review were insightful and strategic, including the specification of a standard dataset for the recording of verified academic attainment in the Report.

Burgess's recommendations were sound but ineffectual as, yet again, important innovations for the student experience were sacrificed on the altar of institutional autonomy. Where confident strides towards implementation should have been taken, there was instead a fanfare followed by *gentle encouragement*. Over a decade later, the Higher Education Achievement Report is far from universal and the guidance on a minimum dataset remains exactly that. There remains, therefore, a huge opportunity to achieve commonality in credit practice in the UK higher education sector by standardising the data captured and reported in the consistent verification of a student's academic attainment. We stress that the success of digital learner mobility must be built upon the cornerstone of the standardisation and recording of credit-related information.

A decade ago, the UK Credit Forum published *Making Sense of Credit and Qualification Frameworks in the United Kingdom*. Editors Paul Bridges and Mark Flinn discussed in their preface that 'the purpose of this book is to make sense of the frameworks: to clarify, elucidate and explain. It also suggests how we might begin to reduce some of the current complexity' (2010: v). Many of the issues and complexities discussed by Bridges and Flinn in 2010 remain evident today and some of their efforts to reduce such complexity will be eerily familiar: 'The inclusion of credit in the FHEQ [Framework of Higher Education Qualifications] in EWNI [England, Wales & Northern Ireland] ... would address this shortcoming in the future' (2010: 38). It can only be hoped that the progress towards a coherent and cohesive credit framework in the UK will advance further in the next ten years than it has over the last decade.

Note

1   For details see, https://www.turing-scheme.org.uk.

References

Bridges, P. and Flinn, M. (eds.) (2010) *Making Sense of Credit and Qualification Frameworks in the United Kingdom*. Derby: University of Derby.

Burgess, R. (2004) *Measuring and Recording Student Achievement*. London: Universities UK/SCOP.

Dearing, R. (1997) *Higher Education in the Learning Society*. Report of the National Committee of Inquiry into Higher Education (The Dearing Report). London: HMSO. Available at: http://www.educationengland.org.uk/documents/dearing1997/dearing1997. html (accessed 2 July 2021).

Erasmus (2017) *Erasmus+ Annual Report 2017*. Brussels: EU. Available at: https://op. europa.eu/en/publication-detail/-/publication/4e5c3e1c-1f0b-11e9-8d04-01aa75ed71a1/language-en/format-PDF/source-search (accessed 18 July 2021).

Higher Education Quality Council (HEQC) (1994) *Choosing to Change: Extending access, choice and mobility in higher education*. The Report of the HEQC CAT Development Project+ Executive Statement & Summary. London: HEQC.

Higher Education Statistics Agency (HESA) (2021) *Non-continuation Summary: UK Performance Indicators*, 24 February. Available at: https://www.hesa.ac.uk/data-and-analysis/performance-indicators/non-continuation-summary#outcomes (accessed 18 July 2021).

Kennedy, H. (1997) *Learning Works: Widening participation in further education*. Coventry: Further Education Funding Council.

Robbins, L. (1963) *Higher Education: Report of the Committee appointed by the Prime Minister under the chairmanship of Lord Robbins 1961–63* (The Robbins Report). London: HMSO.

The Guardian (2005) Obituary of Gordon Oakes, 22 August.

Turnbull, W. (2020) *A Brief History of Credit in UK Higher Education: Laying Siege to the Ivory Tower*. Bingley: Emerald Publishing.

Index

Page numbers in italics are figures; with 't' are tables; with 'n' are notes.